DANGEROUS SKIES

WAR EVENTS and FAMILY LIFE - 1941

Peter Angus Anderson

DANGEROUS SKIES

WAR EVENTS and FAMILY LIFE - 1941

A War Diary

by

PETER A. ANDERSON

(with John N. Anderson)

Raydon Wings Ltd

First Published in 2007 by
Raydon Wings Ltd
Raydon
Suffolk

www.raydonwings.co.uk

British Library Cataloguing-in-Publication Data
A catalogue record for this book is available from the British Library.

ISBN: 978-0-9556066-0-1

Published by Raydon Wings Limited

Printed and bound in Great Britain by Biddles Ltd, King's Lynn, Norfolk

Acknowledgements

Imperial War Museum Records.

Mr Gordon Ramsey.

Mr Gordon Smith.

Mr David Page, Navy-photos.

Mr Peter Swarbrick, Ships Pictures.

Mr Jamie Wilson, Spellmount.

The Coggeshall Museum.

Mrs S.A.Dickinson – Air Historical Branch – MOD.

The Franklin D. Roosevelt Presidential Library and Museum.

A&C Black Publishers – Noel Coward poem, 'Lie in the Dark and Listen'.

Roy Conyers Nesbit & Georges Van Acker.

Mr Jerry Scutts.

Mr Jason Pipes, Feldgrau.

Mr Geoff Slee, Combined Operations.

Essex Record Office.

Mr Ken Delve.

Mr Andrew Pirie.

Mr Tony Gearey.

Mr Dilip Sarkar.

Material has been accessed from a number of sources, including the internet, and in some cases it has not been possible to determine copyright ownership - all material has been used in good faith. While I have endeavoured to follow the path of complete accuracy in all sections of this journal, I request to be forgiven for straying into unknown territory. It has purely arisen from my efforts to seek fact.

I am most grateful to all those who have given advice and assistance in my efforts to expand my father's diary. My thanks must go to Kimberly, my daughter, and Tyson, my son, for their support and help during the construction of this journal, and I would also like to extend my thanks to my cousin Sue Bronniman for enlightenment concerning our family history - most interesting!

I am most grateful to my mother, Ena Anderson and my uncle, Hedley Pudsey, for digging into the depths of their fading memories to help fill in the gaps of our family life during 1941. I must also thank those who care for them and help to massage their memories of the past.

Finally, I must thank my wife Priscilla, for her eternal patience and understanding, as I have forsaken my household tasks in this labour of love.

John N. Anderson

FOREWORD

This is a story very close to me, and one that I could not ignore. It started when looking through some of my father's papers a few years ago as I was seeking correspondence my mother had requested, but had forgotten the location. In a hidden section of our family bureau I came across a very small diary - no more than three and a half inches by two inches and a mere half an inch thick. But it was the content that interested me and rapidly raised the awareness of the traumas and constant stress that everyone lived through during the dark and dangerous days of World War II. My parents lived in Coggeshall, and indeed, at the time of writing, my mother and her brother and sisters still live within the proximity of this small Essex town. Although there were incidents recorded in and around the town during the course of the war, it could never be claimed as being in the front line. However, it was the route for many of the German bombers. With their harsh unsynchronised engines they forged relentlessly to their targets to drop their deadly loads on the helpless citizens in many towns and cities across the British Isles. For that reason it was the war in the air that scared them the most as it brought the conflict frighteningly close: virtually on a daily basis. Father took his responsibility as an Air Raid Precautions Officer very seriously, and even though he took his turn at his workplace, my mother told me that he also managed to fit in his duty locally. In fact, she confirmed that when an alarm was raised, he used to bundle her and my sister Jane into the shelter at the bottom of the garden and then go off to do his rounds.

Consequently, the war did have its moments; especially on one occasion when bombs dropped on the church and demolished a large proportion of the tower. Coggeshall folklore claims that only 150 yards away in the 'Woolpack' those who were enjoying a leisurely evening were totally unaware that any incident had occurred! It was argued that because the bomb went into the tower, the blast

The devastation at St Peter-ad-Vincula, Coggeshall, 16th September 1940.
(Source: Coggeshall Museum)

went vertically and not horizontally and although unlikely, it bore a modicum of credence, as the weak beer served during those traumatic days was not the strongest to have caused inebriation! May I assure the reader that the bombing was a genuine happening, and not, as well known in legend, a 'Coggeshall job'! Today, both the pub and the renovated church stand testament to the value of pleasure and religion - and long may they both prosper!

However, this book is more than a record of isolated happenings. It is a journal of an 'ordinary' man and his family during 1941; their hopes and fears, their work and leisure, and a view of the progress of the war through the eyes and ears of a member of the British public whose only avenue for information came from the 'wireless', newspapers, cinema and local happenings. The diary cannot claim to be a literary masterpiece, as it is nearly always restricted to one sentence for every event, but it surely gives an insight into the progress of the war and the daily happenings in Britain and around the world. For that reason, the contents are valid for many who survived the ordeal, and offers a record of the terrible events that shaped and changed our world as we see it today

I hope that the reader will understand that, in the light of the carnage experienced by many, my father and family did not suffer as others did during the blitz periods of destruction in the towns and cities, but as an observer he has managed to give an insight as to what did happen. I have purely endeavoured, with the benefit of hindsight, to expand and enlighten the reader of the actual events as they unfolded in his diary during that momentous year - 1941.

John Anderson
2007

PROFILE

Born on the 1ˢᵗ November 1908, Peter Angus Anderson was a bonny babe. His parents, Peter and Helen, eventually had four children, two boys, Peter and Jack, and two girls, Doreen and Helen. In his earlier years their home was in Scotland where his father ran a brewery - in fact, I was told it was the first nationalised brewery in that country! My paternal grandfather (who had passed away before I was born), very much enjoyed his work, so much so that he had a gregarious disposition and had many friends. It was quite well known that on frequent occasions, after socialising and imbibing of the amber nectar, and dressed in his best outfit with spats, bowler, and an umbrella over his arm, he would be led to his front door to lean and wait for my grandmother to open up and let him in. She must have been very patient.

However, my father had a tough but enjoyable early life, and at the age of seven had just started school at George Herriots School - a very notable teaching establishment, which still flourishes today. Even at an early age he began to excel in sports, and was also blessed with an artistic streak that regretfully was never to emerge beyond his youth.

But, within a very short period, there appeared to be problems associated with my grandfather's business, and consequently my father had to leave the school into which he had settled and enjoyed. Work for my grandfather was hard to find, and the difficulties of obtaining a job in Scotland led the family to seek other avenues of employment. So, the Anderson family packed up their home and headed south.

Initially, they moved to Coggeshall for a few years, and then finally relocated to Cressing Road, Braintree, where my grandfather was employed as a clerk at the Crittall Manufacturing Company, at that time one of the largest employers in the region. Upon leaving school, my father settled into what was to be a working lifetime with Crittall's, a very modern and progressive company who had already employed his father.

It was while he was at Crittall's that he became the sportsman. The Company certainly had the facilities for young working people to thrive in all forms of sport, and it soon became evident that Peter Anderson was going to become a brilliant footballer. Playing for Crittall Athletic from their home ground at Cressing Road, Braintree, he eventually achieved many honours; first from the County of Essex, then playing for the FA Eleven fifteen times, until he reached the pinnacle of his game by playing for the English Amateur International side against Ireland in Belfast. Back in those

England v Ireland – Belfast, November 15th 1930. Peter Anderson is back row, right. The photograph is inscribed on the reverse side 'A memento of an auspicious occasion'. Signed by Frank Hobson 15/11/1930

days in the early 1930's the professional game had really yet to emerge, and the fact that he played many times for the FA team, which consisted of the best players in the country, was a mark of his stature in the game. Although he signed for Tottenham Hotspur, it was the intention to keep the other clubs at bay, for those were the days when virtually no-one could afford to be a professional as the wages were so poor. So it was necessary for him to carry on his work at Crittall's, which he enjoyed, and he eventually became a leading expert in the galvanising process that retained him in 'reserved occupation' for the duration of the war. But before that terrible conflict came upon this country, he still had the benefit of playing the sport he loved so much. However, 'our Pete' as he was affectionately known, was also an excellent cricketer and tennis player, and it is fair to say that the rumours were rife that he could have made county status in the former, and high status in the latter. At that time, the seasons for these sports did not overlap as they do today and were very defined, thus allowing time to be spent improving other sporting skills through the seasons.

Work and sport was not all his life. He courted and married Ena Pudsey, the eldest daughter of Reginald and Beartrice Pudsey of Coggeshall. At that time it was a high profile wedding, as my future mother was well known in the locality for her singing and dancing ability and also for her sporting prowess at tennis. She also achieved the high honour of being the Coggeshall Carnival Queen on one occasion, which must have alerted my

father to the fact that theirs could be an ideal match! It certainly was. Perhaps there are parallels of a similar match today? Well…maybe not! Whatever the case, theirs was a happy and fruitful marriage.

However, during 1938 my grandfather became very ill and sadly died, leaving my grandmother with virtually no money. Grandmother (who later would become 'Nan' to all the family), being most resilient, survived the considerable shock of losing her husband;

Father and Mother on their wedding day – 25/7/1936.

much aided by the love and support from her now grown family. She was intensely proud of her four children who had matured into adulthood, who were married, and had by then been well integrated into the community.

It is at this point I will finish my profile, as the war, which had appeared imminent, then broke out. By that time my mother and father had been blessed with my sister Jane, born on the 10th January 1939. Like all babies, she was beautiful, and she carried that blessing through until her untimely death at the young age of forty-four years. Her loss was a tragedy for my parents, her husband and two young daughters, and myself.

So, with the background set, the diary begins.

The Diary 1941, actual size

The Family - 1941

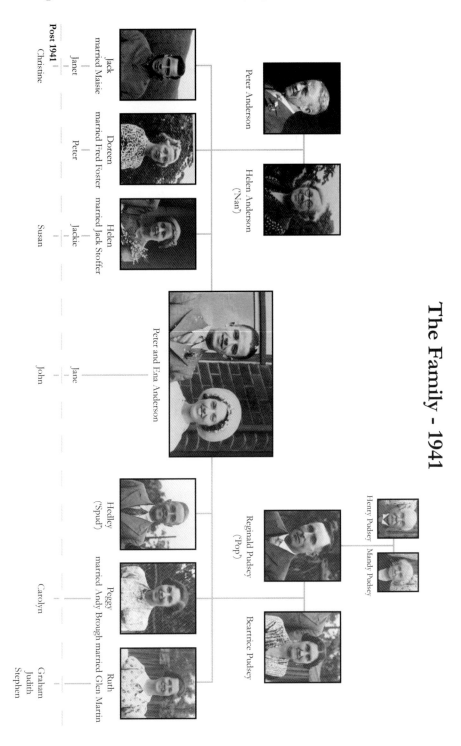

Peter Anderson

Helen Anderson ('Nan')

Jack married Maisie
Doreen married Fred Foster
Helen married Jack Stoffer

Post 1941
Christine
Janet

Peter

Jackie
Susan

Peter and Ena Anderson

Jane
John

Hedley ('Spud')
Peggy married Andy Brough married Glen Martin

Carolyn
Graham
Judith
Stephen

Reginald Pudsey ('Pop')
Beatrice Pudsey

Henry Pudsey
Mandy Pudsey

Ruth

Diary - 1941

PREFACE

On the 3rd Sept 1939 war was declared against Hitler, the Nazi fanatics of Germany.

He had already taken over the Rhineland, Austria, & Slovakia, and was threatening Poland, when Britain warned Hitler that an invasion of Poland would mean war.

Hitler did not reply but marched into Poland.

We declared war and within a few hours, France again became our allies.

Germany, by stages, overthrew Poland, Norway, Belgium, Holland, Denmark, and to the rest of the worlds horror, France, after terrific fighting, went under.

We were left alone.

Hitler had been assisted in all the campaigns by 'Quislings' and traitors. He will not be helped by these against Britain.

After the B.E.F.'s epic retreat from Dunkirk, he started his air Blitz on Britain. After terrific losses in planes – he failed to break Britain.

Things looked very black.

Mass raiding on the country started Sept 1940. Night raids were ghastly – bombs falling everywhere. Our church was demolished one night.

Coggeshall & district had dozens of bombs.

I was in Birmingham when the blitz started there.

London had terrific raids.

Morale everywhere excellent.

We soon stopped Hitler's mass day raiding – bringing down as many as 200 in one day. Night bombing more difficult to check.

Preface written by Peter Angus Anderson
January 1st 1941

Galvanising

The following memorandum that my father made at the start of the diary is presumably a reminder for setting performance temperatures.

Zincing (?) Pot solid
Lower to 780d F & hold for 1 day (24 hrs).
Then drop 100.
Flue Temp should be kept about 20d lower than pot temp. until zinc has gone solid.
Melting point 787F.

Then a further memorandum:-

Per F.C.W. to Mr Parker, Braby's.

Father almost certainly made an error in the initials as this entry in the diary appears to be written with undue haste. Later in the diary he mentions visiting customers with 'Pink' Crittall, and with **'WFC'**. After some research into the Crittall family history, it appears that 'Pink' is Walter Francis Crittall, son of Francis Henry Crittall who founded the steel window manufacturing business at the turn of the century. WFC had a creative and artistic talent and brought to the business design flair and innovation. He would also take a deep interest in manufacturing processes, and for that reason, and from the entries later in the diary, I am sure that he would have involved himself with the development, and marketing to potential customers, of the improved galvanising process on which my father was working.

The Process:

Galvanising is a zinc finishing process to protect metal windows and other products and components made from iron and steel that are susceptible to rust and corrosion.

The process of galvanising in the year of 1941 had been used for nearly 100 years, and varies little today in application. Initially, the component to be treated has dirt and grease removed by dipping in a hot alkaline bath, and then surface impurities such as rust are removed by dipping in sulphuric or hydrochloric acid. This process is called 'pickling'. It is then immersed in liquid flux - generally a zinc ammonium chloride solution - to prevent oxidation prior to immersion in the molten zinc bath. The bath temperature of zinc is set between 815F and 850F, and at that stage the zinc bonds to the component, covering it with very resistant zinc alloy layers, which are usually finished with a layer of pure zinc giving the component a resistance to impact. On removal the excess zinc is drained off and the component is vibrated, processed, and cooled in air or liquid. It is then ready for inspection.

JANUARY 1941

Wednesday 1   New Year's Day
Yesterday full of excitement. Got first bombs (3) on works. Rest fell in fields.
Dornier 215 300ft. Too close to be comfortable.
Spotter put us in holes.

This raid occurred during the morning of the 31st December 1940, as bombs were reported, in some records, as having fallen 'near Chelmsford'. More precisely, as my father has stated, they fell on Crittall's in Witham! It was not a good start to the year.

The raid was officially recorded in a *'Situation Report'* on the 1st January 1941, and signed by Superintendent Sheppard of the Essex County Constabulary. It covered the period from *'09-00hrs on 31/12/40 to 09-00hrs on the 1/1/41'*, and listed together with one or two other reported incidents, it stated: *'At 11-10hrs 9 HE* (High Explosive) *bombs were dropped over Crittall's Works, Witham. Two fell on a workshop causing some damage and one slight male casualty. The other bombs fell in fields.'*

The weather was most inclement with extensive low cloud, which confirmed the observation that the German bomber had been very low when the attack was initiated. At least it appears that the spotters were able to offer some warning prior to the attack, which gave the opportunity for the vulnerable Crittall employees to head for the 'holes' *(shelters)* - my father included!

As a result of the worsening conditions, no enemy air activity was recorded on the night of the 31st/1st January as adverse weather cancelled all Luftwaffe operations.

At the end of the *'Situation Report'* entries that were concluded on the morning of New Years Day, it was recorded by Superintendent Sheppard that: *'The total number of evacuees from London now in this county is 34,106. 20 have returned to London during this period.'* The logistics of coping with this growing mass of humanity must have been quite awesome for the authorities. Where do we send them? Where do we house them? Would they be safe? It was a tremendous and heartbreaking problem.

With frequent falls of snow hindering German raiders on the night of the 1st/2nd January, London, the Midlands and north-west England experienced small raids where destructive parachute mines were dropped, and airfields in the east of England also received some unwelcome attention.

~~~~~~~~~~

Ena gave me a whiskey this evening.
I needed it!

Father's favourite tipple was Drambuie, and it would be extremely hard to obtain during that period of the war. However, at least it was whiskey to calm the frayed nerves!

Thursday 2
General cleaning up of mess.
Shouldn't take long.

There is no record of the size of bombs that had fallen, but it is evident from this observation that no serious damage had been sustained, and the bombs may well have been reasonably small. However, they were still very dangerous with potential to maim and kill - Crittall's were lucky this time.

Friday 3
Still cleaning up in Main Shop.
Galv. Dept still running.

Father's main preoccupation had been the galvanising department. My guess is that he had offered a sigh of relief that his area of operation was still intact.

Night raids not so heavy.

Hitler saving up for something.

In fact, the very poor weather conditions throughout Britain and the Continent had curtailed operations by the Luftwaffe. Heavy snow, poor visibility and extensive low cloud cover had not offered the most ideal conditions for enemy bombers to find and attack targets.

Invasion appears to be the general opinion, tho' all convinced it could not succeed.

By this time the British Government was reasonably confident that the acute danger of invasion had passed for the time being, however, there was still the possible threat of an invasion in the spring, and it had been deemed wise by the Government to keep the public on their guard.

Roosevelt declares all aid for Britain.

In 1940, in spite of considerable resistance from certain sectors within the Senate, America had been edging towards assisting Britain with the struggle against Nazi tyranny. However, there were limits at that time as to how far

Roosevelt could proceed with the help Britain so desperately needed. Although there were severe restrictions, intended to keep America 'neutral' and not be drawn into war, in August of 1940 Roosevelt signed an executive order approving limited but valuable assistance, such as repairs for shipping, and the covert approval of the RAF 'Eagle' Squadrons, consisting of RAF (American) fighter pilots on the front line in England. However, in November, having further authorised substantial arms and materials, it became obvious that Britain lacked the means to fund the increase in assistance. It was shortly after that situation occurred, during December 1940, that Lend-Lease was first muted as a solution - but the urgency was growing for help immediately. Britain was crying out for food, general supplies and war materials. They had successfully beaten back the Germans during the Battle of Britain and had sacrificed many young pilots' lives. But now, at this stage of the war, the major threat to Britain's survival, apart from the receding possibility of invasion, was the threat to our vital supplies so desperately needed. It had been well documented by the British Government that its deepest concern was that our ships were constantly being tormented by U-boat 'Wolf Packs', which were taking an ever-increasing heavy toll on our Atlantic shipping.

To receive this declaration of assistance from Roosevelt was a major response to the current situation. Help was near at hand, but not as much as Churchill wanted. He wanted America in the war - and as soon as possible!

Saturday 4
Very cold.
Ruth started skating.

All the Pudsey daughters, and son Hedley (Spud) could be termed as 'sporty' types, and my Aunt Ruth was especially keen on horses. However, with the extremely cold winter, and unable to ride safely, she picked the only solution available!

~~~~~~~~~~

Ena, poor darling, has a rough time of it these days.
It is not bombs which keep her awake, its our little imp (my big sister, Jane) who wakes up calling for orange-juice about 6 times per night.

~~~~~~~~~~

There had been many bombing raids around the country during the night, with London, Derby and various Eastern Counties receiving unwanted attention, but no local incidents were reported.

Sunday 5
Works got 3 bombs.
Dornier 215.
Upset things a bit.

In an Essex County Constabulary *'Situation Report'* for the period *'09-00hrs on 4/1/41 to 09-00hrs on 6/1/41'*, it was reported that on the 5th January a further raid was made on Crittall's, and on a different location at similar times. The report stated: *'At the same time 10 HE bombs were dropped at Witham. Extensive damage was caused at Messrs Crittall's Works, and a branch railway was slightly damaged. The plane responsible for this attack afterwards machine gunned the town and broke a few windows. No casualties.'*

There was a further communication from the Police Headquarters at Chelmsford, to Essex County Control. It stated: *'Owing to air raid damage, the siren at Crittall's Works, Witham, cannot now be operated but the warning will be supplemented by the sounding of whistles by Police and Wardens.'*

As with the previous attack on Crittall's, weather conditions had restricted raids by large formations of enemy aircraft, and single aircraft attacking British targets during daylight hours carried out these 'nuisance' raids.

Heard above news at Doreen's (Father's sister), where Ena, Jane, & I went to tea.

Weather heavy & cloudy – ideal for low flying attacks.

As previously observed, there had been limited raids in other areas - certainly more than can be recorded in this journal. In fact, when researching the 'local' incidents, I was staggered by the amount of raids that were conducted by single enemy aircraft in our part of Essex over an extended period, and I have generally only been able to draw attention and expand on those of local, personal (to my father) and operational relevance and interest. For taking this course I must apologise, and although possibly insufficient, I trust that the reader will gain a 'feel' for the destructive offensive conducted by the German Luftwaffe and the tremendous tension and stress it placed upon the citizens of Great Britain.

It is quite probable that the local raids, including those on Crittall's, were carried out by low-flying Junkers Ju88's or Dorniers based with Luftflotte 3. Flying from the near continent, they were tasked to bomb targets of opportunity.

Monday 6
Gerry had another go but Home Guards had a pot at him & he dropped his load in fields 200 yds away. Think he was hit.

The *'Situation Report'* for this incident stated: *'At 15-20hrs 20 HE bombs fell in fields and allotments at Witham. Two failed to explode. Slight damage to roofs of 12 homes. No casualties.*

At the time, the District was under 'yellow' alert.'

It was almost certain that, as a manufacturer of war materials, Crittall's, would retain the attention of single raiders - but once again they were fortunate. However, it would have been an extremely lucky shot for a single Home Guard .303 bullet to bring down a German bomber!

Tuesday 7
Gen. Wavell taken Bardia. (Aussies) on to Tobruk.
Going strongly.

During 1940, after the French/German armistice, it was absolutely vital that Britain should protect its position in the Mediterranean. If Hitler had been able to control that essential area of operation, and had it been sealed from British forces, he would then run roughshod over Vichy France and Spain. Gibraltar would fall at the western end, and at the eastern end Egypt and the Suez Canal would fall under German control. Britain's last base within striking distance of Europe would not exist. The road to oil in Syria, Iraq, Iran and ultimately the Caucasus, would be wide open to the Nazi invaders.

There was one bastion of Allied territory that held on for the entire duration of the war - Malta. In the early years of the conflict Malta was isolated, but had a vital role in keeping an Allied presence in the Mediterranean when all looked lost during the darkest days. Constantly bombed and strafed by Italian and German bombers and fighters, the magnificent and brave defenders of this island were able to repel and eventually turn aggressor against the Axis forces. The horrific losses of ships and lives tasked to supply Malta, and the bravery of the fighting forces and the islanders under extremely desperate conditions eventually earned Malta the George Cross from King George VI. It was well deserved, as the sacrifices were great.

It was therefore essential that Britain should protect all those vital interests, and the key to that problem lay with the French Navy. It had to be neutralised to ensure that Britain's seaways, and the gateway to the Atlantic and Britain, remained open. For that reason, Winston Churchill issued an ultimatum ordering that the French navy fight together with the British, or be neutralised to ensure that their ships did not fall into German hands. The French ships were in many different locations, a few even in British ports, and there were several unsavoury incidents when some French sailors refused to fight with Britain, and yet others remained to form the basis of a Free French navy later in the war.

Several key French ships were harboured at Mers-el-Kebir on the coast of French Algeria and also some at Oran. On the 3rd July 1940, Admiral George Somerville, in charge of the British naval force based in Gibraltar, issued Churchill's ultimatum to his French counterpart, Admiral Gensoul. This was refused, and the British warships opened fire on the French, and consequently sunk one battleship and severely damaged two others together with a destroyer. It is sad to report that nearly 1,300 French sailors lost their lives. Eventually, those ships that remained in other locations were either taken by the British or scuttled by the Vichy French.

At a stroke, Britain had eliminated the threat of Germany using the Vichy French ships to clear the Royal Navy out of the Mediterranean. However, Hitler did not intend to cease his endeavour to remove British forces from that pivotal area.

Mediterranean, North Africa and the Balkans - zones of conflict 1941.
(Source: Gordon Smith, naval-history)

When Italy declared war on Britain in June 1940, the North African country of Libya was under Italian control, and Mussolini, possessing over 200,000 troops at his command in that colony, had decided to mount an invasion of Egypt. The offensive would take place in September of that year under the command of Marshal Graziani. To guard the gateway to the oil-rich countries around the Persian Gulf, and to defend their position in Egypt, Britain could only count on about 30,000 troops, led by General Archibald Wavell.

Having initially been successful in entering Egypt, the Italian forces were halted at Sidi Barrani.

By December the small British force, strongly supported by the RAF, had attacked the entrenched Italians, capturing many thousands, and sending the rest into full retreat, as it was Wavell's intention to neutralise the Italian forces by pushing them back into Libya. There were now two main routes open to Wavell; one to the Italian frontier through Sollom, and the other through Bardia, then on to Tobruk and Derna to Benghazi. On the 3rd January, the Australian 6th Division attacked Bardia, and with the Royal Navy providing heavy fire, and with mixed resistance from the Italian forces, the town surrendered the next day. Over 40,000 prisoners were taken, together with vast amounts of weapons and vehicles.

Greeks still pushing Musso thro' Albania.

The invasion of Greece by Italy had begun in October 1940, although, before that occurred, it was not a forgone conclusion that Greece would be dragged into war together with other Balkan states. It was known that the Greek King George was pro-British, although the Greek dictator, General Metaxis, was more inclined towards the fascist mentality. Although this situation had been difficult, it was by no means certain that Greece would commit itself to the war as it was assumed that the country would remain neutral.

Hitler, with the Rumanian oil fields in his grasp, and other Eastern European alliances under control, did not wish to see this balance changed. However, Mussolini had the Balkans in his sphere of operations, and wanting to gain more kudos within the Axis alliance, he invaded Greece - Hitler being unaware of his intentions until the invasion was in progress. Britain soon declared its support for Greece: support that would involve military action, and eventual disaster for the Allies.

From their base in occupied Albania, nine Divisions of the Italian Army were alerted to carry out the invasion. Mussolini also sought the aid of Bulgaria in this deed of deception, but they declined, and with winter approaching and with a paucity of planned air support, the invasion was not a success. Communications were poor, and deployment for attack was very difficult in the mountainous regions of the country. There were initial successes, with the Greek Army slowly retreating in some areas, however, the Greeks were noted for their tenacious and fierce fighting nature, and soon a disoriented and chaotic Italian command structure was struggling to survive.

In November 1940, the Italian 9th and 11th Army, supported by a further four Divisions, prepared for another offensive, which soon failed miserably in the bad winter weather. Fierce counter-attacking by the Greek forces, advancing into Albania, enabled them to capture key positions. It was at that point that Mussolini sought the assistance of Hitler who was, by that time, not deliriously happy with 'Il Duce', his strutting Axis ally. In January, with the Italians in disarray, Hitler started moving troops into Romania in preparation for the assault on Greece.

Wednesday 8
Everyone appears to have one eye on work & one on lookout for raiders.
He won't come so low next time & get away with it.

Low flying raids would continue. Arriving over England below the radar screens meant that little warning was possible, unless the eagle eyes of the Royal Observer Corps had been able to pick up the raider and track it inland visually.

It was on this day, the 8th January 1941 that Roosevelt sent his emissary Harry Hopkins to England, to establish just what Britain's requirements were to win the war. The goods and weapons that started as a trickle, eventually much later became a flood to feed the insatiable demands of the British people at war - but it would be at a cost, for, with the lethal U-boat 'Wolfpacks' waiting, the potentially wild and forbidding seas of the Atlantic had to be crossed.

Bren guns & 2 Bofors guarding works.

Bombing had been reported at Ipswich in Suffolk during the morning, but nothing had been reported locally.

Thursday 9
Took plaster off my arm & put another on.
Been on 10 weeks today.

The accident was probably caused at work. Although unable to confirm the circumstances, it may have occurred next to the galvanising bath. I vaguely recall my father telling me of an accident he had sustained when the zinc surface on the galvanising bath solidified. When he tried to release it some molten zinc sprayed out, and in trying to avoid it he fell and badly injured his wrist.

Had a quiet night.
Rough weather.

Clear skies tonight.
We're off again.
Heard bumps but nothing close.

There were widespread raids by several hundred enemy aircraft on many towns and cities throughout the country with Manchester and London receiving major attention. The Eastern Counties had many raids, but nothing significant was reported locally. It is quite possible that the 'bumps' reported were bombs being dropped on Hatfield Peverel during the night.

Friday 10
JANE'S BIRTHDAY (2)

My sister Jane was indeed a very pretty little girl, and my parents were so terribly proud of her. She had yet to grow up to be the extremely attractive woman who married Peter - an ex-RAF pilot. The delight was compounded when they brought two beautiful daughters into the world - Amanda and Claire. But that, as they say, is another story. The war goes on.

Jane

Closed down plant for repairs and alterations.
Letting pot go solid.
Stopped fans & stoker 2-0PM (835dF)

W.F.C. asked for programme, giving promises, material, etc.

Obviously keen to promote the galvanising process within Crittall's, and also for potential customers, WFC appeared to be pushing for a date when they could commence production.

Quiet night.

As a result of bad weather, the German target of Manchester was changed to a major attack on Portsmouth by 153 bombers. The raid caused considerable damage, particularly around the dock areas.

Nothing of significance was reported locally.

Saturday 11
Temp. of zinc 785dF (9-0am).

Shooting in afternoon. Pictures with Pop (Grandfather) *at night ('Typhoon'- Dorothy Lamour)*

Quiet night.

London again attracted a total of 145 bombers causing damaging fires in many locations. A multitude of smaller raids were recorded throughout the country, but none had been reported locally.

Sunday 12
Doreen, Mum, Fred, Aunt N. & Peter came to tea.

Father's sister, mother, brother-in-law, Aunt Nellie and nephew Peter. The stories about Aunt Nellie are legion - but not to be repeated here!

Raid on London 3½ hours.

Targeting the docks for the second night in a row, London was the recipient of a major attack by 141 bombers of Luftlotte 3. Many areas received bombs and there was significant damage caused by large conflagrations and explosions. A wide area around London was attacked, with Chelmsford and Southend being the nearest to home.

Monday 13
Pot now at 700dF 8-30am.
Opened up doors & vents in furnace and flues.
Pot 665dF at 5pm

Quiet night.

All quiet locally, but Plymouth and Devonport received the brunt of the enemy attacks that night, causing many fires in the docks and in the vicinity of the town.

Tuesday 14
Pot 535d at 8-30am. Zinc now solid and leaving sides of pot.

R.A.F. have started daylight bombing & appear to be causing considerable damage to enemy 'dromes and harbours in occupied France, Belgium & Holland.

During the previous day and the night of the 14th January, RAF Bomber Command sent 24 aircraft to bomb Wilhelmshaven, Dunkirk and Boulogne. Also 12 aircraft were mine laying off Brittany ports. Unusually, this kind of operation was called 'Gardening', where the mine laying aircraft dropped their 'Vegetables' in areas where enemy shipping movements were prolific. There were successes, but also many crews failed to return from those dangerous low level operations. Often operating on pitch-black nights, and occasionally in foul weather, the ability to find and lay the mines in the correct locations took great skill, a lot of luck, and frequently on longer trips, significant demands of endurance by aircraft and crews. It was a lonely and difficult task.

There were no RAF losses during night operations on this date.

Jane now making habit of waking at 8pm and asking to come in other room with Ena & I. She usually wins.

Quiet night.

There was very little enemy activity due to fog over Britain.

Wednesday 15
Pot 400d at 9-0am.

Tho' we know we will stick it to the last, Ena & I miss our evenings out and peaceful evenings by the fire. They'll come again – soon, we hope.

Little news.
Raid on London.

According to Ministry of Home Security records, bombing was widespread over London and the Midlands with 'no serious damage done', although as a tragic footnote at least 60 persons lost their lives. It was to be expected that, even though significant damage and casualties may have occurred, it would be in the interest of the 'authorities' not to spread alarm to the citizens by over-emphasising the effect of the bombing - although sometimes the truth could not be avoided. Keeping up morale was a key feature of their policy and probably understandable, but not entirely accurate in certain instances.

Thursday 16
Little news

~~~~~~~~~

Where on earth Jane gets her new words – beats me. She says 8 nursery rhymes right thro'.

~~~~~~~~~

Raid on Midlands.

Note: Some of these reports and observations from the 'wireless' and newspapers will have been taken, and these diary entries in most cases will probably have been written, on the next consecutive night to reflect what happened on the previous day. The raid quoted on the Midlands occurred on the night of the 15th/16th January.

Friday 17
Little news.

~~~~~~~~~

Forces in Libya still pressing on Tobruk.

Living off materials and supplies left by the retreating Italians, and by stealthily gathering intelligence, Wavell's forces were aware that Tobruk was very heavily defended, with extremely good fortifications around the perimeter. Although the conditions were tough and the defences apparently formidable, Australian troops of the 6th Division, and tanks of the British 7th Division had encircled the town and the estimated 30,000 defenders within a few days.

~~~~~~~~~

Greeks still advancing.

As a result of a prior agreement made in 1939, Britain had given a guarantee to come to the aid of Greece if her territory had been threatened. Although reluctant to take valuable forces from North Africa, in November 1940 Britain had committed a small number of RAF squadrons to assist Greece. They had also allowed some troops to be deployed in Crete, thus releasing Hellenic military resources in Crete to support Greece in her fight against Italy.

There was no doubt that the Italian invasion was in deep trouble, and aided by squadrons of the RAF, the Greek strategy of 'holding the line' in some areas and advancing in others was working successfully. It could not go without note that the RAF, fighting with almost obsolete Gloster Gladiator biplanes, had been inflicting severe losses on the Italian Air Force, and were a vital component giving protection to forces on the ground. However, there was also no doubt that very soon Hitler could not avoid intervening on behalf of the arrogant Mussolini and his incompetent army command, and therefore, to reinforce and support the Italian military effort, Hitler moved troops into Italy on the 20th January 1941.

Raid on South Wales.

There had been very heavy attacks on Swansea and Avonmouth reported on the night of the 16th/17th January with the dock areas being the main targets. However, there were also scattered and minor bomb attacks in the South, South-East and Midlands.

Jane's latest:- 'Goodnight Pete – goodnight Ena', with a saucy look.

Saturday 18
Not much air activity, but bombs fell a few miles away.
Bombs were reported having fallen at Chitts Hill near Colchester.

Snowing & blowing heavily.

America definitely for helping Britain – money no consideration.

It was not exactly 'money no consideration', for nothing was or is free between countries. I think that what my father meant was 'live now - pay later'! The Lend-Lease Act was in the making, and the arrangements were being defined for Congress to approve in March. Britain was at last getting sustained assistance from America, although there wasn't yet an abundance of war winning material finding its way to Britain.

Newest American bombers being flown over to Britain under own power.

That would have been the Boeing B17 Fortress 1, as it was reported that 20 were flown from America to Britain early in 1941. Based on the USAAF version of the B17C Flying Fortress, the bomb load was poor, and the

USAAF advised that they should be used for training purposes only in preparation for the more reliable and more effectively armed USAAF version, the B17E. However, the RAF did not heed the advice, and carried out raids during the summer. These were not successful, although they gave aircrew some indication of what to expect in combat at high altitudes - if they survived.

Should alter things a bit when we get these in quantities promised.

The Flying Fortress and Liberators would be seen in abundance in England when America joined the war and was committed to the offensive in 1942, carrying out very expensive daylight raids that resulted in devastating losses in valuable crews and aircraft. However, they always somehow managed to reach and bomb their targets whatever their losses, for on occasions those could be almost overwhelming.

Ena got rotten cold.

Quiet night.

As a result of snow falling in most parts of Britain, there were only limited attacks on airfields in East Anglia.

Sunday 19
Worked on shop alterations most of the day (at Crittall's).

Several Gerries about.
Put in dugout once.

There were raiders around and about the north of the county as an incident was reported at Clacton in Essex, which would have been sufficient to send Crittall workers to the dugouts. An early warning could save lives.

Went to Mrs J. to be with Ena & Jane.

Mrs Johnson was our next-door neighbour. Her husband, Claude, owned the cycle shop in Coggeshall. On the other side of our house lived Major and Mrs Burroughs. He had been soldiering in India before he retired to Coggeshall and had retained some of the 'eccentricities' of living in the days of the Empire. Often feeling vulnerable and sometimes scared, my father and mother could not have been surrounded by better neighbours.

Warning sounded at 7pm. Several bumps heard – London I think.

That was correct. There were heavy raids on London and Southampton. 54 bombers dropped 48 tonnes of bombs on London and the Boroughs, and a further 62 bombers dropped 57 tonnes on Southampton. Bombs were also widely scattered around the Hampshire area.

All clear 11-40pm.

Still got plaster on my arm. Sick of it – nearly nine weeks.

Monday 20
Horrible weather – rain, snow, & sleet.
Driving getting risky.

Everyone, inc. Ena & self, reading, talking & dreaming of German invasion, expected anytime now.
If attempt is made issue will be decided sooner.
I may be wrong, but apart from a few dropped by planes, they will not land, but will be beaten in the Channel.

Father's view had probably been gleaned from newspapers and the 'wireless'. There had been no doubt that the country was preparing, but it seemed pretty inconceivable that the invasion would be carried out during the severe weather conditions of January.

Quiet night.

A few bombs were dropped in Norfolk, Kent and Cambridgeshire, but it was only during the day as bad weather cancelled German raids at night.

Tuesday 21
Scattered daylight raids. Put in dugouts twice by spotters. Little damage.

It had been another incident at Clacton that had probably caused the alert. The German raiders were sliding in under the foul weather and doing their best to disrupt industry and not allowing the population to relax. It was a nervy time for everyone.

Hitler & Musso meet in 'friendliest spirit'. Rome radio state invasion in 7-70 days from now.
Sooner the better.

On the 19th January, Adolf Hitler and Benito Mussolini met at Berchtesgaden to discuss several contentious issues. All was not well with the relationship, although the veneer of friendship was evident to watching parties. With Ribbentrop present at the conference, the 'Duce' had been seeking German assistance with his conflicts in Albania and Cyrenaica, and they also discussed the proposed attack on Greece. One can only deduce that Rome radio had been fed the information of the invasion (which presumably was to be England) to keep the pressure on Churchill. However, Hitler's thoughts had moved to the East - and Russia.

Poor Ena cannot think of anything else.

To this day my mother still worries. She even worries when she has nothing to worry about!

~~~~~~~~~~

Horrible day – ideal for raiders.

As previously mentioned and as a result of poor visibility during this period, there were only isolated incidents during daylight in East Anglia and the South-East, and they were enough to disrupt normal activities. But, if the raids occurred at night, they would prevent that valuable commodity so desperately sought by the weary population - sleep!

Wednesday 22
Tobruk falling. Allied troops on the outskirts of the port.

Having first carefully reconnoitred and placed his forces in suitable strategic positions for the battle, Wavell's troops attacked Tobruk on the early morning of the 21ˢᵗ January. By the end of that day, after fierce fighting, virtually the entire town had fallen and Italian resistance had collapsed.

The Australians lost nearly fifty soldiers and several hundred wounded, but the victory had left Wavell with 30,000 more Italian prisoners.

~~~~~~~~~~

Put in dugouts twice. Nothing occurred.

The warning was due to a few isolated raiders sent over during the day.

~~~~~~~~~~

Quiet night.

~~~~~~~~~~

Quiet for several nights now.

The lull had been the result of bad weather. It was the opportunity for blissful, uninterrupted sleep!

Thursday 23
Tobruk is ours.
20,000 prisoners.
This brings total Italian prisoners in Africa to 100,000.
Things appear to be moving.

Marshal Graziani's army had been defeated, and there was no doubt that Hitler had to take action. That such a small force of British and Australian troops could rout an army of over 200,000 with such a small force of 30,000 was a severe blow to the aspirations of Italy and Germany in North Africa. On the 3rd February, Hitler told his Army staff that '...the loss of North Africa could be withstood in the military sense but must have a strong psychological effect on Italy. Britain could hold a pistol at Italy's head.... The British forces in the Mediterranean would not be tied down. The British would have the free use of a dozen divisions and could employ them most dangerously in Syria. We must make every effort to prevent this.... We must render effective assistance in North Africa.'

Went to hospital to see about my arm.
Plaster to stay on for a week or so longer.

Quiet night.

There was still virtually no enemy activity due to the very poor weather. This period must have been a blessing for a vast number of people living in Britain, as constant alerts and raids frayed the nerves. Unfortunately, it also gave the enemy a chance to rest and prepare for better weather and more damaging attacks.

Friday 24
Jane has rotten cold & losing a lot of sleep.

Lord Beaverbrook wires to C.M.C. (Crittall Manufacturing Company) **to say 'in view of threatened invasion it is hoped firm will work each Sat. & Sun.**

There was little doubt that this 'request' would have to be taken as an order, and Crittall's were swift to respond. Regarding weekend work; this has been confirmed by the daughter of a local businessman who reported recently that her father had been working at Crittall's on Sundays by assisting in the manufacture of Bailey bridges for the war effort. Although the development and production of these bridges in 1941 was limited, the demand would grow as the war progressed. It will also be noted that several of my father's entries refer to him being at work on the 'day of rest', so it was already becoming evident that the war effort would not stop at Crittall's on Sundays!

There was also no doubt that Beaverbrook 'galvanised' industries to do their utmost to produce all that was needed to repel the anticipated invasion should it materialise. His organisational skills were exceptional. However, it was those below him who had to bear the wrath of his tongue should the words 'it can't be done' be uttered. He took no prisoners. If a man was not up to the task, he had to go, and someone else was appointed who assured him that he would get the job done - and did it! Far from perfect in his manner and actions, he was however, a man for the time, and one who very ably partnered Churchill in 'getting the job done'.

Quiet night.

No enemy activity again this night. The nation sleeps.

Saturday 25
Everyone, including press, government officials & my darling wife, attempting to explain reason for sudden slackening in German Luftwaffe.

Very concerning, and something more for my mother to worry about!

Weather – sending his planes to Mediterranean – lull before invasion – any of these may be right.

It was almost certain from the records that bad weather was the cause of very little activity - generally poor visibility caused by snow, fog and low cloud, which was definitely not suitable for mass raids by the Luftwaffe.

No night raids for 6 nights.

After constant raids, this period of inactivity by the Luftwaffe was a massive boost to Britain. Constant interruption of sleep could be most debilitating, and those who worked during the day could ill afford being disturbed at night.

Working on Galv. Dept alterations all day.

Quiet night.

Sunday 26
Work all day.
Ena & Jane went up to Pop's. Jane's cold getting better.
She has just started asking her first questions – what you doing – who's that – where's Daddy etc.

Our African forces still forging ahead. Now at Derna.

Having taken Tobruk, Wavell's forces advanced to Derna, which fell a few days later. However, the North East African campaign was also securing the attention of the media.

In 1935, with Mussolini in power and wishing to show to the world that he could raise the spectre of another 'Roman Empire', he ordered his troops based in Italian Somaliland and Eritrea to attack Abyssinia. The evil intent was highlighted in their methods of warfare when the barbaric use of mustard gas on innocent inhabitants was revealed. The result was that the League of Nations did very little to stop this incursion, and only issued punitive sanctions. Major powers, including Britain, did not appear interested in the event, other than to recommend a plan to give Italy most of Abyssinia. However, in Britain there was a national outcry at this outrage, and the British Foreign Secretary, Samuel Hoare, resigned. The League of Nations proved to be a failure, which effectively encouraged aggressive nations like Italy and Germany to pursue their misplaced agendas. In 1936 the King of Italy deposed the Emperor, Haile Selassie, leaving Italy in control of Abyssinia.

North East Africa - zones of conflict.
(Source: Gordon Smith, naval-history)

In August of 1940, Italian forces, led by the Duke of Aosta, invaded neighbouring British Somaliland, forcing the defenders to retreat to Aden.

In January 1941, from bases in Sudan and led by Lieutenant General Platt, British forces counter-attacked the Italians and advanced into Eritrea through difficult and mountainous terrain. They took the garrison town of Agordat and headed for the town of Keren. Whilst Lt. Gen. Platt was leading his forces through Eritrea, a mixed force of South African, Nigerian and Ghanaian troops under the command of Lieutenant General Cunningham were attacking Italian territory from the south in East Africa.

British troops training Africans in anti-aircraft units.
(Courtesy of the Franklin D. Roosevelt Library Digital Archives)

Furthermore, crossing the border from Sudan, a group led by Major General Orde Wingate had been harassing Italian forces with the aim of assisting in the liberation of Abyssinia and finally reinstating the Emperor Haile Selassie.

Italians rioting in Tunis and other Italian towns.

Whilst I can trace nothing of these riots, it could be possible that, on about this date, Axis forces were taking over airfields near Tunis and the port at Bizerta from the Vichy French, thus possibly causing unrest within the towns in Tunisia and Italian Tripolitania.

During the recent month, General Wavell's Western Desert Force had captured Cyenaica and was on the border of Tripolitania at El Agheila. There they halted, as the situation in Greece demanded that troops from his force be sent there pending the forthcoming conflict with German forces. Two Australian Divisions were despatched, leaving one Division to hold the line in Cyrenaica.

Still quiet.

Monday 27
Associated Press Correspondent say's Germany will shortly launch biggest attack ever thought of, but we will beat them back.
In doing so, he predicts we will suffer tremendous losses – half our airforce, ¾ of our navy, & about 250,000 men.

If this report had been interpreted correctly, as the world's oldest and largest newsgathering organisation, Associated Press had obviously been of the opinion that an invasion had been imminent. Was this a warning to Britain, generated by pressure from 'dubious' propaganda sources within the German Reich? Regardless of the origin of the claims, Britain's defences were growing stronger by the day, and an invasion attempt that early in the year would probably have caused the enemy fleet to founder or be destroyed by the RAF and the Royal Navy in the Channel.

This, the British are prepared to sacrifice for our cause.
I wonder how far he is out in his calculations.

Originally scheduled for the summer of 1940, Hitler's preconditions for the invasion had never been fulfilled, as the prime requirement had been the destruction of the Royal Air Force. That did not happen, and it was the RAF's heroic fighter pilots who fought that vital battle, and turned the odds decisively in Britain's favour. As a result, Hitler postponed 'Operation Sealion', the invasion of England, on the 17th September 1940, and, following that dictate, most of the transport barges were dispersed, or more fortuitously, they had been systematically destroyed in their Channel ports by RAF bombers. Hitler rescheduled the invasion for the spring of 1941, but the omens were against him, and he had that other priority - Russia.

Quiet night.

Tuesday 28
Finished alterations at work.
Lit furnace fire midday & gave it a run till 5-0pm.
Let out fire ready for tomorrow when I will 'give it the works'.
Should take a week to melt the zinc.

Very little fresh news. Shipping sunk during last month 58,000 tons including allied losses.

The British fleet of merchant ships had been suffering, especially in the latter part of 1940. Half of Britain's food and two-thirds of its raw materials were being imported from overseas, and German Naval Command (Kriegsmarine) had decided upon an aggressive attacking policy to destroy those valuable commodities on ships destined for our shores. Vizeadmiral Donitz, who commanded the fleet of U-boats, initiated the plan for the campaign, which would continue until the end of hostilities.

When France had fallen in June of that year, U-boats began to operate from their coastal ports and the Luftwaffe had sent four-engine Focke-Wulf 200 Kondor aircraft to bomb the convoys from French airfields, thus giving both aggressive raiding components a greater ability to range further out into the Atlantic to seek our shipping. At that time, RAF Coastal Command did not have the ability to fly far out into the Atlantic and the Allies lacked sufficient quantities of escort vessels, so the German offensive was still in the ascendancy with their submarine 'Wolfpacks' and Kondor bombers mauling our convoys. The situation was becoming extremely critical, although with the arrival of winter, U-boat strength had temporarily declined and bad weather had assisted the convoys as they crossed the Atlantic.

However, during that quieter period of aggression from the submarines there would be no respite for the ships struggling through turbulent and heavy winter seas. The very serious situation had also been compounded by the presence of the German pocket battleship 'Admiral Scheer'. Since October of the previous year this massive ship had been ranging across the Atlantic sinking several freighters, as it carried out it's deadly cruise. As if that wasn't enough, since January 1941, the battle cruisers 'Scharnhorst' and 'Gneisenau' had also been disrupting and sinking ships in the convoy system. These two warships would remain at sea, harassing the convoys, until March.

There were few British Navy surface vessels to offer continuous cover to the merchant ships, and the time for long-range aircraft protection by Coastal Command had yet to come. The situation was becoming dire, and many brave seamen were losing their lives. The time was approaching for the Battle of the Atlantic. If this battle was lost, Britain was lost.

~~~~~~~~~~

There had been an incident near Braintree. The *'Situation Report'* stated that: *'Single raider. 4 HE's (failed to explode) fell near farm at Rayne. Number of incendiaries scattered in locality at same time. Slight damage to cottage and cattle shed. No casualties.*

District under 'yellow' at the time.'

Wednesday 29
Started up furnace in order to melt zinc in pot ready for production.
Should get good results from furnace for a month or two.

~~~~~~~~~~

Day raids by single planes. Sent to dugouts.
Incidents were reported in Essex, but none locally.

~~~~~~~~~~

Night raid on London. Planes steaming overhead as I write. 4 bumps
heard. Learned they fell at Witham. Little damage. Few casualties in
London.
The *'Situation Report'* stated that: *'At 20-05hrs, 2 HE bombs and 100 incendiaries fell at Witham, causing extensive damage to a large dairy and 48 houses, and slight damage to 27 houses. A minor road was partly blocked and damage caused to overhead electric cables and telephone wires. 1 person (F) was slightly injured.'*
This raid approached from the direction of the Dutch Islands. It is recorded that 37 bombers and 7 night-fighter/bombers came in two waves; the first wave by night-fighter/bombers probably causing the Witham report, but the main heavy bomber formation centred their attack on East London.

Thursday 30
Low clouds brought more single raiders than usual.
Sent to dugouts at times between 1-15pm & 4-15pm. Heard one or two bumps fairly close but nothing dropped within 2 miles of works.
Yet again, single German raiders targeted the South-East of England and East Anglia. Incidents were reported at Finchingfield and Clacton in Essex, and other locations in the region.

~~~~~~~~~~

Works now well away on 'new products'.
Begin to feel we are really contributing to war effort.
As previously recorded in the entry on the 24th January, the Crittall's site at Braintree built Bailey bridges during in the war, and it is probable that my father would have been involved in the galvanising process of components for them. However, Crittall's produced many other products for the war effort. In the early years of the war, there was a demand for metal windows destined for camps and government properties, pressed steel ammunition boxes, and pickets for holding down barbed wire. Late in 1940, 25lb high explosive shells were being produced, and later still, supporting ribs for temporary hangers. They made landing mats that were used when the terrain

was not suitable for normal aircraft operations, and also components for the Admiralty. Finally, later in the war, and to assist the landings at Normandy on the 6th June 1944, a large quantity of pontoons and other equipment had also been produced, demonstrating that Crittall's had certainly been doing their bit for the war effort.

The emphasis on 'new products' implied (correctly) an element of secrecy, and that would remain throughout the war. However, the Luftwaffe had to be aware of the capability of the Company, and for that reason, Crittall's would always be at risk from enemy bombers.

Will Hitler invade or try to push thro' Balkans?

It had been Mussolini and his invasion of Greece (through Albania) that had threatened the strategic stability sought by Hitler in the Balkan area. He had secured Germany's oil in Rumania, and had put on hold his plan for the invasion of Britain. His sights were now firmly on Russia, where he was intent on breaking the Non-Aggression Pact. However, Greece was more than holding its own against Italy, and Germany would soon be sucked into the Balkan conflict.

Friday 31
Few more single raiders.

At work for a few hours.

Shooting in afternoon.

There are several occasions in diary entries where my father records he is 'shooting'. When rationing began to affect the availability of essential foods, the need to supplement the basic requirement wherever it could be obtained became very important. Our family was fortunate, as my maternal grandfather's (Pop's) farm became the means to supply fresh game for the table. The ability to walk round the fields and shoot rabbits and game birds was a great bonus, but even so, each cartridge was very valuable, and my father became a good marksman. It is rather curious that, my grandfather, having been in the Army in India in his early years, was never seen to hunt for game with a gun. My earliest memories of walking the fields with him were with his ever-faithful dogs - the labrador to flush out the game, and the greyhound to hunt down the kill.

Quiet night.

In fact 95 German aircraft were plotted 'in-coming' and the main target was again London, with further smaller incidents reported in other areas, including East Anglia. It was a sad reminder of war that 28 fatalities occurred in the bombing of the capital, although far worse was yet to come.

FEBRUARY 1941

Saturday 1
Worked in morning.

~~~~~~~~~~

Shooting after dinner.

~~~~~~~~~~

Quiet night.
No activity recorded.

Sunday 2
Called at works for hour or so.
At Beaverbrook's request!

~~~~~~~~~~

Up to Griggs for dinner & tea.
This is 'Grigglands', the Pudsey house, still in the family today; not to be confused with Griggs Farm half a mile to the south, then operated by my grandfather, but now a small country industry complex.

The meal this day may well have consisted of game shot previously, which was probably rabbit, although my grandfather always insisted that birds should be 'hung' to enhance flavour. They were always 'hung' in the outside toilet! Personally, as a small and impressionable lad, I never liked utilising that essential abode in my younger days after the war, as the requirement to use that unwelcome facility was always tarnished by the sad and limp bodies hanging from the wall above, and the eyes just staring…at me!

~~~~~~~~~~

Air raid.
Several planes over.
There had been small-scale raids, with East Anglia reporting incidents during the day.

Monday 3
Still getting single day raiders.
5 times in dugouts today.
Altho' we heard bombs – nothing very close.
Single enemy aircraft dropped bombs during the day - again in East Anglia, but still on a small scale. It is certain that these 'nuisance' raids were beginning to annoy and disrupt the workforces in all industries, and play on the nerves of those of unsettled disposition. To the majority it would be a

severe annoyance, but to an unfortunate few came instant death or serious injury.

~~~~~~~~~

Raid on London.

The raid was recorded as being carried out by 15 German raiders penetrating inland during the night, with several bombs falling once more in East Anglia.

Tuesday 4
3 times in dugouts. No incidents.

These frequent daylight warnings were caused this time by Luftwaffe fighter sweeps over the East Coast. RAF fighters destroyed 2 of the enemy raiders; probably attacking allied shipping in the Channel, or inbound seeking targets of opportunity.

~~~~~~~~~

So far, U.S.A. have sent Britain 400 bombers.

One type of aircraft shipped over had been the Lockheed Hudson. They were a reconnaissance/bomber and were operated in quantity by RAF Coastal Command during 1941. Used extensively for maritime patrol, they were a potential deterrent against U-boats and other enemy craft. However, being lightly armed, they could be easy pickings for any German fighter that happened upon them. Also sent in reasonable quantities had been a light bomber, the Douglas Boston, which was well armed and could carry up to 2,000lbs of ordinance. In time of need, both had been gratefully received by the RAF.

Douglas Boston, American twin-engine bombers provided by Lend-Lease, are shown being hoisted aboard ship in an unnamed American port.'
(Courtesy of the Franklin D. Roosevelt Library Digital Archives)

~~~~~~~~~

Raid on Midlands.

There were 159 bombers reportedly involved, with London being one of the main targets. Also the Rolls-Royce factory at Derby was the target concentration point for 40 aircraft, but bombing was widely scattered and mixed results were observed.

Scores of planes about including our fighters.

Scouring the darkened skies for enemy aircraft, 60 night fighter patrols were flown by the RAF. This resulted in one enemy bomber being destroyed.

Wednesday 5
Pot now at melting point.
Looks as if I'll have to work thro' the night.

Night fire raid on London. 6 bombs dropped just outside Braintree.
I was at work & we were sent to holes 6 times before 12 m/night.

This incident occurred at Rayne on the outskirts of Braintree. As it was the second to be reported within a few days, it would be interesting to know exactly what target at that reasonably isolated location was so magnetic for the Luftwaffe - or was it just a bad miss? In which case, where were they aiming?

Although Chatham appeared to be the main target for 26 aircraft, raiders were widely scattered and were dumping bombs on any target of opportunity. There were a number of incidents reported in East Anglia.

Thursday 6
Worked thro' till 3-30am.
Drove home in snow storm. Snow a foot deep in places.

Went to hospital about my arm. Not healed yet – new plaster. This makes 14 weeks today.

Pot now OK for production. No snags so far.

Ena in bed now with flu! Temp 102½ d. Jane much better.

It was reported that no bombs were dropped in Britain during the day or night - a very rare occasion. The weather was almost certainly the cause.

Friday 7
Ena pretty bad. Temp 103½d.
Jane a wee bit brighter.
Doctor calling later.

It was Doctor John Moffat who, with Peggy, his wife, became close family friends. Father must have been considerably worried about my mother's condition, as that was some kind of temperature!

When I was 18 months old, near the end of the war, this fine man saved my life when I had an exceedingly serious stomach complaint which, had it not been operated on within just a few short hours, would have proved terminal. My deepest gratitude for his perception and diagnosis remains to this day.

It must have been a very worrying time for my father, with both mother and Jane very poorly, but having an excellent doctor in the town was also a great benefit to the people of Coggeshall during those troubled times.

~~~~~~~~~~

Quiet night.

Several bombs fell along the coast of East Anglia, but there were no reports of incidents locally.

Saturday 8
Ena's temp. normal. Feels very weak.
Jane about the same as yesterday. Sleeps most of the day & night.

~~~~~~~~~~

Quiet night.

Nothing reported locally as fog and drizzle persisted in many areas.

Sunday 9
Ena & Jane about the same.
Doc says Jane has had a flu germ.
Peggy (Mother's sister) is coming up each day to look after them.
I had dinner at Griggs.

With mother and Jane being poorly, it was 'café in-laws' for a welcome meal. While their condition must have been most concerning, my father had to eat and my grandmother's cooking was good - very good! I can testify to that!

~~~~~~~~~~

Raids at night.

There was little damage recorded as a result of various raids on airfields and industrial targets after dark; these included incidents in the Home Counties and East Anglia.

Monday 10
Ena & Jane improving. Jane getting saucy again.

Invasion still the topic of the moment, tho' I am still convinced old 'nasty face' won't try it. He is moving several divisions to the Balkans. I suppose to protect Yugo-slavia & Bulgaria.

Note: Father continues to mention the growing crisis in this region as the year progresses. Whilst he spells Yugoslavia with a 'Y', sometimes it is with a 'J' but most often it is spelled Yugo-Slavia.

Raids at night.

There was enemy activity over East and South-East England; notably Ipswich where there were 2 fatalities.

Tuesday 11
Ena & Jane still in bed but now OK.

Spotlight now on Japan. Will they move on behalf of Axis, or use common sense and keep out.
America particularly interested.

Having gained power between the two wars, and pursuing an expansionist policy in the Far East, Japanese extremists had ruthless aspirations to elevate Japan into being one of the great nations of the modern era. Therefore it demanded its 'fair' share of raw materials, land, and domination equal to those countries that had influence around the world. A key target of this greed would be the British Empire. With the rise in influence of the German nation, Japan could see and sense an alliance that would destabilise the world order and thrust itself into the major league of nations by this aggressive and potent policy.

To commence this national policy, Japan had waged an undeclared war against China from July 1937. Requiring domination of Asia and the Pacific, Japan was relentless in its desire for conquest, and although China resisted, the aggressors were not to be deflected from their evil intent. The outcome of the continuing Japanese policy for dominance was leading inexorably to war with other nations throughout the world, and the inevitability of conflict was sealed when the Tripartite Pact of September 1940 was signed by Germany, Italy and Japan. The Pacific region was in turmoil, and international justice had been severely shaken.

~~~~~~~~

Quiet night.

Wednesday 12
Ena up for a while. Jane up most of day.
Jane now her cheeky little self, but very thin.

~~~~~~~~

My job seems to be a real chance, if I can keep hold of the rudder and keep other hands off. We'll see.
My salary £350, is more than I expected from CMC at this stage tho' I didn't refuse it – nor did my darling wife.

As always in industry there is a competitive spirit amongst the workforce; and especially so in war-time, but I am sure that my father, who understood the galvanising process, was reluctant to let others of (perceived) less calibre start to interfere with his program for getting the plant up and running. It is also apparent at this stage that Crittall's were beginning to appreciate him for more than his football skills. It also sounds as if he was going to need all those skills to stop my mother spending too much money!

~~~~~~~~

There had been very little air raid activity recorded in the UK as a result of bad weather blanketing the country.

Thursday 13
Busy day.

~~~~~~~~

Short raid at night.

Bombs fell in London and the Eastern Counties with an incident being reported at Great Wigborough, near Colchester.

Friday 14
Hitler creeping into Bulgaria. Things on verge of storm.

There had been little doubt that Hitler was preparing for war against Greece. If my father gathered this information via the media, censured as it was, events would show that the British Government had already been taking steps to assist Greece in the coming conflict.

~~~~~~~~

What is Japan going to do?

~~~~~~~~

Turkey seems to be straight enough.

In October 1939 Turkey signed a Tripartite Alliance with Britain and France. However, following the invasion of France and after the devastating defeat by German 'Blitzkrieg', France eventually surrendered to Germany in June 1940. Turkey subsequently decided not to take sides in the conflict and declared itself 'non-belligerent', for, with France defeated, Turkey claimed that it was no longer bound by the Tripartite Alliance. Having taken that stance and eager to retain neutrality, it sat on the fence to see what would happen.

~~~~~~~~~~

Load of bombs dropped about 6½ miles away.

With London once more a target, other towns and cities were also singled out for attention, including the important port of Great Yarmouth. Various other locations recorded incidents but the raids were not concentrated, although the Luftwaffe again visited Great Wigborough; the site of the crash of a mighty Zeppelin that had been shot down by local defences in the First World War.

Father recorded the results of the local incident in the next diary entry.

Saturday 15

Bombs we heard last night were at Braintree. Lloyd's Bank and surrounding buildings badly damaged by one bomb, and second bomb fell in High School lawns, damaging school & setting fire to eastern Garages. 3 killed, 15 injured, reported so far. Lad in R.A.F. & his girl were two of those killed. They were getting married today. Small boy was the other – killed by flying glass.

It had been a serious and fatal incident in Braintree, as the *'Situation Report'* stated: *'At 22-00hrs 2 HE bombs fell in the central part of Braintree, completely demolishing a bank, 2 shops, 1 house and a garage. 3 persons (2m, 1f) were killed, 5 seriously injured and 17 slightly injured. The High School was extensively damaged, 200 business and private premises badly damaged and water and gas mains also damaged. Roads, A131 and A120 have been closed. The remote control system for sirens at Bocking and Coggeshall was put out of order but both sirens can be operated manually.'*

It was a distressing and destructive day for the town.

Simultaneously reported in the *'Situation Report'* was a further incident only a few miles away. It stated that: *'At 22-00hrs 1 HE bomb fell at Pattiswick, slight damage being caused to a cottage.*

The incidents occurred during an alert period.'

~~~~~~~~~~

Although bombs fell on airfields in East Anglia, it transpired that Liverpool Docks had been the main target for a sizable night raid by 79 enemy aircraft. Bombing was quite widespread, with many other areas throughout the country experiencing incidents.

Sunday 16
Ena & Jane now OK.

Uncle Tom very ill. Pleurisy and pneumonia.

My grandmother Beartrice Pudsey's sister Bess, was married to Tom Winterton. The Winterton's were a well known Braintree trading family, and were respected and admired. Their daughter Diana (Auntie Di to us kids post-war) married Hamish Barron, who was incarcerated in a Japanese concentration camp after the fall of Singapore and Malaya. He was Scottish by descent and tough with it - but he survived.

E (Ena), J (Jane), & myself went up to Griggs to dinner.
Shooting after dinner.

The more you eat the more you have to shoot! At least the family had the benefit of hunting for game on 'Pops' farm, whereas those in the cities did not have that advantage. However, I am sure that poaching was rife during the difficult period of shortages, and the addition of a rabbit or pheasant for the pot would have been a luxury for those brave or foolish enough to try and outwit the local gamekeeper.

Raid on London, 8-15pm – 7-0am, but planes few & far between.

Whilst there was mine laying by German aircraft during the night, it was off the coast between Clacton-on-Sea and Skegness. No other activity had been reported locally.

Monday 17
Germany putting pressure on Bulgaria & Yugo Slavia. Position uncertain tho' Hitler already has several divisions in Bulgaria.

Turkey still stand firm.

Japan & Russia still a query. Pro-axis Japan attempting to particularly harass Britain & U.S.A.

As early as 1937, Great Britain and the United States had been holding private discussions regarding the emergence of Japan as a possible hostile nation. As a result of the meetings, an accord was reached between their naval chiefs (the US Navy having been instructed by Roosevelt personally), that provided a mutual agreement, which stated that the waters of each nation would be used by naval forces of either country 'in the event of the two fleets being required to work together in a war against Japan'.

America had been adamant that the neutrality of China should be protected, and was most insistent that Japan should accede to the demands to withdraw from the aggression in China. Indeed, sanctions on many vital materials and components had been activated by America since 1939, which alienated both countries and raised the pressure to find a solution. However, Japan was not going to be tamed or intimidated by USA and Britain. Quite to the contrary, it was raising the stakes by being more open with its motives and had increased industrial and military production to incredibly high levels during 1940 and 1941.

Anti-everybody Russia still waiting to see what will happen.

The unholy alliance between Germany and Russia, effectively known as the Non-Aggression Pact, had been signed by Foreign Ministers Molotov for Russia and Ribbentrop for Germany just prior to the latter's invasion of Poland in 1939. These two countries were never destined to be 'friends', as their cultural and ideological positions were completely opposed - fascism and communism were totally incompatible. There had always been a mutual suspicion between the two countries, and with each in the hands of a dictatorial tyrant, all the signs were pointing to an eventual conflict. However, to meet their own ends, and to suit their own temporary convenience, the Pact was signed. Initially, it was able to offer some mutual trading, but their ambitions for world dominance were greater than the short-term benefits.

Britain confident.

Airfields in East Anglia were attacked during the night by a great number of Luftwaffe bombers and night-fighters. London was also the target for 40 German bombers; with the worst incident recorded being a direct hit on a shelter at London Bridge where, tragically, 90 people lost their lives.

Tuesday 18
Turkey & Bulgaria sign non-aggression pact. Hitler's next move.

Bulgaria heavily relied on Germany for exports and imports, as they commanded well over half of Bulgaria's trade; therefore the country was economically dependent on the fascist state. Although very well attached to Germany when WWII commenced, King Boris III had elected that Bulgaria would remain neutral. Despite pressures, he was able to negotiate terms to try and avoid joining the Axis, although he did relent and agree to have a pro-German Prime Minister. It was this latter move, which eventually resulted in Germany having effective control in Bulgaria. Following these negotiations, the government then agreed to support the Axis, finally ceding Bulgaria, which then became part of the alliance.

It is recorded that the Turco-Bulgarian Non-Aggression Pact was signed on the 17th February 1941. This reflected the new 'status quo' in the Balkan region, and consigned both to roles of neutrality. However, Germany occupied 'neutral' Bulgaria at the end of February.

In 1943, King Boris died suddenly after a fiery meeting with Hitler. It was a mysterious death.

We have dropped several (about 20) parachutists in Italy whose duty was to upset transport. They did – successfully.

Designed as a raid to test the accurate dropping of parachutists by the RAF, 'Operation Colossus' had been carried out by 38 highly trained volunteers from No. 2 Commando led by Major T. Pritchard. In difficult winter conditions, they were flown to the objective by 6 Whitley bombers on the 10th February. Although the danger was so acute that few were expected to return, they were tasked to blow up an aqueduct spanning the Tragino gorge in Southern Italy. This they succeeded in doing, although the Whitley bomber transporting the men who were carrying the explosives overshot the drop, and caused a two hour delay before the team had been able to pack their explosives around the structures and finally detonate the charges.

In destroying the aqueduct and a small bridge, their success was only partial, as all but one was captured. They had been heading for a pick-up by a British submarine but, due to one of the bombers making an unfortunate forced landing next to their pick-up point, the submarine was scared off; subsequently it did not appear, and shortly after they were apprehended. One, an Italian national, was executed; the one that escaped eventually managed to get back to England. The rest were interned as POW's *(Prisoners of War)* for the rest of the war.

This raid helped to form the famed Parachute Regiment, and created the germ of the idea that went on to become the SAS (Special Air Service).

Bomb dropped in Clare Road, Braintree. Little damage – no casualties.

The *'Situation Report'* for the *'Period 09-00 18/2/41 to 09-00 19/2/41'* stated that the Luftwaffe was: *'Confined to daylight attacks by single aircraft'*, and continued: *'At 16-30hrs 1 HE bomb fell in a garden at Braintree. A glass house was destroyed and a number of windows in dwelling-houses were broken. 2 females suffered slight shock.'*

Altogether, it was noted that there were 8 separate reported incidents in the locality during this period.

Quiet night

Together with the incident previously reported, and with the enemy operating in poor weather, the South, South-East and East Anglia still continued to experience attacks, and it appears that most raiders in our region were targeting airfields. They were probably night-fighters with limited bomb capacity - hence, it appears only one bomb was dropped in what was called a 'nuisance raid'.

Wednesday 19
Little snow fell during morning.

Uncle Tom about the same.

Have not mentioned this before, but for last few months thousands of troops have been moving by convoys all over the country. The roar of motor engines, tanks & motor bikes, lasts for hours as they travel by day & night.

Quote by US source:

'In February there was still much talk of invasion, spurred on by a statement made by the US Secretary of the Navy to the Senate Committee at the beginning of the month. It was reported that he had been informed authoritatively that the Germans were studying weather conditions with the object of seizing the first available fine spell in which to attack. All the signs were that the crisis would occur within 60 to 90 days (i.e. March or April) and there were indications that the Nazis might use gas on a large scale'.

Churchill was aware, via decrypted messages from the German code machine Enigma, that certain changes in German Air Force dispositions in Belgium and Northern France during January indicated no immediate cause for concern. A German broadcast in February added to the war of nerves when the announcer spoke of the special training of Nebeltruppe *(fog troops)* equipped with 'fog shrapnel' and fog grenades'. Fuel was added to the speculation when Hugh Slater, ex-Chief of Operations in the International Brigade in Spain in 1938, published his handbook 'Homeguard for Victory' illustrating seven invasion possibilities. 'Plan 1 - Encirclement, with vast numbers of landings by troop carriers and strong naval forces.'

My guess is that the other six possibilities would be equally as concerning to Britain, but Plan 1 was enough to scare anyone! However, the quote by Hugh Slater was written in 1938 - and Britain was considerably better prepared to repel all invaders by this period in 1941.

Raid on Swansea.

This raid was carried out on Swansea by 61 aircraft of Luftflotte 3, resulting in extensive damage being inflicted by the bombers. London, together with other unfortunate targets, suffered again from a further destructive raid. East Anglia experienced continued attacks during the night and several bombs were reported dropped by single aircraft.

Thursday 20

Went to hospital about my arm. Plaster to stay on for another fortnight at least. 16 weeks today since I broke my wrist.
While at Colchester I heard a Heinkel raider machine gunning the station. It was chased off by 2 Spitfires & believed shot down.

Although there were the usual reconnaissance flights by German planes, and one or two bombs were reported dropped in East Anglia, the only record that I can trace for this incident occurred at 11-25hrs, when a Bf110 fighter-bomber was shot down on a raid on Harwich. It was destroyed by AA *(anti-aircraft)* fire from the Royal Navy minesweeper HM 'Bramble'. It is possible that it may have strafed Colchester Station before heading to the coast. Records show no further losses during the day for the Luftwaffe.

America telling Japan to get off. She will fight for her rights in the east.

There was no doubt that, at the highest diplomatic level, America had been endeavouring to put pressure on Japan to cease its expansionist plans and warn them off the path of confrontation against American interests in the Pacific region. Although showing considerable restraint, America could no longer tolerate the Japanese stance in the Far East and had begun to sense that they must exert greater pressure, or the path to war would probably be inevitable. But, the diplomatic initiatives continued.

Another raid on Swansea.

Although a few bombs fell on East Anglia, the main target was again Swansea, which suffered considerable damage from a sustained attack by 64 bombers. Chatham Docks had also been attacked with serious fires and explosions reported.

Friday 21
America & Britain sending re-enforcements to Pacific. Doubtful about Japan.

By the autumn of 1940, America had already issued orders that the Pacific fleet should remain at Pearl Harbour, while other vulnerable bases were to be reinforced. Japan was placing pressure on the Dutch to release their resources in the Dutch East Indies, but with pressure from British and American diplomacy, this was resisted. Obviously the British and American governments were sensing that their Far East interests were now at a higher risk, as the Japanese were intransigent in their dealings with countries that they viewed as vulnerable to aggressive diplomatic pressure.

Uncle Tom still very ill in hospital. Very weak.

Gerry seems to be a little more active at night, of late, tho' the weather is still very bad. Raiders over East Anglia 9 nights out of 10.

Single raider dropped 3 bombs at Broad Green 8-30pm.

The incident file in the records of Essex County Council, Colchester Division: Lexden and Winstree, states that the bombs were dropped at Little Tey. A Ju88 operating from Gilze-Rijen in Holland may well have carried out this attack.

A further incident occurred and was recorded in the *'Colchester Division: General'* file, which reported bombs had been dropped at Thorpe-le-Soken.

Raid on Swansea.

Once again there was another damaging attack on Swansea and many other locations throughout Britain. Varying damage and several casualties were reported.

Statistic: It was reported by the Ministry of Home Security on this day that, from the start of the war, with figures quoted to the 15th February 1941, the following damage for domestic properties had been:-

Destroyed and damaged beyond repair   -   93,865
Seriously damaged but repairable   -   298,915
Slightly damaged but repairable   - 1,094,190

Of this total more than half were in London. Figures for Scotland were not included.

Saturday 22

Went to work in morning. Drove Ena into Braintree after to see Auntie Bess after dinner. Uncle Tom seems a wee bit better. Still very weak.

Lovely day today – no sneak raiders. Will probably get'em tonight.

Japan, Bulgaria, Hungary, Russia – position still obscure. Japs hesitating.

The Japanese were busy at this time with 'negotiating' their interests with Vichy France and the Dutch, and beginning to feel the effects of sanctions placed upon them by America. Furthermore, the agreements recognised in the Tripartite Pact with Germany and Italy was seen as an act of aggression against the 'neutrality' of America. Therefore, to protect its own strategic interests, Japan also needed to establish a consolidated relationship with Russia.

Regardless of the Pact between Russia and Germany, it had always been Hitler's intention to expand to the East where Germany could benefit from so called 'living space' providing labour, food and vital raw materials. In Russia, there was always a natural suspicion that Hitler could not be trusted, and as early as January 1941 he had issued confidential orders to invade Russia in a directive designated 'Operation Barbarossa'. Originally planned for execution during May, world events in Greece, North Africa and Yugoslavia forced a postponement until June. Hitler was over confident. His view that Britain was on her knees and Russia was vulnerable induced him into thinking that an invasion would be over in just a few weeks, and that the result of defeating Russia would mean that Britain would sue for peace.

Raids in North.

Hull was the main concentration point for enemy aircraft, with other locations in the North-East also receiving small raids. There had been no incidents reported locally - and there were no sneak raiders! It was a peaceful night for the Anderson family.

Sunday 23
Lovely day. No raids.
Gardening in morning.

The weather must now have been sufficiently settled for my father to make his first attempts at starting the growing season and preparing the garden prior to seeding. It must have been exceedingly difficult for him with plaster on his arm to 'Dig for Victory'. That was the phrase given to the scheme, and encouraged by the Government, for every person in Britain to put aside areas in their gardens and allotments to grow food for themselves and the nation. With rationing beginning to bite, the search had commenced for every possible spare piece of land in the country to enable food to be grown. Areas down to grass were cultivated, and Britain was geared so that every able body would be available to gather up the harvest in the coming year. The scheme would consist of all those persons who were not on military or other vital service to assist in all forms of work on farms and smallholdings throughout the length and breadth of Britain. The force would become known as the famous 'Land Army', and it would be those determined land workers who would carry out that vital task.

With his arm in plaster, my father could certainly have found a use for just one volunteer!

~~~~~~~~~~

Shooting & then tea at Griggs.

~~~~~~~~~~

6 Hurricanes roared in circles 3 or 4 times round Coggeshall after blackout. They were only 200ft up and gave us quite a scare before they switched on their lights. Night training, I expect.

Father's aircraft recognition must have been superb at night! However it is more likely that they were Defiant night-fighters according to records! With similar profiles and both powered by the remarkable Rolls-Royce Merlin engine, they would look and sound the same in a darkening sky.

At this point in the war, many people could discern the different 'sound' of aircraft engines and get a certain amount of reassurance if the aircraft were identified as 'friendly'. The simple rule was that if a multi-engine aircraft had engines that sounded de-synchronised or discordant then it was German. If the engines sounded like a steady 'growl', they were British. To those who could not tell the difference or just plain got it wrong, every aircraft was a potential threat!

~~~~~~~~~~

Short raids generally at night. Little damage.

There were scattered raids mainly in the Humber area, but also London and the South-East. Nothing of significance had been reported locally.

Monday 24

Was congratulated by W.F.C. (Director) on my report of alterations in Galv Dept.

That was indeed a feather in my father's cap. To receive praise from W.F. 'Pink' Crittall must have been well deserved after the earlier traumas of bombing, and the trials and pressures of getting the galvanising plant up and running as quickly as possible. He was certainly achieving, but of more importance he knew his contribution to the war effort was appreciated. Not sufficient praise, however, to warrant a letter of thanks from Beaverbrook! Never mind, the praise from W.F.C. was excellent for morale.

There is now doubt as to who will do the invading – Germany or Britain.

My guess is that he means Britain! Probably benefiting from a good night's sleep, my father must have been in an optimistic frame of mind at this point, as some indications still existed to suggest that Germany might yet invade - unlikely but still possible.

Submarines likely to be the only chief problem, altho' I have no doubt that we will overcome it.

It was ominous for the Allies that U-boat production began to increase significantly in early spring. However, British Ministries of Shipping and Transport (on the 9th May these Ministries would be amalgamated and known as the Ministry of War Transport) were also devising tactics to counter the submarine threat to Allied convoys. It was agreed that the best defence against submarine attack was a broad front formation with several columns of ships consisting of up to five ships per column. The columns were about 1,000 yards apart and the ships in each column had a quarter of a mile separation. In this way, the escort vessels job was made easier and it enabled more ships to sail in each convoy. Originally, those ships with inadequate or incompatible speeds sailed independently, but such was the loss rate, the ruling was changed in November 1941 to again include them in convoys, resulting in losses of those slower vessels being significantly reduced. The Allies were beginning to learn - but so were the Germans!

Raid from 9-15am – 12-20pm. Few overhead – small scale.

It was reported that a few HE *(High Explosive)* and incendiary bombs fell widely scattered during the night - mainly in East Anglia.

Tuesday 25
Uncle Tom slightly better.

Weather fine – can work in comfort – suffer at night.

The Germans – altho' doing a lot of shouting – do not appear to be quite as sure of the outcome of the war, as they were a few weeks ago.
Our raids on Germany are leaving their scars.
We certainly have ours.

80 RAF bombers targeted Dusseldorf during the night, although only 64 crews managed to bomb through complete cloud cover. Of only 7 loads of bombs that landed on the city, there was one claim for compensation for damage to a barn, and one civilian and two flak gunners were injured. That result really summed up the difficulty of finding targets in poor weather. Electronic aids and Pathfinder techniques were a long way from being available to Bomber Command, and many Allied bomber crews were lost during this phase. However, the vital point was that the RAF was taking the battle to the German 'Fatherland', and not all raids had been that unsuccessful. Of greater pertinence, the problem of accuracy had to be addressed.

Raid from 7-30pm – 12-20am.
Raid was on Suffolk & North Essex. Mine fell at Gosfield.

A total of sixty enemy bombers and four night fighters carried out raids, with Hull being the main target and East Anglia being attacked on consecutive nights. Three people perished in the local raids. Although 40 of our night fighters were operating, they only managed to destroy one enemy aircraft.

The *'Situation Report'* for the *'Period 09-00hrs 25th to 09-00hrs on the 26th instant'* records that: *'At 22-57 2 PM (1 UX) fell at Gosfield and High Garrett, near Braintree. A farmhouse and part of the farm buildings were demolished. Two serious casualties (1 male, 1 female) and one slight (female). Roads A131 and B1017 were closed owing to UXPM (Unexploded Parachute Mine) and local alternatives arranged.'*

Wednesday 26
Tired after last nights' raid. It was a bit hectic.

Altogether, during the attack the previous night, the authorities recorded 13 incidents locally. It was a busy time for the rescue services as they sought to bring some semblance of organisation to the increasing number of incidents. As the weather improved, so did the number of German bombers - and that situation was going to get worse.

Poor Ena is very nervous. Sends me to report on direction of every plane.

On this date, mother had every reason to be nervous, as the German bombers were preparing a ferocious assault on the residents of the county, and more significantly the town of Coggeshall, during the coming night.

It's a blessing Jane is too young to appreciate what it's all about.

Still waiting for Hitler's next move in the Balkans.

At about this time, Hitler had decided to move several of his bomber 'Gruppen' for anticipated operations in the Balkans, and thus away from bombing operations over Britain. But, to the inhabitants in our cities, towns, and villages, it was not evident.

We are ready for him.

Raid 7-5pm – 11-35pm.
Awful night – mines, bombs & 2 flares in Coggeshall.

During the night, parachute flares were used in abundance to illuminate a great number of targets for the Luftwaffe, as they spread their bombs and mines over many locations throughout Britain.

London and Cardiff received the main concentration, but North Essex suffered intense and destructive attention from the enemy raiders. The 'mines' described wreaked havoc as a result of their devastating blast effect on detonation, and it was on this night that the war came ever closer to the inhabitants of Coggeshall as they were dramatically positioned in the front line of the assault to receive those deadly weapons.

Thursday 27
Last night was a terror.
Several bombs fell near Holfield Grange. 2 mines near Gatehouse farm.
2 mines at Rivenhall. 2 flares hung over Coggeshall for 10 mins, Gerries hovering over them looking for targets.

The *'Situation Report'* for the *'Period 09-00hrs on 26/2/41 to 09-00hrs on 27/2/41'* records that: *'At 20-45hrs, 1 Parachute Mine fell in a field at Coggeshall, causing slight damage to farm buildings.'*

There appears to be a slight discrepancy in the number of weapons dropped by the raiders, but it was an incomplete report, as another parachute mine was discovered later.

However, Coggeshall was not the only place to suffer that night as bombs and mines were reported having dropped at Feering, Rivenhall, Abberton, Peldon, Great Wigborough, Clacton, Walton and Harwich. In total, 32 separate incidents were recorded, and it seemed like the whole German air force had targeted North Essex. It had been a terrifying night for the inhabitants of the county, and one they would remember for a very long time.

I grabbed Jane and told Ena to follow me to the dugout. First time we've used it since early December.

As was recently explained to me by my mother, as soon as the air raid warning was sounded, they would grab Jane and bolt down the garden to the shelter. When inside, my mother would place Jane in a basket on a shelf perched on the side wall, and hope that the cacophony of explosions would not disturb her too much and allow a little sleep. She

An overgrown, but typical dugout photographed recently. Substantially built and topped with earth, it would take a direct hit before casualties resulted.
(Source: Coggeshall Museum)

also informed me that my father would be at the door of the shelter checking the sky for any sign of imminent danger in their proximity. There was plenty to worry him that night.

12ft unexploded bomb found near Gosfield.

There was no report of any incident near Gosfield as a result of the raids on the previous night. However, it was very probably a mine that had been dropped on the night of the 25th/26th February as reported, but only came to light a day later.

~~~~~~~~~~

Quiet night. Low clouds & high wind.

Obviously, the bombardment on the previous evening had made it a tough night locally, and bombs also continued to fall in many parts of Britain. London and Cardiff were again the principal targets, where considerable damage and many casualties were reported.

Friday 28
Weather slightly better.

Somaliland practically ours. Italian resistance finished.

Splitting his fighting strength, with one party going north towards Abyssinia, Lt. Gen. Cunningham took his force and entered Italian Somaliland; the capital being Mogadishu, which fell to them on the 26th February. All resistance was over by the 5th March.

However, at this stage, the British forces in British Somaliland were isolated, and it would not be until April, when the Italians were fatally weakened in Africa, that a small force was despatched from Aden to recapture the British protectorate.

Musso's African airforce now wiped out. About 2 dozen only left. This should release some of ours.

As a result of Cunningham's advance and the taking of Mogadishu, the Italian Air Force *(Regia Aeronautica),* had been rendered virtually impotent. They were no longer capable of mounting any meaningful attacks and were a severely depleted force. In the drive through Somaliland, the South African Air Force Hurricanes and Gladiators of No. 3 Squadron, supported by four squadrons of antiquated bombers of the SAAF, played a major role in the decimation of Italian forces. During their skirmishes with Caproni bombers, and Fiat CR42 biplane fighters, a great number of enemy aircraft were destroyed, as the aggressive pilots and crews of Air Commodore Sowrey's SAAF squadrons created havoc in the air and on the ground, leaving wrecks and carcasses of burnt out Italian planes throughout the country. Mussolini's grip on East Africa became virtually non-existent.

Unexploded mine & parachute – dropped Wed. night – found hanging in tree, in Witch Wood.

The *'Situation Report'* was able to expand slightly on the note that my father had made. It stated: *'Period 09-00hrs 28/2/41 to 09-00hrs 2/3/41'* that *'No enemy act reported over the county during that period.'* That was quite unusual and probably the result of continuing poor weather as reported by him on the previous night, and was to benefit most citizens of North Essex on this night. However, as a conclusion to the raid late on the 26th February the following report was added: *'With reference to item 5 (g) Situation Report 49/41 of 27/2/41 an unexploded parachute mine which was found in a wood at Feering on 27/2/41, was dealt with by the Admiralty on 28/2/41.'*

Note: I believe that there may be a discrepancy in this report, as it is my understanding that Witch Wood is nearly 2 miles from Coggeshall just off the road to Earls Colne and therefore not at Feering However, both locations are on the B1024, but on opposite sides of Coggeshall - Witch Wood to the north and Feering to the south. But could there have been two mines? Father is quite clear when stating the location, which is also confirmed in a further incident officially recorded on the 12th May. Coincidentally, the same possible error occurs on that date also.

There is absolutely no doubt that the bomb disposal squads, whose job it had been to render harmless all types of explosive devices, were a breed apart. The Germans were constantly scheming to invent new ways to ensure that these extremely brave men could not defuse the weapons, and thus make them safe, by changing the standard method of disposal. Throughout the war, the teams safely defused many thousands of unstable or delayed action bombs, but sadly, on occasions, they were fooled. The outcome would be immediate and catastrophic for the individual whose job it was to protect the community from these potentially lethal weapons.

However, it is fair to say that during the war all protagonists employed delayed action devices, as this was a deliberate and potentially deadly way of casting fear and doubt among the recipients of the unwelcome weapon. For tactical and safety reasons it was also necessary for low flying aircraft to use delayed action bombs to ensure that they had sufficient time to escape from the blast of the weapon - but there were many occasions when, accidentally, the bombs would explode immediately and blow the raider out of the sky. Conversely, there had also been many instances when weapons that malfunctioned did not explode and the outcome would be an extremely dangerous and lethal situation if handled incorrectly by the disposal team. The mine at Witch Wood appeared to be the latter example.

To summarise, it was not a job for the faint-hearted!

2 short raids on London at night.

Although the raids were few, East Anglia again received some attention from the bombers, and there had been one reported incident of a lone raider dropping bombs at Stisted near Braintree.

MARCH 1941

Saturday 1
Bulgaria join Axis. This will not help Hitler much, but will hurt Bulgaria a lot.

On this day Germany moved into Bulgaria in preparation for the attack on Greece. The invasion would commence just a few weeks later.

~~~~~~~~~~

Gardening in morning. Took Ena into Colchester after dinner.
Bought new Mac, suit, & shoes for me – out of my money.

This must have taken a big chunk out of the family budget. Fortunately for my father, clothes were not yet rationed, as that would not take effect until the 1st June 1941. After that date, every person would be allowed 66 clothing coupons for each year, and that would have meant that a new Mac (raincoat) would have taken 16 coupons, a suit would have taken 13 coupons for the jacket and 8 coupons for the trousers, and finally, the shoes would have consumed another 7 coupons - a grand total of 44 coupons. So, even if one could afford the clothes, it was not possible to buy beyond the total allocated after that date. Consequently, many people made their own clothes from all sorts of materials, and ingenuity was needed to keep the family well protected. Although it was possible to be reasonably fashionable for the day, it was increasingly difficult to 'keep up appearances'. Some succeeded, but the vast majority of people had to 'make do and mend'.

~~~~~~~~~~

Navy officials exploded the mine in Witch Wood this afternoon.

This was presumably the mine that had been dropped on the night of the 26th/27th February. It appears that the official report differed slightly from the actual event, as it stated that the mine was '...*dealt with by the Admiralty on 28/2/41*' when in fact it was a day later. It is possible that it had just been rendered harmless *(dealt with)* and then exploded on site as the bomb disposal squad thought it would not be safe to move.

~~~~~~~~~~

There had been widespread activity throughout the country, with enemy aircraft harassing and bombing East Anglia's bomber airfields, as well as several other raids on towns and cities during the night.

Sunday 2
Poured in the morning. Tinkered on car before lunch.
Mr & Mrs Pudsey & Hedley came up to tea.

Everything stopped for tea!

Pop, Spud & I walked to see the mine crater at Gatehouse Farm.
86ft across 41ft deep.
The mess it made in the meadow was incredible. Lumps of earth 6ft diam. Thrown all over the place.

The Germans had possessed many different types and weights of bombs and mines by 1941. Judging by the size of the crater, the land-mine dropped near Gatehouse Farm was probably a parachute mine, 8'8" in length and designated 'Luftmine B', which weighed 1,000kg *(one tonne)*. Due to the weight of the weapon, it had to be dropped by parachute with a descent speed of no more than 40mph, or else the clockwork fuse would not operate as the mine struck the ground. It was a terrifying weapon.

The explosive effect of a mine was catastrophic, and it can only be imagined what terrible destruction would result from the detonation of one of those weapons in built up areas. It would be a massive explosion, inevitably leading to devastation and carnage. In the above incident, Coggeshall and its inhabitants were lucky - others would not be so fortunate.

Raid at night. Bombs fell near Waltham.

As a result of poor visibility, only a small amount of enemy activity was recorded in the South-East.

Monday 3
Spring weather.

Bulgaria join Axis. They are already under the Nazi boot.

Russia advised Bulgaria that they were not giving them any assistance, even though the Bulgarian government had effectively elected to join the Axis alliance.

Eden & Dill see Turkish Minister.
Talks very satisfactory.

The aim of the visit by the British Secretary of State for Foreign Affairs, Anthony Eden, together with General Dill, had been to persuade Turkey to enter the war with the Allies. They failed in that endeavour.

Raid at night 9-30 – 10-45
Very little about.
Some bombs 15 miles away.

Cardiff and Newcastle were the main targets this night, with multiple incidents reported in many places including East Anglia.

Tuesday 4
Weather still fine. Little fear of day raiders.
They can't get far inland when our Spitfires & Hurricanes have a chance of getting at them.

This is a fair comment in respect of our fighters challenging the German daylight raids, but at night the RAF 'day' fighters were far less successful. It was predominantly left to the twin engine Blenheims and the single engine Defiants to carry out this thankless task at night, and very few victories were recorded until the more suitable and heavily armed Beaufighter, equipped with radar and cannons, claimed greater success.

~~~~~~~~~~

More German troops moving into Bulgaria.

~~~~~~~~~~

Quiet night.

It may have been so in Coggeshall, but there had been bombing reported in many areas throughout Britain, with Cardiff once more being targeted, together with smaller raids on London and Southampton. At this time, many night raiders were also patrolling over our airfields in Eastern England, looking for returning bombers and harassing and disrupting operations.

Wednesday 5
Russia & Turkey obviously displeased at Bulgaria's weakness.
Juga slavs may be next victims, unless Russia's & Turkey's attitude encourage them to stick out against Hitler.

On the 1st March, when German forces in Rumania crossed into Bulgaria with no resistance and were thus threatening Greece, Churchill instructed Eden to make an appeal to Yugoslavia to continue with its policy to resist any aggression and not to allow the movement of foreign troops on its territory. However, Yugoslavia did not protest to this incursion, and it therefore became a concern to the Turkish government that their own neutrality was being threatened.

This was a blow to countries that had protected their position of neutrality, and did not sit well with Russia as a so-called ally of Germany. The warning signs were apparent to most - except Stalin.

~~~~~~~~~~

Not so many night bombers coming in lately. May be the weather has been against them.

Raid 7-30 – 10-30pm
  Due to unsuitable weather conditions, there were very few raids during the night, and those only by single intruders.

Thursday 6
Britain breaks diplomatic relations with Bulgaria.
Does not necessarily mean a declaration of war.

Constable Lewis called about registration of my car. I omitted to inform council of transfer.
  There was certainly a great deal of 'authority' regarding procedures during the war in the interest of security. I doubt that this personal visit by a constable regarding his car registration would occur today, and it can only be presumed that, at some time in the recent past, my father had changed his car.

Early raid 7-0pm – 7-30pm.
Nothing heard.
  There was limited Luftwaffe activity on East Anglia's coastal towns during the evening, although little damage had been reported.
  This was also a significant date, for, although small by comparison with what had previously occurred and what would happen later, it would be the last daylight raid on London until the 17th July 1942.

Had new plaster on my arm today. (41/2 months).

Friday 7
Mucky day. Raining all day – low clouds.

Several A.R. warnings. Sent to cover once.

100 Enemy planes raid Malta. 17 shot down & a number unlikely to reach home. R.A.F. lost 1 fighter.
  With regard to the raids reported in this entry, the Luftwaffe caused great damage to airfields and aircraft. Against heavy odds, RAF fighters and ground defences accounted for 16 of the enemy raiders.

The number and intensity of raids on Malta by Axis aircraft proportionately exceeded those carried out during the Battle of Britain. Predominantly targeted by Italian aircraft during the early stages of the war, the vital strategic importance of Malta to the Allies in the Mediterranean encouraged Germany to reinforce support for the flagging Italian air force with growing numbers of bombers and fighters. But, Malta held on, as limited numbers of RAF fighters continued to resist with increasing desperation.

Navy raids German occupied Norwegian island. Sink 18,000 tons shipping – do great damage – take 215 prisoners.

It had been Winston Churchill's directive to harass all west coast shores that had become German occupied territories. The Lofoten Islands, adjacent to the Norwegian coast and close to the Arctic Circle, evolved as a base contributing to the German war effort by producing herring oil, which was processed into glycerin used in the manufacture of munitions. Therefore, realising the importance of that commodity, it was vital to disturb the occupying forces and their installations.

With the Royal Navy providing cover, a Combined Operations raid designated 'Operation Claymore', consisting of No. 3 and 4 Commando, assaulted the Islands and destroyed herring oil factories, 11 ships and petrol dumps. There was also an unexpected bonus. The raiding parties were able to relieve the occupiers of spare rotor ciphers for the German Enigma coding machine, which was a valuable find to assist the British Ultra code-breakers at Bletchley Park.

Many bombing incidents were recorded in East Anglia during the day, with Clacton in particular receiving the attention of enemy raiders. None were recorded at night.

Saturday 8
Went to hospital in morning. To Braintree pictures after dinner with Pop, Spud, & Ruth, to see 'I love you again' (Myrna Loy & W. Powell)

Balkan situation nearing crisis. Hitler settled in Bulgaria may make a move to help Musso out of trouble.

It would not be long in coming. German forces were poised to strike at Greece within a month.

Big raid on London. 8-30 – 11-45 P.M. Real ol' timer. Planes overhead all the while, but ended before midnight.

125 aircraft bombed London during darkness. Significantly, it was the night that Buckingham Palace was bombed. Fortunately, the King and Queen were not in residence at the time. It was also the night that the Café de Paris, supposedly the safest restaurant in the City, was bombed, killing 34 people who were trying to enjoy a little London nightlife. Whether or not this was reported in the newspapers the following day, father has not seen fit to record it. South-East and Eastern Regions also had their fair share of raids, including Halstead and Colchester locally, so it is understandable that there was so much aerial activity.

He111 flying over Surrey Docks, London, 1941
(Source: Southwark Library Collection)

Although Spitfires shot down one aircraft during the day, over 50 RAF night fighters were on patrol during the night, but no raiders were claimed.

Sunday 9
Miserable day. Drizzle. Two warnings before breakfast.

Garden waiting to be done but can't get on it yet.

Father foiled again by rain and the threat of bombs from the skies. It was becoming increasingly important for him to prepare the garden for his 'fruits of the earth'.

Altho' big events are expected any moment, there is very little fresh news yet.

Raid on London at night. Ena & Jane & I in dugout 8-45 – 11-45 P.M. Mr & Mrs J.
Nothing dropped close.

This would be Mr & Mrs Johnson, Claude & wife Agnes, who I explained earlier were our next-door neighbours in St. Peters Road, Coggeshall. Our two families shared the bunker at the bottom of our garden. I remember it well. Just after the war, it was used for storing garden equipment, and also used as a rather dank and dirty play area for us small people. However, we were not very popular with my father and Mr Johnson who always tried to chase us out - after all, it did have some strange bottles stored in it occasionally! Home made brew perhaps? Moonshine in the moonlight?

~~~~~~~~~~

While 94 bombers raided London during the night, resulting in significant damage to utility services and dwellings, there had also been widespread bombing in Essex (notably Dedham reporting an incident), East Anglia and other areas, with varying levels of damage called in to reporting agencies.

Monday 10
Foggy in morning but cleared up – beautiful day.

~~~~~~~~~~

Hitler crouching for his spring in the Balkans. Turkey says she will resist. She appears reliable.

It had become very evident that Germany was threatening Greece. However, Hitler had given a guarantee to Turkish President Inonu that no hostile action would be taken against Turkey, although, with the dishonest and ruthless methods adopted by Hitler, who was well known for betrayal, that message could not have been too reassuring.

~~~~~~~~~~

Japan quieter.

The confused and complicated political situation was to become more complex as the German/Russian accord stumbled towards disaster as the year progressed. However, in April, Japan succeeded in negotiating a non-aggression pact with Russia. This was also to the benefit of Russia who possibly anticipated the German intent to break their accord, and considered the agreement a tactical benefit to keep Japan away from their borders. This would change when Germany eventually invaded Russia in June, and although they did not exploit the resulting opportunities, it released Japan to consider advantages on their northern borders once more.

~~~~~~~~~~

Lease & lend bill passed in America. Good news.

At last America was committed to support Britain and other allied nations with all forms of aid for the extent of the war. It empowered the President of the United States to lend or lease, sell or transfer all war supplies, which included food, military equipment, essential materials and all forms of weaponry. The Office of Lend-Lease Administration was formed to oversee the implementation of the program when the recipient country had agreed to the terms of the Act set by the President. Eventually, as the war progressed, this task was administered by the Department of State. America was being drawn inexorably towards war, and the preparations to assist Britain would ensure that their own requirements to pursue an active war industry were also efficient and effective. America was not yet committed to war, but there was a certain inevitability as the year progressed.

Raid on London & North. In dugout 8-45 – 11-30 P.M. All clear at 1-30 A.M.

According to records, it was the Portsmouth area that bore the brunt of the night bombing, which was carried out by a large enemy force of 244 aircraft. The dockyard areas were the main concentration points, where extensive damage was reported, although other surrounding areas, including Gosport, received a severe mauling. Nearly 50 people lost their lives during this raid.

Locally, an incident was reported at Little Saling.

Tuesday 11
Hitler appears to have started his blitz on Merchant shipping. Tonnage lost last week third highest since war began. 148,000 tons inc. allied losses & 1 neutral.
Looks as tho' we are in for a rough time, but confident we can win thro'.

Since the fall of France the previous summer, nearly 900 British, Allied and neutral ships carrying vital goods for Britain were sunk. The German battle-cruisers 'Scharnhorst' and 'Gneisenau' were causing great concern as they sunk or captured Allied vessels, and there was the threat of further ocean raiders, the 'Bismark' and her sister-ship the 'Tirpitz', yet to come. Our lifeline with America was in great jeopardy. As a result of this increasingly critical and dangerous situation, Winston Churchill issued the instruction for Bomber Command efforts to be directed against targets that were the source of the threats to British shipping, which included U-boat bases and raids on German occupied naval ports. That directive had been given to Bomber Command on the 9th March and was put into action a few days later.

As from January, escort vessels were beginning to be fitted with radar, which enabled them to detect U-boats on the surface. The reason for the decision was that Asdic *(ultrasonic underwater sound detection)*, targeted to pinpoint submarines below the surface, could not detect them above. The convoys were susceptible to both methods of attack and until radar was fitted, the Allies were losing ships to surfaced submarines. The Navy, now reinforced by destroyers that had been on standby against an invasion on the British mainland, could still only manage two of those warships as escort protection for every convoy crossing the Atlantic. The destroyers, together with a small number of corvettes of the British and Canadian Royal Navy, were the only protection that could be offered to the poorly defended merchant ships at that time. Consequently, ranging further into the Atlantic, the enemy was still sinking ships.

America will now openly assist our shipping.

During the autumn of 1940, the British Government agreed a contract with the USA to provide the Royal Navy with 50 mothballed First World War destroyers.

Naturally, in that condition, they required renovation and re-equipping to bring them up to an acceptable standard. By the start of 1941 only a handful were in service. This would rise to 30 by May - but it wasn't enough. The US Navy as yet were not belligerent, but confined themselves to patrolling constantly expanding sections of the Atlantic. Confrontation on a greater scale would come later.

Destined for new duties under the British flag, one of 50 old destroyers crosses the Atlantic in rough seas.
(Courtesy of the Franklin D. Roosevelt Library Digital Archives)

~~~~~~~~~~~

Raid on Midlands somewhere. 8-30 – 1-30 A.M. In dugout till 11 P.M. Several planes about.

Birmingham and Southampton were the main targets, although many raids were recorded throughout the country, including East Anglia and the South-East. Once more there had been significant damage and many casualties. It should be noted that, at this time the Luftwaffe were paying great attention to dock and shipbuilding areas in towns and cities across the country in an endeavour to disrupt shipping allocated for convoys, and the distribution of valuable supplies at home ports necessary for Britain's survival.

Wednesday 12
7 Bombers brought down on Monday. This is best result for night raiders down for several weeks.

One Bf110 was lost in the Channel during the morning, but only two raiders were destroyed during the night of Monday the 10th/11th March - both Ju88's; one a night intruder, the other shot down by AA fire when attacking Portsmouth. It appeared that over-claiming continued to occur.

Roosevelt signed Lease & Lend Bill yesterday. Should be turning point in war.
Gallons of stuff ready to come over right away.

There is no doubt that America had anticipated the unique opportunity for their industries, and had responded accordingly. When the Act was signed, so the flood of goods and military equipment began to cross the Atlantic, with a few aircraft making the direct crossing, but the greatest quantity of supplies coming most dangerously and vulnerably by sea.

Troops in Africa still pushing ahead.

Fighting in the extremely wild and difficult Abyssinian countryside and supported by RAF air strikes, the British forces, led By Lt. Gen. Platt, gradually extricated the enemy from their entrenched strategic positions, and slowly progressed towards Keren.

Raid at night 8 P.M. – 5-30 A.M. Biggest this year but not much damage.

The main target was Merseyside where over 500 inhabitants perished. Although South Coast airfields were attacked, many other locations were bombed throughout the country, and five enemy bombers were shot down by RAF night fighters.

Combat Report, Defiant N1801, March 12, 1941

'Plater 35 left Tangmere at 1945 hours and was vectored from Beachy Head to the Inner Artillery Zone. No contact was made with enemy aircraft so returned to Beachy Head and orbited. Was then vectored on to a second raid and after a second and third vector Sgt. Gash picked up a bandit at 800 yards, about 700 feet above and flying on a parallel course on the port beam. The enemy was approached under the starboard wing and identified as a He 111. Enemy Aircraft was then engaged from 50 yards from this position with a series of one second bursts. First burst started a small fire in the starboard engine whilst the next two bursts set the engine thoroughly on fire. At this juncture, the reflector sight went out. Carrying on with night tracer Sgt. Gash transferred his attention to the cabin and fired several more one second bursts. The de-Wilde ammunition could be seen bursting in the cabin, which forthwith filled with flames. The bandit then fell off in a left hand spiral dive and plunged to earth where the bomb load exploded. The position of the aircraft has now been traced to Oakwood Hill, south of Dorking, and it turns out that one of the crew baled out and is now at Horsham. Another member of the crew baled out but his parachute did not open. The new ammunition was extremely good and the controller reports this was partly a C.L. interception. My gunner fired with his Perspex closed. I landed at Biggin Hill at 2125 hours having expended 1000 rounds.'

Report by Flying Officer F. Hughes with gunner, Sergeant F. Gash.

Thursday 13
Biggest raid of war on Berlin and other German towns. Cheering!

Both Berlin and Bremen, and also Hamburg dockyards were targets for the RAF during the night of the 12th/13th March. The bombing of Berlin by 72 aircraft was scattered and several buildings were hit causing a few casualties, however, little damage resulted from the raid. At Bremen, 86 aircraft bombed factories and the town centre with reasonable success. At Hamburg, 88 British bombers attacked the Blohm & Voss yards causing severe damage and large fires. The RAF lost 7 aircraft.

9 Gerries brought down last night over England.
Secret devices helped.

In the early 1930's there was a theory that if powerful radio waves could be pointed at an aircraft, there was a possibility that the so-called, and much sought after 'death ray' could destroy the aircraft. It was when this was being disproved that the researchers realised that they could get a return signal from the target, and radar was borne - or so the story goes!

Is my father alluding to radar? As the 'ordinary' working man, this information could only be obtained through the media - unless, of course, he was involved in some way in the production of components. Even if that were the case, which I doubt, the procuring authorities would not inform the manufacturer how the components would assemble to complete the eventual end product; this to retain security. Of course, if it had been reported in the media, it would not be detailed in any way and just related as 'a device'. More likely the successes will have been put down to eating carrots to enhance night vision as described later!

As recorded in last night's entry, only five bombers were brought down.

Lovely weather – full moon so must expect big scale night raids.

Big raids at night. 8-30 – 11-45 P.M.

Glasgow and Clydeside, Liverpool, Birkenhead, and Hull took most of the 380 raiders attention during the night, with significant damage and heavy loss of life being reported. In North Essex, further incidents were reported in Marks Tey and Clacton. 9 enemy aircraft failed to return; the result of nearly 300 RAF night-fighters despatched to intercept the raiders.

Friday 14
13 planes brought down last night. Good work.

Although only 9 bombers were destroyed over Britain during the night, it was subsequently recorded that 2 German raiders crashed into the Channel and 1 crashed in Europe returning from the raids.

Big raids by R.A.F. over Germany.

The German U-boats were causing havoc in the North Atlantic. To try to hit their navy at source, the RAF sent 139 bombers during the night of the 13th/14th March to bomb the docks at Hamburg - again hitting the Blohm & Voss shipyard. The raid was recorded as a success, although 6 of our bombers failed to return.

Hitler sending over shoals of planes now – taking advantage of the moon.

Were in dugout from 8-0 P.M. – 1-30 A.M. Big Raids. Glasgow appears to be getting it now. All clear at 3-30 A.M.

The intensity of the raids was increasing, and the heavy attacks continued as the Luftwaffe despatched 203 bombers to Glasgow, and a further 117 bombers to Sheffield - the latter attack spilling over as far as Leeds. During these raids, many inhabitants lost their lives and significant areas were devastated by the sustained and destructive attacks.

Further raids took place across the country, where again East Anglia had been targeted and 17 separate incidents were reported. A *'Situation Report'* for the *'Period 09-00hrs 14/3/41 to 09-00hrs 15/3/41'* recorded that: *'At 22.25hrs 3 IB* (Incendiary Bombs) *fell in fields at Coggeshall.'* Further incidents occurred at Feering, Stisted and Cressing, which showed it was quite a busy night for the organising authorities locally, and rather too close for comfort for the residents.

The RAF shot down 3 of the raiders during the night incursions.

A fine group picture of Coggeshall Air Raid Wardens – location probably behind pub. From left to right, back row: Brown, Sellers, Arnold. Front row: Pease, Browning, Shelley. The equipment is interesting!
(Source: Coggeshall Museum)

Saturday 15
Spent morning in garden.

At last the weather had allowed my father to attend to his garden and prepare the seedbeds for sowing. Depending on the type of vegetables he would be growing, the first shoots would be on show if he had been raising the crop under glass (if there was any spare!). However, if it were the formidable wartime standby, the brussels sprout, then he probably would be sowing at about that time of the year, and could even still be picking the remnants of last years crop. He would also be looking forward to picking spring cabbages during April - as well as sowing the winter cabbage seeds for the next year at the same time! As for potatoes and onions, they would be cast to the earth for their growing phase with whatever other variety of vegetable he considered suitable.

So, whatever he was planning to grow in the garden, it appears that the middle of March was going to be a busy time. After experiencing a cold and wintry period during the recent months, I am sure that he would have been relieved to be making some progress to feed the family.

~~~~~~~~~~

Took Peggy Moffat & Ena to Colchester shopping. Ena bought new coat.

With clothes rationing still to happen, my mother was able to buy a new coat. However, after the 1st June, this would have consumed 8 of her valuable coupons.

~~~~~~~~~~

Jugo Slavia does not seem to be falling to Hitlers plans. Turkey is behind her. Hitler hesitating.

Yugoslavia had continued to resist resigning neutrality, and had earlier indicated to Eden and Dill through the British Minister in Belgrade that if Britain was prepared to assist Greece, then it could also assist Yugoslavia! With the uncertain attitude of the Yugoslav government, British resources could not be stretched that far, as Britain's commitment to Greece and their ability to resist Germany was paramount. It was the gateway to the Mediterranean and fascist forces in North Africa - and oil.

~~~~~~~~~~

Foggy at night. Raid from 8-45 – 11pm. Small scale on London.

Over 100 bombers reached their target of London, again causing great damage and loss of life. Essex was among many other targets experiencing the effect of bombs during the raids, with an incident noted at Great

Bardfield. As a result of fog, only 20 RAF night-fighters were able to operate and the Germans lost one aircraft.

Note: It must be observed that, in many instances the air raid warnings would have been given to the public to enable them to seek shelter even though German aircraft were en route, but targeting other locations. The logical reason was that it was unknown where the raiders would finally eject their bombs; thus safety was paramount and caution advised. As it was, some enemy aircraft just dumped bombs anywhere deemed suitable by the crew, so any random locations might have received destruction from the 'dangerous skies'. Therefore, it paid to be cautious.

Sunday 16
Gardening most of day. Jane 'helping' me for some of the while.

At 2 years of age, my guess would be that much of my fathers' attention would have been directed at keeping the 'imp' occupied without her damaging any emerging vegetable plants! However, I am sure that Jane's busy little hands would have helped him; still struggling to carry out garden work with his broken wrist.

Roosevelt makes brilliant speech. Sending all help to Britain. Some already on the way.

It was announced that Harry L. Hopkins had been officially appointed to administer Lend-Lease.

This should assure our victory altho' we expect a rough time ahead.

Whilst the situation was appearing slightly more optimistic for Britain, there would be desperate times ahead for the Allies. It was only the decisive catalyst at Pearl Harbour, finally bringing the American nation into the conflict, that would ease the burden for the beleaguered British nation.

We appear to be having a little success against night bombing, using secret devices.

The 'boffins' were struggling with this problem. In fact, the early radar installations in RAF night-fighters had been quite unreliable and difficult for the operator to interpret height and relative position, and the range was too short to calculate distance accurately. It must also be pointed out that the operators themselves had yet to become proficient with the new technology. Consequently, the radar technicians had many months of continuous experimentation before greater success could be achieved with more advanced equipment, which would ultimately provide operators with improved results. However, the important point was that they were improving. That would become more evident as the year progressed.

~~~~~~~~~

Raid on Bristol. Quiet over here.

Bristol and surrounding areas experienced widespread damage, with more than 200 people losing their lives during the raids.

Monday 17
Cold & cloudy

~~~~~~~~~

Hitler & Roosevelt made speeches yesterday.
H. (Hitler) said Britain will fall this year.

Not according to my father!

R. (Roosevelt) said 'Aid on an ever increasing scale will be given Britain and so seal the defeat of Nazism'.

It must now have been apparent to Hitler that he had missed the prime opportunity to invade England. It must also have haunted him to think that America would come to the aid of Britain, and potent weapons of war would be hurled at the German infrastructure. However, not having the most rational of intellect, his fear may not have been in evidence. Roosevelt had no such illusions; he had fear, but he also led a nation about to be awoken from slumber. The American war machine was stirring, and Britain would be the primary beneficiary.

~~~~~~~~~

Jugo Slavia & Turkey still defy Hitler.

The situation regarding neutrality had become extremely tenuous. Yugoslavia was weakening, but Turkey, with its uncertain assurance from Hitler appeared comparatively safe from invasion. The complexity of alliances, agreements, and unreasonable demands, together with the ruthless efficiency of the German military machine throughout the whole region was a recipe for total instability, and a potential disaster for the Allied cause.

~~~~~~~~~

Troops in Africa routing the Italians.

Lt. Gen. Platt's force had arrived on the outskirts of Keren in Abyssinia, and launched an assault on the town on the 15th March.

Cunningham's forces were still progressing forward and approaching the town of Jijiga.

~~~~~~~~~

Gen. Wavell appears to be awaiting Hitler's next move.

I am sure that Wavell was more concerned about Rommel, who had recently arrived in North Africa! What would <u>he</u> do next?

~~~~~~~~~~

Raid 12pm – 3-30am.

German night bomber operations were cancelled due to mist, fog and drizzle, but in East Anglia and the North Midlands it appeared that enemy reconnaissance flights had taken place. There was no record of any bombing locally.

Tuesday 18
Hitler not yet moving in Balkans, tho' it is expected any moment.

As previously stated, the region was in a very difficult situation, with many inter-related alliances and agreements. It must be remembered that Hitler was a poor advocate of such arrangements, for if the situation did not suit him he would have his way by force. It was the ultimate aim of Hitler to cover the map with swastikas.

~~~~~~~~~~

98,000 tons of shipping sunk last week. Bad news, but it is lower than previous week. Hitler has definitely started the battle of the Atlantic.

On the 6th March, Winston Churchill had officially christened the campaign 'The Battle of the Atlantic'. In reality, it had been in progress for a considerable time, but the situation was becoming increasingly critical for the survival of Britain, and consequently the pursuit of the war against Nazi Germany and Italy. Meanwhile, it suited Russia to be the passive bystander in their 'unholy' alliance. No less evil than Hitler, Stalin was biding his time, for he also wished to capitalise on the eventual defeat of the Allies.

~~~~~~~~~~

Heavy raid on Hull. 9-20pm – 1-30am.
Planes overhead all the while.

Hull was the main target for 378 bombers. Many conflagrations were started, but with mixed and scattered results due to mist over the city. London again was an alternative target, although many other areas experienced raids. Locally, it was High Garrett, Abberton and Holland-on-Sea that had received unwelcome attention from enemy bombers.

Fog hampered RAF night fighters and the Luftwaffe lost no aircraft during the raids.

Wednesday 19
Moon is on the wane & we are not bringing so many down at night.
Our pilots can bring them down if they can find them.

We all wait patiently but anxiously for the device, which might stop night raids.

By that last statement, there must have been some indication leaked by the media that 'eating carrots' had not been the only aid in the efforts of RAF night-fighters to destroy German bombers. I cannot imagine that my father was privy to the secret of airborne radar - at least, not in his capacity at Crittall's.

The British public at large would have to wait until June before the secret was eventually revealed.

~~~~~~~~~~

Biggest raid of war on London. 8-20pm – 2-20am.
Awful night.
2 mines at Tiptree.

A total of 479 German bombers dropped 470 tonnes of bombs and over 122,000 incendiaries on London during the raid - the largest number of incendiaries yet dropped on a single raid in Britain. Parachute flares preceded the attack, with parachute mines and HE's inflicting heavy damage in many areas - especially the Docks. Numerous conflagrations and many explosions were experienced. It was a horrific night with over 630 Londoners suffering the ultimate fate.

'This was our home'. Victims of the bomb damage on the Home Front.
(Courtesy of the Franklin D. Roosevelt Library Digital Archives)

Further incidents occurred in the Home Counties, with bombs falling again at Great Bardfield. Also, Tiptree had been the unfortunate recipient of two mines, but it was the people of London who suffered the greatest during that terrible raid.

Although a few RAF night fighters were patrolling, no claims were made and no enemy aircraft were reported lost.

Thursday 20
Everybody wants the raids on this country avenged.

Bomb Berlin is the general cry. This would be good news, but our bomber command know best where to hurt Germany most.
They certainly have got these raids to come to them on a bigger scale than they ever raided Britain.

This prediction certainly came true - eventually. The great fury of the nation was avenged on the night of the 30th/31st May 1942 when Air Chief Marshal A.T. Harris, Commander-in-Chief of Bomber Command, instigated the first '1,000 bomber' raid on Cologne, and from that day forward the die was cast for the destruction of Germany. Following that massive raid, the enemy could expect continuous and unabated bombing during night and day by great and lethal armadas of bombers. But tragically, in doing so, it cost the lives of tens of thousands of young aircrews, the fine youth of all the Allied nations. Today, in retrospect, many question the value of the result of that destruction, and many question the moral implications of the decisions that cost the lives of great numbers of German citizens. Hindsight offers excellent conclusions, but unless you lived during those times, and unless the complete evil of the Hitler regime was understood, true values cannot be comprehended. A predominantly military war was very cruel, but all-out war against civilians was horrendous - and it was Hitler who initiated the carnage.

Short early raid 8-20 – 10pm.
Did not hear anything.
A good nights sleep was very welcome.

Tonight it was the turn of Plymouth to be hit by the Luftwaffe, and it was hit hard and a great deal of damage resulted. A secondary attack was repeated against London, but not with the intensity and damage of the previous night. Again, Fighter Command had no success.

Friday 21
Italy still being pushed back everywhere, but Keren (Africa) is still holding out, tho' our troops are besieging the town.
It's the Germans we want to see pushed back.

The town of Jijiga fell to Cunningham's forces on the 20th March. Their next destination was the Abyssinian capital, Addis Ababa.

Big talks again about invasion.
We have been told on the wireless what to do should the Germans arrive.

It wasn't until May that Winston Churchill issued a statement, and notes were produced for all householders on what to do in the event of an invasion. Whilst verbal advice over the 'wireless' was useful, the action should have been initiated much earlier.

~~~~~~~~~~

No raiders about over our way.
Very heavy raid on Plymouth.

Yet again Plymouth received the weight of enemy activity by 168 bombers claiming to have hit the naval dockyards. Subsequently, great areas of the town and dockyards were severely damaged, and coupled with the raid on the previous night, over 300 people perished. As a result of the multiple bombing raids, Plymouth was having a rough time.

Saturday 22

Internal trouble in Yugo Slavia. Some ministers went to make pact with Germany, others threaten to resign unless she stands out against Hitler's demands.

It had become evident that Yugoslavia was most unstable, and that the factions within the government were under severe pressure to capitulate to the pressure from Germany. Hitler was impatient, for he was preparing for the invasion of Greece.

~~~~~~~~~~

Russia encouraging Yugo Slavia & Turkey to resist the Nazis.

As a result of Stalin's vicious and unprecedented purges of the military hierarchy during the late 1930's, the Russian armed forces were severely weakened. He had a paranoia regarding the power of the military and considered that it was conspiring against him, and many high ranking and capable leaders were slaughtered to ensure that he remained in control. That decision to purge the ranks of the military proved to be almost fatal when it came to Russia's ability to defend itself in the coming months.

Stalin was now becoming increasingly disturbed by the actions of Germany, and although Hitler had given Turkey an assurance of neutrality, it would soon become evident that Yugoslavia would not be so fortunate. Whether it was his awareness of the obvious lack of strategic planners with the ability to co-ordinate his fighting forces, or his wish to retain trading arrangements with Germany, Stalin still showed distaste at any flagrant breach of neutrality, and thus he offered his support to those who would defy Hitler. However, he was not prepared to commit to a military confrontation with his Axis partner.

~~~~~~~~~~

Rotten weather – had four daylight warnings, but were blessed with quiet night.
No activity at all at night.

A small amount of activity in Essex during daylight unfortunately resulted in two persons being killed in Brightlingsea. In a *'Message Report'* sent from *'Essex County Control to Regional Control Cambridge'* it stated that a HE bomb caused damage to boats at Aldous shipyards and there were: *'5 or more casualties'*. It continued by observing: *'One naval drifter badly damaged 1 naval rating and one other unidentified killed. Sub Lieutenant of naval base conveyed to Essex County Hospital.'*

Sunday 23

Very little concrete news, nowadays. Papers full of various peoples' opinions, suggestions, & hopes, regarding the war.
A number of prominent people say we will win the war this year – others say 1942.
I think, personally, Hitler will be on the run at the end of this year and that the war will finish in 1942 – early in the year.

I do not know how my father could have arrived at this conclusion, other than a certain amount of optimism engendered by the media at the time. Surely those with the 'inside' information and intelligence in government and military agencies would know the true situation was still extremely serious and far from optimistic. They obviously kept their silence and let the media and others engender hope: although realism would only come after America joined the conflict, and even then the situation could only be viewed with cautious optimism for the future.

Quiet night. Clear, starry night.

This is strange, because research reveals that extensive low cloud with rain, drizzle or mist was covering most of Europe and the UK, but it is recorded here as a clear, starry night! One can only presume that the clear skies were a local phenomenon and that the general situation elsewhere was as stated in the records. However, apart from one or two isolated incidents, the weather conditions appear to have enabled much of the country to have a quiet night.

Monday 24

We raided Berlin, Kiel & Hanover, last night. Ought to be every night.

Altogether, 87 RAF bombers raided these cities, with very little damage recorded. The results were not satisfactory, as Bomber Command desperately needed to improve 'on target' performance.

Yugo Slavia resisting slipping towards Hitler, tho' internal feelings are fast proving anti Nazi.

The situation was very fluid, with factions working for neutrality and factions with pro-German leanings. Events would soon be taken out of their hands.

Turkey as firm as ever.

A little pickling drum I worked out had a very successful trial today. W.F.C. very pleased.

As previously explained, this is the process of removing scale and rust in a diluted solution of either sulphuric or hydrochloric acid. Father obviously valued the support by 'Pink' Crittall.

Quiet night.

Although recorded as a quiet night, a few bombs caused damage and casualties in Ipswich.

Tuesday 25

Yugo Slavia sign with Nazis (Non aggression pact)

It was on this day that the government of Prince Paul signed the Yugoslav Alliance with the 'Three-Power Pact', therefore becoming allies of the German, Italian and Japanese Axis. The Tripartite Pact was signed on the 27th September 1940 ostensibly promoting peace throughout the world, but preparing to 'receive the space to which it is entitled'. These words gave all parties in the Pact carte blanche to take the 'living space' that they required, and by force if necessary.

Went to Birmingham with Mr 'Pink' Crittall. Visited their Galv. Plant, then went over to see Mr Crispin at Kings Norton. Saw little of the blitz damage.
Got puncture 60 miles from home – raining, no torch, very dark. Changed wheel by touch. Got soaked. Home 11-45pm. Slept at Griggs.

This episode must have been particularly difficult, especially as my father still had his arm in plaster. I sincerely trust that Mr 'Pink' Crittall was assisting in changing the wheel, but it certainly sounds as if my father had to do most of the work. Rank has its privileges!

~~~~~~~~~~

Quiet night.

No activity during the day and night as a result of bad weather.

Wednesday 26
Big disturbances in Yugo Slavs. Majority of people want pact rejected.

The signing of the pact had been deeply distressing to many Yugoslavs who wished their country to remain neutral, and the situation would soon become critical.

~~~~~~~~~~

Libya still quiet.

With a growing military force, General Erwin Rommel had arrived in North Africa to plan and execute the offensive against Wavell's army. It would not take long before he made his presence felt, as the British and Australian forces were soon overcome at Beda Fomm, and the German military machine rolled onwards to threaten Benghazi in Cyrenaica. The Allied armies were now in retreat. However, the RAF and RAAF squadrons had been receiving more Hurricanes to replace the Gladiators and Gauntlets, and they began to assert their authority during the many air battles with Italian and German fighters *(predominantly CR42's and Bf110's)* and dive bombers *(Stuka's)* as they clashed over the bitter fighting below. But, as yet, the Luftwaffe had not sent Bf109's into the fray. In a couple of weeks that would change, and threaten the balance of air power in North Africa.

~~~~~~~~~~

Keren not yet fallen to our men in Abyssinia but likely to any time now.

The fighting for Keren continued, being heavily resisted by entrenched Italian forces.

~~~~~~~~~~

Hitler not yet moving in Balkans.

He was coming!

~~~~~~~~~~

Quiet night. Weather has been bad the last few nights.

There had been limited activity during the day only, with enemy aircraft bombing and machine-gunning targets in South and South-West England causing several casualties.

Thursday 27
Great news today. Revolution in Yugo Slavia. Prince Paul has fled and the minister who signed pact with Germany has been arrested.
Prince Peter takes over and is forming new cabinet.
Yugo Slavia now likely to repudiate pact as the new minister & Prince Peter are pro-British.
Nasty smack for Germany which may have far reaching effects in the Balkan situation.

The Yugoslav Army had overthrown the government of Prince Paul, and declared Prince Peter as king. The Three-Power Pact was rescinded immediately.

~~~~~~~~~~

Quiet night.

However, during the day, raiders were again over Britain and 29 people were killed in Poole.

Friday 28
Keren is captured at last. Abyssinia will soon fall.
We seem to be getting better news lately.

After eleven days of bitter fighting, Keren fell to the forces of Lt. Gen. Platt. They then proceeded to the coast with the aim of capturing Massawa.

~~~~~~~~~~

Yugo Slavia have formed new Government and there appears to be little or no internal opposition.
Germany very annoyed & have started with threats, but these will be ignored.

General Simorich had formed a new cabinet committed to neutrality. However, this was not acceptable to Germany and severe repercussions were to follow.

~~~~~~~~~~

Weather has been bad over Germany lately.

Due to inclement weather, there had only been predominantly RAF coastal sweeps for the previous four days.

~~~~~~~~~~

Another quiet night.

Saturday 29
Went into Colchester with Pop, Spud, Peg & Ruth.
Went to Pictures in the evening with Pop.

Grandad has been very queer of late, but seems a shade better today

My great-grandfather Henry Pudsey was greatly loved by all the family. It must have been very concerning that his health had been suffering. I was never fortunate enough to have known Henry and my great-grandmother Mandy, although my father and mother told me on numerous occasions how lucky they were to have them as their grandparents; '…they were kind, loving and gentle people'.

We have at last drawn part of the Italian fleet into battle in the Mediterranean.
Little news of the scrap.

The Royal Navy had been tasked to protect shipping taking Allied troops to Greece. As a result of an intelligence report received from intercepted messages via 'Ultra' decrypting code breakers at Bletchley Park, the Royal Navy was alerted that the Italians had sent a fleet of warships to intercept the shipping. Involved was the Italian battleship 'Vittorio Veneto', together with six heavy and two light cruisers and several destroyers.

Sailing from Greece, with Vice-Admiral Pridham-Wippell in command, a Royal Navy force consisting of four cruisers and a few destroyers left port on the 27th March. Sailing from Alexandria in Egypt was a separate force under Admiral Cunningham. This consisted of three battleships and the aircraft carrier, HMS 'Formidable'.

On the morning of the 28th March, the Pridham-Wippell force intercepted and went into action against some of the Italian cruisers, but due to the appearance of the 'Vittorio Veneto', the Royal Navy ships were fortunate enough to be extricated when a torpedo carrying Fairey Swordfish aircraft from the carrier 'Formidable' attacked and distracted the Italian battleship. Eventually gaining the upper hand and with the Italian force in retreat, it was then the intention of Cunningham's more powerful force to chase them back to Italy.

In the early afternoon, the Italian battleship was attacked yet again by Swordfish, but although damaged, was able to make port. A further torpedo strike by Swordfish crippled a heavy cruiser, but by the evening, the big guns of the British battleships HMS 'Warspite', HMS 'Barham' and HMS 'Valiant' had caused havoc amongst the Italian fleet, and by the morning of the 29th March the battle was over.

Quiet our way, tho' Gerry has broken the lull. Heard several thumps.

Very limited Luftwaffe operations during the day saw some damage in Norfolk and Suffolk. Bristol and Avonmouth were the recipients of the main attacks, and although there were a few casualties, damage was slight.

Sunday 30

When I mention 'quiet night', it does not mean peaceful nights for the menace is always existing.
We cannot concentrate on anything after dark, when most of the time is spent listening for planes or the siren.
It's marvellous how poor Ena, or anyone, can stand the constant strain, with little hope of relief for a long time to come.

It appears that my father's view of the war situation tended to vary daily, and it is evident that it had been influenced by several factors, such as the lack of sleep due to constant air raid alerts, the general war situation, the media, and his concern for my mother and Jane.

~~~~~~~~~~

2 raids at night. 11-15 – 12-30am. 3-30 – 5-30am. Heard no planes or bumps. Small scale.

Long-range enemy bombers carried out attacks during the night, with East Anglia reporting a small amount of damage. Both Great Horkesley and Holland Haven received the unwelcome attention of enemy raiders.

Monday 31

Great news of Mediterranean battle. Italians lost 2 Cruisers & 3 destroyers, possibly 2 more, and one battleship very badly damaged. We suffered no losses, & no damage.
We have got a navy.

This was a decisive battle, which effectively weakened the Italian navy to such an extent that it was no longer a force to be reckoned with for the rest of the war. It would be up to the German Luftwaffe to do battle with the Royal Navy in the Mediterranean - and it would be devastating for the Navy.

~~~~~~~~~~

Greeks still giving Musso what-for in Albania.

On 9th March, reinforced by a further 28 Divisions, the Italians embarked on a spring offensive, which very soon ground to a halt, with heavy casualties having been inflicted by both the Italians and the Greeks. The Italians had been humiliated yet again, and the way was now open for the fascist German military machine to start rolling once more against the free world, only next time it would be the Greeks who would suffer.

~~~~~~~~~~

Quiet night our way.
Raid on North East towns.

There were attacks on Hull and Great Yarmouth with substantial damage reported at both locations. Other areas were attacked by night-fighter/bombers, with some further widely scattered bombing activity over East Anglia.

Note: Civilian casualties since the start of the bombing until the end of this month had been 28,859 killed and 40,166 severely injured – a terrible price to pay for peace. This is not to forget the many tens of thousands in military service who also sacrificed their lives, and yet the war was to continue for four more dreadful years.

APRIL 1941

Tuesday 1
Horrible day. Raining all day.

But the farmers would surely call that good growing weather in April?

~~~~~~~~~~

Now disclosed that Italian fleet was lured out of it's nest by one of our cruisers. They chased our ship for 4 hours but did not hit it once. When well out our navy closed in & let them have it. One broadside from the Warspite blew one of the Italian cruisers to bits.
It is now thought the Italians lost 8 boats.
This reduces their navy to 2/3rds of what it was at the outbreak of war.

Apart from the damage to the battleship 'Vittorio Veneto', records show that three Italian cruisers and two destroyers were sunk, with the total loss to the British force of just one aircraft. It was a substantial victory. However, there had been one serious loss on the 31st March when the cruiser HMS 'Bonaventure', escorting a convoy to Greece, was sunk by an Italian submarine.

When the time came for the Allies to evacuate Greece and Crete, the Royal Navy would lose many more ships to vicious and unrelenting air attacks by aircraft of the German Luftwaffe.

~~~~~~~~~~

It was reported that bombs fell harmlessly in East Anglia during the day. However, bad weather put a stop to night incursions due to inclement weather conditions at German bases.

Wednesday 2
Went to Mitcham (Surrey) to see Mr Wilson of Wireworkers Ltd regarding galvanising his work.

As with one or two other enterprises mentioned in the diary, the company of Wireworkers Ltd in Mitcham no longer exists in business directories. It may well have ceased trading, but also may have been subject to a take-over, and thus be trading under a different name. Whatever the case, the company must have been of sufficient size and importance at that time for my father to pay them a visit.
Saw some of London's damage. Ghastly sight. Row upon row of houses & flats in ruins.
Familiar places now unrecognisable.

The description was very vivid, and to go beyond those comments and explain the obvious tragedies of loss of life, destroyed homes, disrupted and ruined services and businesses, cannot be adequately comprehended two-thirds of a century later. It is obvious that my father sensed the complete catastrophe of the moment as he viewed the smashed and burnt out shells of once prestigious buildings - no longer bustling with busy business people, or, more tragically, in destroyed properties that had once been the carefully tended homes of the much threatened population of London. It must have been a most distressing and demoralising sight, but I am sure that it would have

London devastation 1941 - life goes on.
(Courtesy of the Franklin D. Roosevelt Library Digital Archives)

spurred him on to ensure his own contribution to the war effort would not falter.

Our advance forces in Libya retreating in face of superior German & Italian forces.

Although still with limited forces, Rommel's 'Afrika Korps' virtually wiped out the inferior British tanks of the 2nd Armoured Division, thus opening the route to Mechili.

A lot of our forces were withdrawn for the East Af. Affair.

As the conflict in Abyssinia had drawn to a close, and the Italian army was close to surrender, it had been the senior Allied commanders' intent to support the deteriorating position in Libya by releasing troops from this area of operation; either directly committing men and military equipment, which they did by sending an Indian Division, or releasing others in an endeavour to reinforce the North African battlefront.

Quiet night.

Bad weather resulted in virtually no enemy activity.

Thursday 3
3 more Italian destroyers sunk

There were still some elements of the Italian Navy at sea, and although this recorded incident may have occurred during the aftermath of the sea battle on the 28th March, I can only trace the final destruction of two destroyers during that period: the 'Alfieri' and the 'Carducci'.

As a final footnote to the battle, over 2,300 Italian sailors lost their lives.

We are now nearly on Addis Ababa, capital of Abyssinia. Note has been sent to the Duke of Aosta asking him to surrender.

Lt. Gen. Cunningham was now at the gates of the city, but still meeting stiff resistance from the Italian army.

Yugo Slavia remaining calm under threat of German aggression.

The repercussions resulting from the overthrow of the government had created a critical situation, which yet again put the security of the country at severe risk from German aggression.

Raid on South West. (Bristol).
We had warning 9-15 – 11-15pm.
No planes came our way.

There was a large raid on Bristol and Avonmouth, and those targets suffered serious damage at dock and residential locations. Other areas in the South received attention from enemy aircraft, and further raids were reported in the North. RAF night-fighters destroyed 2 aircraft.

Friday 4
German forces take Benghazi (Libya). I think this was forseen. We will hit back hard shortly when the Abyssinian affair is settled.

Elements of the 'Afrika Korps' entered Benghazi on the 4th April, and some of the Allied forces withdrew towards Tobruk, while the armoured element headed for Mechili where unfortunately a number were captured. The remaining formations were able to retire through Derna.

We can control the number of Germans getting into Africa.

Unknown to the British public, Rommel's forces had been reinforced on the 3rd April with heavily armoured and superior tanks of the 15th Panzer Division that had recently been offloaded at Tripoli. I can only deduce that my father had been influenced by the conjecture of the media insinuating that the Allies could control the flow of war materials destined to support Rommel's advances. As it turned out in the final analysis this would happen, but it was a desperate struggle for the Allied forces to control the Mediterranean routes. Eventually, as the war progressed, and after losing a great number of supply ships, Germany was forced to try and reinforce Rommel's army by air. The lumbering Ju52 tri-motor transport aircraft were shot down in great numbers by RAF fighter aircraft based on Malta, and the supplies and troops to enable German forces to consolidate their gains did not materialise. However, that situation was very much in the future, as Wavell's forces on this day were now under severe pressure.

4 of our bombers lost in night raids over Germany & France.

These reported losses appear to have occurred on the night of 3rd/4th April during a raid on Brest, which had been attacked by 90 aircraft of Bomber Command. The intention was to bomb the warships 'Scharnhorst' and 'Gneisenau' that had located back in Brest harbour following their destructive Atlantic operations. The raid was not successful. However, a further raid on the 4th/5th April by 54 aircraft on the same targets proved to be vital.

The threat of these lethal ocean raiders to our convoys and ships in the Atlantic was critical to our survival, and it was imperative that they be neutralised as soon as possible to help our hard-pressed merchant fleet. It had been, therefore, fortuitous that one bomb fell in the dry dock in which the 'Gneisenau' was lying. The following day, the ship was moved as it was considered to be safer in the harbour, but while finally anchored it was attacked by a Coastal Command Beaufort torpedo bomber. Severe damage was inflicted, which caused the ship to be under repair for 6 months. Unfortunately, the Beaufort was shot down when carrying out this attack and all aboard were killed. For that heroic feat, the Victoria Cross was posthumously awarded to the pilot, Flying Officer K. Campbell.

Raid from 10pm – 2am.
Heard only one plane. It was right overhead. It dropped a few bombs a few miles away.

A large force of enemy bombers continued targeting Bristol and Avonmouth, and widespread destruction occurred. Great Yarmouth also received the attention of the Luftwaffe, but sustained little damage.

Minor raids were reported elsewhere, although I cannot, in Air Raid Precaution records, trace a plane having dropped bombs locally. The aforementioned occurrence noted by my father must have been one of those isolated incidents that remained unreported, as the lone raider may have dropped bombs harmlessly in an isolated area; there to await location at a later date.

Saturday 5

Bristol had another raid last night. It has had its full share of raids since the blitz started.
The raids are not quite so heavy as they were.

May be that Hitler is flying them to the Balkans where it appears he may start against Yugo Slavia any moment now.
Yugo Slavs will fight.

The invasion would start in the early hours of the next day. As previously observed, Hitler was not an advocate of freedom and neutrality.

Drove Ena & Jane to Chelmsford to get shoes for Jane.

A good day to choose as there was virtually no enemy activity.

No record exists of how much they paid for the shoes! However, after the 1st June it would have required 3 coupons to purchase these items.

Sunday 6

Germany has declared war on Yugo Slavia. He has already bombed Belgrade twice altho' it was declared an open city.

Having seen the pro-neutrality government taking control, Hitler decided to invade Yugoslavia to secure the position of the Axis powers in the Balkans.

On the early morning of the 6th April, the German Luftwaffe commenced the attack on Belgrade. Bombers, dive-bombers and fighters soon overwhelmed the Yugoslav Air Force, and in the horrendous and devastating assault an estimated 17,000 innocent people perished in the wreckage of the city, where the bombing negated all forms of communication and counter-attack for those brave enough to resist.

In parallel with the Luftwaffe attack on Belgrade, Hitler's heavily armoured ground forces entered Yugoslavia from their bases in Hungary and Rumania.

No news yet but he has started against Greece. Greeks resisting strongly.

Hitler will not have it all his own way.

In February, as a result of Greek concerns and the worsening situation in the area, Britain had agreed with the Greek leadership to send an expeditionary force as a deterrent against the Axis threat. Therefore, to support the Greek struggle against fascism, the 'British' Expeditionary Force *(BEF)*, eventually comprising in excess of 55,000 British, Australian and New Zealand troops, began to arrive in Greece during March.

However, within the military alliance with Greece there were disagreements on deployment of the forces. The Greeks had favoured fighting on the fortified Metaxas line, but the BEF had favoured the Kleidi line directed to the south-east. Although far from strategically satisfactory, the two lines of defence were dictated and reluctantly agreed.

Hitler had deployed his troops and aircraft on several fronts, and on Sunday the 6th April his forces attacked Yugoslavia from their bases in Hungary and Rumanian. Simultaneously, German forces also invaded northern Greece from their temporary bases on Bulgarian soil.

No news of Turkish reaction.

Although Turkey must have been severely shocked by the events, it remained rather subdued, and still fearful for its own neutrality.

Russia have signed pact of friendship with Yugo Slavia.

The Russian media accused Germany of expanding the war by aggression. Their reservations regarding the strength of the Non-Aggression Pact had been shaken - and stirred!

Quiet night.

There had been little activity recorded, but German aircraft patrolled East Anglia's airfields looking for bombers returning from operations over Europe. With tired and hungry crews; some shot up and barely able to make it home, the last thing that the bomber crews wanted was to be intercepted by a deadly German night-fighter. Tragically, many were.

Monday 7
Unable to get much news, but our Air Force have started knocking down German dive bombers in Greece & Yugo Slavia.

It was reported that 20 Yugoslav Air Force planes were shot down and 44 were destroyed on the ground, with the Luftwaffe losing only 2 fighters. No RAF planes were in that region.

Greeks offering stubborn resistance.

As a result of Greek troops being stubbornly committed to their fight against Italian forces in Albania, the Metaxas line of defence was not as strong as it should have been. Lacking in weapons to neutralise tanks and armoured vehicles nevertheless, the Greek forces managed to inflict severe casualties on the attacking German forces in that difficult and mountainous terrain. However, the rapid and aggressive German advance through Yugoslavia would be an ominous sign for the Greek defenders.

The RAF was carrying out a spirited defence over the skies of Greece. Hurricanes were now their front line fighter in the conflict, but it was an uphill task for them to master the Messerschmitt Bf109's of the Luftwaffe, although in the initial stages of the invasion the Hurricanes gave an excellent account of themselves.

B.E.F. are in Greece.
British, Australian, & New Zealand, troops are in Greece in large numbers.
Hitler has a tough job in front of him before he reaches his objective – Salonika.

As previously noted, there were now over 55,000 British and Commonwealth troops in Greece, plus RAF fighter and bomber squadrons. They would, however, be fighting at a disadvantage due to the positioning of their forces - some on the Kleidi line, and others deployed in more scattered and remote defensive positions.

Biggish raids generally.
8-45pm – 5-30am.

During the night, many raids were reported at different locations. In excess of 500 enemy aircraft carried out major raids on Glasgow and Clydeside, and Liverpool and Birkenhead. It was recorded that every Civil Defence Region in Britain reported bombing during the night, and for a considerable period nearly every area of the UK was under air raid alert.

Once again Ipswich received several bombs, although limited damage was reported.

Although 5 enemy aircraft were claimed shot down by the RAF, only 3 were in fact lost over Britain.

Tuesday 8
I was on fire watching till 3am. Not many planes overhead.

Germans slowly advancing into Greece towards Salonika & into Yugo Slavia in the South.
He will take a bit of stopping at these points.

Located in northern Greece, the city of Salonika, was being approached by the 2nd Panzer Division and would be taken without a fight the next day.

Early on the 8th April, and supported by Panzers, the German Army entered Yugoslavia from their gathering point near Sofia. Although there had been limited resistance from the Yugoslav Army they were forced to withdraw, leaving the Panzer tanks to roll on towards Belgrade. The blow was brilliantly executed and decisive, and was yet another display of the 'Blitzkrieg' tactics that had worked so well in the invasion of Western Europe the previous year.

~~~~~~~~~~

Italians still collapsing in Africa & Albania.

Addis Ababa, the capital of Abyssinia, fell on the 6th April to Lt. Gen. Cunningham's force. It took many days, however, for the Duke of Aosta to surrender as the Italians fought on in scattered groups.

On the 8th April, the Platt force took Massawa, and with it came the liberation of Eritrea.

~~~~~~~~~~

Big raid on Coventry.
8-30pm – 5am.

During the night, Coventry was overwhelmed by 237 enemy bombers. The industrial, commercial and residential areas suffered considerable damage. Yet more German aircraft, seeking alternative targets, bombed many other towns and airfields, with East Anglia appearing to get off lightly on this occasion.

Fighter Command claimed, and German Air Force records show 6 enemy aircraft destroyed.

Wednesday 9
Germans took Salonika at 4am this morning. Bad news.

Although the people of Britain would not have known at the time, it was a disastrous event for the inhabitants of the city. Consisting of a large Jewish population of over 56,000 men, women and children, it would be the year of 1943 when deportations to the concentration camps would commence. At the end of the war it was estimated that 48,000 had met their fate in the gas chambers and labour camps. The evil that was Nazism could never be forgiven for the horrific murder of so many innocent souls.

~~~~~~~~~~

Greeks & Yugo Slavs being pushed back but fighting bravely.

The Yugoslav defence was crumbling, and as it did so, some of the German Panzers reverted to the command of their Twelfth Army attacking Greece.

At the Greek Metaxis line, the arrival of the German 2nd Panzer Division from Yugoslavia had rapidly swung the fight against the brave Greek troops. Although bloody battles ensued, the Greek defenders were eventually forced to surrender.

Our B.E.F. are not yet in contact with the enemy.
Don't quite know where they are.

In Greece, due to the fluid and rapid movement of events, part of the Expeditionary Force facing the German XI Panzer Corps had decided to attempt a delaying action at the Klida Pass. There they tensely awaited the enemy with the mixed force of British and Commonwealth soldiers spread along the narrow and difficult terrain of the pass.

In Abyssinia there is practically no resistance left. This may release some of our forces for the Balkans, before it is too late.

Although there was resistance in Abyssinia, the British and Allied forces were close to victory. However, it was definitely too late to send reinforcements to the Balkans. The German Army had systematically swamped Yugoslavia with its full destructive military power, and there was no stopping them from achieving total victory in the region. There could no illusions. Hitler had created yet another atrocity, and no one could help Yugoslavia.

Heavy raid on Birmingham and South Coast towns 9-15 – 4-30am.

While there were heavy and damaging raids on Birmingham and Tyneside, there were also secondary raids on other towns and cities. The nearest to home had again been Ipswich, where major conflagrations had been reported in the dock area of the town.

Fighter Command claimed 8 enemy aircraft shot down; a slow but much needed improvement in performance.

Thursday 10
Germans still advancing in Yugo Slavia & Thrace.

The German armies were closing on Belgrade. The Panzer Korps were securing bridgeheads as they progressed to the capital meeting little resistance. The net was tightening around Yugoslavia as the German Army attacked through many regions, taking significant numbers of prisoners as they advanced.

Greeks & Slavs fighting hard but are falling back from Hitler's army of steel.
He has yet to meet the B.E.F.

Hindsight shows that this optimism was misplaced. I can only assume that my father is expecting the British Expeditionary Force to halt the Germans and Italians. As can be seen from the previous day's report, the BEF were not positioned well at the Klida Pass and would soon be fighting for their lives in a delaying action as the German army headed towards the town of Vevi. The ability to carry out the monumental task of halting the fascist forces would take several more years to achieve, as the Nazi jackboot was trampling all in its path in the year of 1941.

German & Italian troops are now in Derna & are nearing Tobruk where we will offer our first real resistance.
Losses on both sides fairly heavy.

Regardless of the rapidly developing and critical situation, Allied command had decided that there would be no further withdrawal beyond Tobruk. It had to be held; for beyond Tobruk was the road to Egypt.

Ordering the Australian 7th Division (originally destined for Greece) to be sent back to Mersa Matruh to reinforce defensive positions in Egypt, Major-General Leslie Morshead assumed control of the defences at Tobruk. Within the defensive perimeter he had nearly 25,000 fighting men in his command, together with a few thousand support troops. Encircled by formidable trenched and wired defences, Morshead had a potent array of anti-tank and field artillery at his disposal, as well as tanks, mortars and machine guns.

Raids on Birmingham & Portsmouth.
11-30pm – 4-45am.

There was a repeat raid on Birmingham; this time by 206 enemy bombers, and much damage was caused to industrial areas with great loss of life, which was exacerbated by the raid spilling over into Coventry. Portsmouth, together with Southampton and Great Yarmouth, was one of the three ports targeted by enemy raiders, where again damage was extensive around dock and industrial areas.

With most victories occurring during the raids that night, RAF fighters accounted for 10 enemy aircraft.

Friday 11   Good Friday
3 or 4 Bombs & some incendiaries fall in Witham.   A few houses damaged but no casualties.
½ hour before writing this, a Gerry plane came over & started machine gunning nothing in particular.

The Essex County Constabulary *'Situation Report'* for the *'Period from 09-00hrs 10/4/41 to 09-00hrs 11/4/41'* stated that: *'At 01-50hrs, 4 HE (1 UX) and about 200 explosive IB fell near Witham. A minor road was closed owing to UXHE. 11 houses seriously damaged and 56 houses, 21 shops, 2 churches, 2 public houses and a school also damaged. A straw stack was destroyed by fire. No casualties.'*

As for the 'Gerry' plane 'machine gunning nothing in particular', it was a very regular occurrence, as both sides carried out those types of random low level attacks for no apparent reason other than a target was rapidly identified and strafed, or, it is just possible that the gunner was bored and wanted to let off steam at an unfortunate subject or object of his choice. There were many incidents reported throughout the war of those kind of instinctive but highly unpleasant attacks, and if targeted, those on the ground had little time to react.

~~~~~~~~~~

Little news of Balkan war.

Compounding the problem that occurred during the fighting in the Balkans had been the issue of ethnic rivalries. It had been especially evident in Yugoslavia. The Croatians were pro-German and many refused to fight against the fascist forces, and when the German Army reached Zagreb they were actually cheered into the city. Meanwhile, the Serbs in the Yugoslavian Army maintained their desperate but hopeless fight against overwhelming odds. Such was the outcome of ethnic disputes - they were bitter and divisive and continue, sometimes with great violence, to this day.

~~~~~~~~~~

Our troops are now in contact with Germans, somewhere in Greece.

A German Waffen-SS *(Schutzstaffel)* battle group began probing the defences of the British, Australians and New Zealanders at the Klida Pass - initially with little success. However, it soon became evident that the Allies could not hold out much longer as the German Army began to bring up tank reinforcements. The Allied defences were stretched too thin in the area, and were suffering in the cold weather and deep snow. Now they had to face the Panzers.

~~~~~~~~~~

No warning tonight.
Heavy raid on Bristol.

It was reported that over 190 enemy bombers attacked Bristol and Avonmouth causing extensive damage and loss of life. The Luftwaffe had again been successful in finding their targets of docks and industrial areas on this night.

Saturday 12
Worked all day today.
Very little news except that we are resisting the Germans in Greece and in Libya.
In the battle for Greece, the Allies had fought fiercely, but in vain. Eventually, as the Panzers took their toll, and against overwhelming odds, the Expeditionary Force at Klida Pass retreated in disarray: later to regroup and lick their wounds. To compound the bitter disappointment, they learned that the Germans had taken Vevi the previous day.

They are being held up west of Tobruk.
With German forces also covering the road to the east of Tobruk, the town was now surrounded and under siege.

We are giving Germany very heavy raids now, - as big, if not bigger, than what we have had. This is not a quarter of what they will get when we get the flood of U.S.A. supplies.
Brest was the target during the night for 66 RAF bombers, but due to poor cloud conditions only 37 found the target, with the balance bombing Lorient as an alternative. A few RAF bombers laid mines off Brest, and others attempted to bomb the battle-cruisers in Brest harbour. Cloud cover hampered accurate bombing and the raid produced little success.

Quiet night.
German reconnaissance planes were reported during the night over coastal areas of East Anglia.

Sunday 13 Easter Day
Very busy in garden.
I remember the layout of the garden very well and my father was always proud of the 'home grown' vegetables for the table. Even after the war, he spent a great deal of time tending the garden, which then became more colourful as flowers began to appear, brightening and lightening hearts after the dark days of the war. As he busied himself with those tasks, I am sure he would have reflected on those pre-war days of peace: days of carefree

happiness and contentment. It would sadly take several years yet to return to normality.

All morning & evening spent cutting lawns.

At that time, only pushed hand mowers were used by ordinary householders, and in post-war summers I well remember my father sweating all day when cutting the lawns to perfection - that is, until it was my turn when I was old enough to do some cutting myself! 'Keep the lines straight' was the constant admonishment by him as he sat sipping his lemonade.

My wrist (still in plaster) has put me weeks behind, but I am now making up for lost time – at the expense of my plaster.

Little news of the Balkans.

On the previous day, the 12th April, the German Army had been on the outskirts of Belgrade and the city was about to fall. Late in the afternoon, the German swastika flag was seen flying, and the Mayor of Belgrade officially handed over the city to the conquerors. Meanwhile, the German Army started its drive to Sarajevo, where the Yugoslav Army leaders had planned to withdraw their depleted forces deep into Serbia - there to carry on resistance against the invaders. By this time, Serbs and Croats were in open conflict, helping to confuse the issue and speed the inevitability of the collapse of the country - a war within a war. Yugoslavia was imploding, and as a sign that the conflict was near the end, Sarajevo fell on the 15th April.

We appear to be at least, beginning to hamper the German advance in Greece.

I think that this comment is reasonably accurate in the light of the actual events that were happening. However, it could not be imagined that the Allies were in any way the aggressors in the conflict, as their limited forces were constantly under pressure from the German infantry, tanks and the Luftwaffe. The signs were already evident that another group of the British Expeditionary Force, although fighting hard and tenaciously, was in serious trouble. By the night of the 14th April with their tanks and guns clashing desperately with German forces, and under severe pressure from the Panzers, they were forced to withdraw to the proximity of Mt. Olympus. There they were able to hold the line for a few more days.

Quiet night.

It was reported that a few bombs fell in East Anglia during the day, but with no significant results.

Monday 14 Easter Monday
Worked in garden all morning. Pictures after lunch. Garden in evening.

For a great many people in Britain, the garden was the main source of food for much of the year, for after the fresh fruit and vegetables were eaten, those that had been preserved would then form part of the 'out of season' diet. 'Digging for Britain' was the famous phrase designed to inspire the nation to produce more food, and the situation became more vital as the loss of shipping, badly mauled by U-boats, placed a greater emphasis on home production.

Germans slowly taking back the towns in Libya which we captured from the Italians.
Difference is:- We took over 100,000 Italian prisoners in the campaign, while Germany are having large losses while we are having few. We will hit back when the time is ripe.

During the night of the 13th April, Rommel ordered an attack on the Tobruk defences with tanks, machine guns and infantry. However, with concentrated fire and the use of anti-tank guns on the advancing German and Italian armour, the enemy was forced to withdraw leaving many dead and several tanks destroyed.

Quiet night.

Only minor air skirmishes were recorded in East Anglia during the day.

Tuesday 15
Tobruk, not quite isolated, altho' Bardia has been taken, was subjected to very heavy attack by the huns. They were smashed back and 200 prisoners taken.

Suffering only 80 casualties, the Tobruk defenders had repelled the German attack, and following their retreat many dead and wounded Germans and Italians were left scattered on the battleground. During the attack, the Luftwaffe supported the offensive, and in the bitter fighting that followed, they lost 10 of their aircraft to the RAF and Tobruk defences.

At Bardia, a small Allied assault by sea involving a commando raiding party was assisted by limited gunfire from British naval vessels. The aim had been to disrupt communications and destroy war materials. Although not entirely successful, it did slow down the German advance.

Heavy reinforcements sent to Greece and Africa.

As far as Greece was concerned, it was too late to save the situation as most of the Allied forces were under severe pressure and retreating in most sectors.

However, Britain was withdrawing troops from East Africa - the situation having been stabilised in Abyssinia - and it was confirmed that some of those troops and fighting weapons would be reinforcing the struggle for survival in North Africa.

~~~~~~~~~~

Russia signs non-aggression pact with Japan.
Don't know who or what this will effect.

It had been reported that, on the 13th April, the Russian and Japanese governments had signed a 'Treaty of Neutrality'. This pledged both countries to remain neutral in the event of a war with a third party.

Modern pacts are made to be scrapped anyway.

This was my father's cynical view, which was justified when it involved Axis powers, and Russia and Japan were both unpredictable nations. However, throughout the war it conveniently kept these two protagonists away from each other and gave some comfort to the signatories - if not to the rest of the world.

~~~~~~~~~~

Quiet night

The main attack for the Luftwaffe this night was directed on Belfast. Of the 327 long-range bombers heading for Northern Ireland, 180 attacked the city, but due to inclement weather conditions those unable to bomb chose alternative targets. However, Belfast suffered gravely, with 475 people killed and 1,500 injured.

While this horrific and destructive raid was in progress, an unusual incident had occurred. It was recorded in a local paper that, 'One night when the Germans were bombing Scrabo Hill, a local inhabitant sat out all night in case his house would be hit with a bomb. He sat under a tree and he had his goat tied to the same tree. He woke up next morning and went back into the town. When he went back later for his goat the tree and the goat were both gone. All that was left where the tree had stood was a great deep hole. When the police investigated the matter, they found that he had been sitting on an unexploded bomb all night.'

I guess that could be called 'the luck of the Irish', but to many of the less fortunate, morning never came.

Liverpool received further casualties and industrial damage, as did other areas in the North, with many hundreds perishing in the attacks, which were widely scattered over the Britain. However, nothing of significance was recorded locally.

RAF fighters claimed 6 aircraft destroyed.

Wednesday 16

Organised resistance in Yugo Slavia has ceased, tho' Guerrilla warfare is still going on. Germans have advanced across Yugo Slavia at several points, splitting up the Slavs into groups.

The Yugoslav command began to seek an armistice. The German High Command was requiring an unconditional surrender, but the fighting elements were so fragmented, with certain Yugoslav factions requiring separate settlements (denied by the Germans), that it was not until the next day that an armistice was concluded.

B.E.F. are fighting with the Greeks in a line from Salonika to the West coast of Greece, and have held the German advance.

On this day, General Wilson, who was leading the British Expeditionary Force, advised his Greek counterpart General Papagos that he had decided to withdraw to Thermopylae.

We have halted the enemy in Egypt.

With Rommel contained at the siege of Tobruk, and the disruption by the raiding party at Bardia, the Allies were beginning to stabilise the line of defence. However, they were still retreating - this time to Sollum.

Heaviest raid of war on London.
9-30 – 5-30am.

It was reported that 685 enemy aircraft bombed London in the heaviest raid yet, with some crews making 2 or even 3 sorties to the target. There were massive conflagrations and explosions, and large areas of residential, industrial and

A West End London Underground 'air raid shelter'. This was the life for many during the Blitz.
(Courtesy of the Franklin D. Roosevelt Library Archives)

commercial property were decimated by blast and fire. It was an inferno, and it was estimated that 1,200 people lost their lives during that terrible night.

Although other areas in Southern England received raids, it was another devastating night for London. Against overwhelming odds, 6 German aircraft were shot down by RAF night-fighters and AA.

Note: The improving night defences gave some satisfaction to Air Marshall Douglas, who was particularly pleased with the improved results obtained by 'cats-eyes' units engaged in 'Fighter Night' operations on bright moonlit nights. Nevertheless, he placed on record, in a report on enemy activity, his firm belief '…that AI (*Airborne Interception*) assisted by GCI control (*Ground Control Interception)* will prove the primary means of dealing with the night interception problem, although good success may be anticipated with 'cats-eyes' fighters on moonlight nights'.

Thursday 17
Took plaster off my arm after wearing it for over 5 <u>months</u>.

This must have been a massive relief, as my father was still at work, and still gardening! Whether or not the time taken to heal was caused by constant work aggravation, or the injury was more serious than was appreciated, the period of nearly 6 months does seem rather extreme.

Last nights raid on London did tremendous damage & casualties were very heavy.
Planes were over all night.

Little change in Africa and Balkans.

Rommel's men were licking their wounds after their abortive attempt to dislodge the Allied defenders at Tobruk.

Meanwhile, the armistice in Yugoslavia was finally signed and concluded on this day by German, Italian and Yugoslav officials. It became effective at 12 noon on the 18th April. The short and bloody war, which took just 12 days from the initial attack to the final humiliation, was over.

However, the Greek forces in Albania were reluctant to withdraw, and were inevitably cut off from the Allied retreat. Subsequently, after a major clash with an SS brigade, they were surrounded and after fierce fighting, they surrendered to the German invaders on the 18th April. The Greek Army's failure to accept the worsening situation with the BEF was their ultimate downfall. It is interesting to note that, after the Greek surrender, and in recognition of their fighting skills, the Germans did not intern their forces - an unusual occurrence, very much out of character with normal Nazi behaviour. Perhaps they just did not want to feed them as prisoners of war?

~~~~~~~~~~

We sank complete Italian convoy of 4 supply ships & 3 destroyers. We lost one destroyer.

It was reported that, on the 10th April, four British naval destroyers of 'K' Force sank five Italian supply ships and three escorting destroyers. One of the British destroyers was sunk by enemy fire.

~~~~~~~~~~

Short raid 12-30 – 4-30am.

Portsmouth and surrounding areas were the main recipients of the attack during the night, with nearly 250 bombers targeting naval installations causing large explosions and conflagrations. The Germans lost 3 bombers this night.

Note: Although Portsmouth had a successful decoy site to attract bombs, and proved its worth by attracting enemy bombers away from the intended target during the raid, this information would not have been reported by the media, as it was vital that the Luftwaffe would conclude the target had been destroyed. Many cleverly constructed decoy sites were now in operation throughout the country, deflecting enemy attacks in vulnerable areas.

Friday 18
Ena & I slept thro' last nights raid. Very little about. Main raid was on Portsmouth.
We gave Berlin the heaviest raid of the war last night.

During the evening of the 17th April and into the early morning of the 18th, 118 RAF bombers were sent to Berlin, but as a result of haze causing poor visibility the bombing was not concentrated. German night-fighters were seen to be co-operating with searchlights, which was an ominous sign for Bomber Command who lost 8 aircraft on this raid. RAF aircraft carried out smaller raids on Rotterdam, Cologne, and Mannheim, with others mine laying off Brest and the Frisians.

The RAF lost 3 more bombers on the Cologne raid.

New H.E. bombs used. Blast 5 times more powerful than anything yet used.

The Vickers Wellington II bombers were the first to drop the powerful new 4,000lb (1814kg) 'cookie' or 'blockbuster' against enemy occupied targets in April. Designed by Barnes Wallis, the strong geodetic lattice construction of the Wellington had been ideally suited to transport these

Vickers Wellington bomber, W5379 – 115 Squadron.
(Source: Ken Delve Collection)

huge bombs to their destination, but still had to be adapted to carry this large unstable weapon. The bomb had no fins or aerodynamic features, as it was a thin-skinned highly charged flying 'dustbin', designed to blast buildings and precede the dropping of incendiaries to cause great conflagrations in the target area. With three-quarters of its weight consisting of explosive, and with a 'twitchy' detonation device, this bomb could be just as dangerous to the aircrew as it could be to those receiving it below.

Eventually the bombs increased in size and explosive capability from 4,000lbs, to culminate in the massive 22,000lb 'Grand Slam', also designed by Barnes Wallis.

Allies dropping back a little in Greece to shorten the front.

The British Expeditionary Force had been under constant attack throughout the withdrawal, and although local commanders were unaware at the time and were preparing to hold their positions, an evacuation was being discussed at higher levels.

We are holding the enemy in Libya.

Despite the constant air attacks on Allied ships by Axis aircraft, the Allies endeavoured to continue supplying Tobruk. However, only the occasional Royal Navy ship would get through, and that situation persisted for a considerable period. Meanwhile, the British and Allied forces had withdrawn through Sollum, and on towards Mersa Matruh; there to hold the defensive line inside the Egyptian border.

Quiet night.

Generally a very quiet day – and night!

Saturday 19
Worked in garden all morning. It is looking lovely now. If only we could enjoy it.

With spring well and truly advancing, I can only imagine that the garden looked superb. Father always maintained a very orderly arrangement with his rows of vegetables, and they will have been carefully and lovingly tended. I could never conceive that a former international soccer player could also be a gardener, but, thinking about it, the cabbages did look as big as footballs! When I happened on the scene later in the war and further into my younger years, I could often be found hiding amongst the greenery and nibbling at the leaves. When my father was about, he would admonish me by threatening that this habit would give my constitution the 'collywobbles' - but it rarely did! I carried on munching any fresh vegetables that happened to be around and always found them to be more tasty and fresh than the over-cooked mush served when I eventually reached school age. Apologies to all dinner ladies, but I have been assured that the meals of today are much improved.

Pictures in evening with Ruth & Hedley.

I am assuming that the films were seen in the local Coggeshall Cinema. It is interesting to note that the German raiders 'passed overhead' commencing at 9-00pm, and by that time my father was in the dugout. Therefore, the pictures must have finished prior to the first warning, as it is likely he would have mentioned the film being disturbed by the raid.

Up to this point I have failed to mention that cinema newsreels would also give my father a view of the war, and this must also be taken in the context and comparison of today's television. However, it was not updated for daily consumption for the population, unlike instant communication as we receive it today, and it was heavily censured and understandably rather patriotic. Current media might benefit from a bit more of the latter, as Britain is still a great country.

Worst night of the war. London was the target. Hundreds of planes passed overhead, 9-0 – 11-45 then 1-15am – 5-15am.

Bombs and guns going off all night, fortunately nothing close. In dugout for first warning.

Yet again, London was the main target. Records show that the entry was indeed correct as the Germans sent over 712 bombers, with some crews returning two or three times. This was Goering's so called 'birthday present' to Hitler by dropping over 1,000 tonnes of high explosives in one raid, but thankfully it was not repeated again.

Although the bombing was scattered, a great deal of damage was inflicted, especially in the East End. Residential, commercial and industrial premises were destroyed, as well as hospitals, churches and museums. Tragically, more than 1,200 people lost their lives and many were seriously injured and made homeless. It was another terrible night for our capital city.

There were further attacks in the Home Counties, one having been recorded near St. Osyth, and although my father observed many aircraft passing overhead, there were no recorded incidents locally.

Sunday 20

Tremendous damage & heavy casualties in London.
Germany says this was a reprisal for our recent raid on Berlin, - not mentioning of course, that London has been raided 10 times to every one on Berlin.

REICHSMARSCHALL HERMAN GOERING, APRIL 20, 1941

'The German people, fully confident of victory are celebrating in earnest mood and high spirits the 52nd birthday of the Führer. The hearts of all Germans go out to the defender of German honour and freedom and the guarantor of the German future, in unchangeable and unextinguishable gratitude.

We look back on the uninterrupted chain of fruitful victories which could only have been achieved under the leadership of one who is not only a statesman and a soldier but also a leader and a man of the people.'

The 'Fat Man', as some of his Luftwaffe pilots irreverently called him, could not be accused of subtlety in his praise for the Führer!

This will be reversed. Our airforce is getting more powerful each day, & has long been more than a match for the Huns.

As the year progressed, the RAF sent over an increasing number of bombers. German flak and improved night-fighting techniques began to take severe casualties on Bomber Command. It was to be a bloody battle of attrition. The time of the great armadas consisting of RAF and American bombers, protected by long-range fighters, was yet to come.

~~~~~~~~~~

2 Quiet raids during early morning.

I am not aware of what a 'quiet raid' should be, as all German raiders were well respected for their malevolence to British citizens!

Activity by the Luftwaffe was recorded on a large scale with fighter sweeps, reconnaissance and anti-shipping operations taking place over many areas. East Anglia did attract a small number of bombs during this night, but no damage was recorded.

Monday 21

The Anzacs & Greeks retiring to new defences in Greece.
The Huns are throwing thousands of troops into the battle & they are being mown down in colossal numbers.
They lost 30,000 in 2 days, but with Hitler's vast army, he has no consideration for the lives of his men as long as he gains ground.
This battle will cost him dearly.

The British, Australian and New Zealand forces were fighting fiercely against growing German pressure. Under constant bombing and artillery fire, casualties were heavy on both sides, however, official casualty figures recorded after the conflict do not confirm the heavy losses that my father has reported: if shown by the press, it was severely inflated, but it could be possible that he may have inadvertently added a '0' to the figure.

~~~~~~~~~~

Heavy raid on Plymouth. We had warning 9-15 – 12-30am. I was on fire watching duty.

Plymouth was selected as an early evening target by the Luftwaffe to 'beat the fog home'. Large fires and explosions were reported in dock areas, and the city centre was also affected. Nothing of significance was reported locally, to the great relief of all concerned.

Tuesday 22

After terrific battle we have retreated to our new defences in Greece.

During the battle against fascism, which started with the Italian invasion the previous year, the RAF had been aiding the Greek Air Force in their fight for the air. In the early conflicts, the British aircraft consisted of Gladiator biplane fighters and Blenheim and Wellington bombers. The Italian fighters were mostly biplanes during that period of the campaign, and the skill of the RAF pilots had been causing severe damage to the Italian Air Force. When Germany invaded Greece, the RAF had managed to convert to a more suitable fighting machine - the Hawker Hurricane. However, they were now up against the elite of German fighter aircraft, the single engine Messerschmitt Bf109, and in spite of battling against terrific odds and constant re-grouping, the RAF was continuing to take the fight to the Luftwaffe.

There was one pilot who became a legend during these battles. Born and raised in South Africa, Squadron Leader M.T. St.John 'Pat' Pattle was, as one fellow pilot called him, 'a fighter pilot par excellence'. It was a fitting tribute. He had been in the thick of the fighting in North Africa

A fine shot of Gloster Gladiator K6132.
(Source: Ken Delve Collection)

and had honed his fighting skills against the Italians in that zone of conflict. He continued to score an abundance of 'kills' with the Greeks as they fought the Italian Regia Aeronautica *(Italian Air Force)*, and Pattle had become a hardened fighter pilot with a respected reputation when the time came to withdraw the British Expeditionary Force.

On the 20th April, Pattle, suffering from flu, was patrolling over Piraeus Harbour, which was being attacked by German bombers, when he became involved with some Bf109's and twin engine Bf110's. He was last seen chasing a Bf110 off the tail of a colleague, but was immediately shot down in flames into Piraeus Harbour.

After the war, it was generally accepted by aviation researchers and historians that Pattle was almost certainly the highest scoring pilot in the RAF during WWII. He had many aerial victories; many say upward of 40, but in the heat of battle and sometimes alone, some unconfirmed claims could not be verified, and it is probable several more fell to his guns. However, his fellow pilots agreed after his death that they were convinced those victories had occurred, and attributed his command of an aerial battle to his magnificent flying and fighting ability and his undoubted skill and bravery. He was an irreplaceable loss.

Although my father had the greatest admiration for all our Allied fighting forces, I always had the impression that he had viewed the RAF as something a bit 'special', and I am certain he would have approved of this story of a great fighter pilot being included in this extension of his diary.

~~~~~~~~~~

Germans being killed by the thousand but they keep pouring up, & the Greeks & Aussies deal out death while retreating.
Can we last out?

The inevitable answer was to come on the following day.

~~~~~~~~~~

No further movement in Libya other than slight patrol activity.

During night patrols at Tobruk, Major-General Morhead was encouraging his forces to retain, and if possible extend, the area of no-man's land around the town in order to keep it in Allied hands.

~~~~~~~~~~

Raid on Plymouth.
9-30 – 11-30.

Once again Plymouth and Devonport received the attention of the Luftwaffe. Significant damage was recorded as many fires covered the entire town and docks, causing further destruction of utility services. One Plymothian Observer reported, 'The civic and domestic devastation exceeds anything we have seen…how much damage had been done in the town centre…(was) brought home to us by the fact that we had no water or gas; water tankers used to come round the streets delivering water every day. For a few days we had to cook the best way we could on open fires, people with electric stoves were very popular as the electricity supply was alright….the spirit of the people was wonderful, taking all the inconveniences in their stride, but the stories we heard were horrific….of people who had been trapped in the town when the raids started and unable to get home until next morning (only) to find their homes gone and all the families killed…'

With Portsmouth again receiving the attention of a minor raid, further incidents were recorded in other parts of Britain, but were small by comparison.

Wednesday 23   St. George's Day
It looks as tho' we are fighting a losing battle in Greece.
Germans, with hosts of men & tanks are forcing our numerically inferior forces to retreat daily, but in good order.
Our difficulty is lack of material – especially tanks.
In hand to hand fighting one Aussie is worth 3 Germans.

The British Expeditionary Force was ordered to retreat to the evacuation beaches, with the exception of some British, Australian and New Zealand troops in various holding positions to enable the Force to commence the withdrawal.

Raid 8-15 – 8-45.

Not having written 'am' or 'pm', this raid appears to be in the morning when a few bombs were recorded having been dropped in East Anglia.

Plymouth and Devonport were the targets for yet another night. This continuous bombing was causing great concern to the authorities in these towns. The inhabitants were close to panic; wanting to evacuate their children and also clearly under severe pressure. Misguided reporting and a certain amount of disorganisation by the authorities did not help the situation.

Further minor raids were reported over several parts of Britain including Ipswich.

Thursday 24
We have made a mess of Tripoli. Our navy & airforce have given it a tremendous battering.

The necessity to stop Axis supplies reaching the major port at Tripoli from the Italian mainland was vital to the survival of all Allied forces in North Africa. On the 21st April, British ships bombarded the port, with the battleship HMS 'Barham' in the forefront of the assault. Allied aircraft and British submarines continued to search out and attack enemy supply ships where-ever they could be located, causing considerable disruption to supplies destined for Tripoli and Rommel's Afrika Korps.

We are taking the offensive in Libya by patrol action.

The Axis offensive had held the line at Sollum and the position remained static until the middle of May. Prime Minister Winston Churchill was concerned about the position at Tobruk, and was initiating a plan to provide relief for the hard-pressed troops under siege.

Abyssinia 'do' still being cleaned up.

It would take considerably longer than expected to finally clear out all the Italian resistance, as many fought on in isolated pockets for many months.

We still fall back in Greece.

During fierce engagements the rearguard troops in their holding positions had inflicted severe casualties on the Germans who had intended to cut off the withdrawal. They held for a day, and then retreated once more to be closer to the evacuation locations.

~~~~~~~~~~

Raid 2-45 – 5-15am.
We did not hear it.

That raid could be the last remnant of the incidents from the previous night - possibly bombs on Ipswich. Scattered raids were recorded on the South and South-East coast by over 80 enemy aircraft, with Portsmouth again receiving the greatest attention. Our ports were definitely the key targets during this period of Luftwaffe activity.

Friday 25
Things look hopeless in Greece. We are not losing many men however, compared with the colossal losses suffered by the Germans.

The evacuation had commenced during the previous night when some of the New Zealand contingent had been able to escape. On the 25th April, with the aid of Australian naval ships, some of the Australian force was evacuated from the beaches - all those able to escape, including many from the Greek contingent, were heading for either Crete or Egypt.

Gerry keeps going till he has a sea to cross, & then our navy has a say in the matter.

With the German Luftwaffe in control over the seas around Greece, it was only the bravery and unceasing commitment of Allied naval crews that enabled the evacuation to commence. It was not possible to bring together a major naval force to cause concern to the German battle command, and the Allied evacuation would remain under severe pressure and constant air attack during the evacuation.

Hitler's next move will probably be Turkey.

~~~~~~~~~~

Raid on Midlands.
Warning 9 – 11-30pm.
Ena stampedes all over my garden in the dark.
(Planes overhead)

So much for all the work that my father had put into the garden! However, it seemed to be for a good cause as 'planes overhead' would be a great incentive to reach the safety of the shelter, and my mother had been known to be quite a sprinter in her youth! The vegetable garden was the direct route to relative safety in the dugout, about 50 yards from the house. On putting this to my mother 66 years later, even with a fading memory, she remembers that night well. Laughing, she said that she was quite fast when she was young! I guess she had to be.

Sunderland was the main target for the raiders, with other cities and towns suffering minor raids. Tragically, there were always casualties in these raids, and several fatalities were reported as a result of the bombing.

Saturday 26
Went to Colchester with Pop, Spud, & Peggy.
Peggy & I had coffee then met Pop & Spud & went to pictures.

The trips into Colchester would have been taken by car. Petrol and oil were becoming valuable commodities since limited rationing had been introduced in September 1939, and each motorist was only allowed 200 miles travel per month. The situation would become much worse as the German U-boats were sinking escalating quantities of supplies destined for Britain, and when Japan occupied Malaya in 1942, petrol became unobtainable to the private motorist. Only those authorised with a license were able to obtain supplies. Gradually, other forms of fuel were utilised to keep Britain moving, such as converting vehicles to solid fuel or gas - and even good old-fashioned horsepower pulling wagons and drays were used by local suppliers to deliver goods.

I am aware that the Pudsey family did some of their shopping for food in Colchester - usually on a Saturday, and it was always a special occasion when they could shop, relax and enjoy one of the latest 'pictures' in town.

~~~~~~~~~~

Germany are in Athens. This finishes us in Greece, but most of them are being moved out by boat.

Although it was recorded that German troops entered Athens on the 27th April, there is no doubt that the German forces were virtually there. With Athens in enemy hands, and against overwhelming odds, the country had surrendered to the might of the German fighting machine. The war in Greece was over. The Allies had lost another critical battle, and the battle for Crete was yet to come.

This is a tragedy but will do Hitler little good.

While Athens was falling, those remaining of the Expeditionary Force in Central Greece had their own problems as the Germans parachuted in troops to try to cut off the route for their retreat to the coast. They were not successful, and some of the remaining troops were able to escape from the town and harbours in and around Kalamata.

~~~~~~~~~~

Raids 8-15 – 10-30.
Little about, but biggish raid on South West towns.

Although it was recorded that Portsmouth had been raided, it was Liverpool and Birkenhead that received the greatest attention from the Luftwaffe, with 92 aircraft reporting many fires and explosions. However, those claims were somewhat inflated, and although residential areas unfortunately suffered, damage to the industrial sector was not severe.

Sunday 27
All morning in garden.

Probably repairing the damage done by my mother in her haste to get to the dugout!

Mr Churchill spoke on the wireless and tried to tell us the war situation without giving information away to the enemy.
His theme was:- the road may be long & hard, but we will win in the end.

Churchill inspired the British and Commonwealth people with his significantly timed and brilliant oratory. The speech on this day was remembered for the phrase 'Westward, look, the land is bright'. This must surely allude to the friends across the Atlantic who would soon be joining the Allies in the more official state of war with the Axis alliance.

'Westward, look, the land is bright' – Winston Churchill.
(Courtesy of the Franklin D. Roosevelt Library Archives)

Raid 8-45 – 10-15.
Little about. Main attack was on Plymouth.

It seems that my father had been misinformed as Portsmouth dockyards had been targeted. They had received a heavy attack by 38 enemy bombers and suffered considerable damage and loss of life.

Nothing was reported locally.

Monday 28
The last town in Abyssinia has been captured by our troops. This practically clears up this part of Africa.

The war was drawing to a close, but the Duke of Aosta was still refusing to surrender his forces to the British.

~~~~~~~~~

Germans are making no progress in Libya and Egypt. Tobruk still holds out causing the enemy heavy losses.

Reinforced by the 15th Panzer Division, Rommel prepared for another attack on Tobruk. The previous incumbents - the Italians - had possessed plans of their defensive positions that would aid his assault, but they failed to pass them to Rommel. It would be a cause for regret.

~~~~~~~~~

We are evacuating Greece. Little news thro' yet.

In spite of continuous and systematic bombing by the Luftwaffe, the evacuation of Greece was completed on this day. The British Expeditionary Force had suffered less than 3,000 casualties during the fighting, and by good fortune approximately 40,000 Allied and Greek soldiers were able to escape. However, they left many thousands of Commonwealth troops, who had been cut off by the fighting, to spend the rest of the war as prisoners of the Third Reich.

~~~~~~~~~

Raid on Plymouth.
No warning here.

It appears that the continuing raids on Plymouth by the Luftwaffe had been to 'deprive the dockyards of labour'. The aim had been to dissuade those offloading ships that had brought cargos of materials and arms to Britain to keep away from dock locations, thus further assisting the Germans in their dominance of the Atlantic.

124 aircraft bombed the dock areas in Plymouth and Devonport and, yet again, many fires and explosions were observed. The suffering appeared never ending for the distressed inhabitants.

Locally, in East Anglia, Ipswich continued to record bombing, as the Luftwaffe had become a regular and unwelcome visitor causing considerable damage to dock areas and the town.

Tuesday 29
Troops still getting out of Greece fighting as they go.

As a result of the confusion and circumstances of reporting, the news had yet to reach the British press that the main evacuation was completed the previous day.

Altho' this was rather expected owing to the limited assistance we could offer, we caused tremendous casualties among the Germans, greatly out of proportion to our own losses.

The actual numbers of German casualties could not be accurately defined. The nearest estimate gave the figure of nearly 12,000 killed, wounded or missing in action. However, the Italian forces, throughout the fighting from 1940 until the eventual cessation of the conflict in Greece, suffered over 100,000 casualties.

~~~~~~~~~

Turkey & Russia are still unknown quantities.

Turkey still hung on to neutrality, but the German pact with Russia was weakening by the day.

Lack of unity caused the fall of the Balkans to Hitler.

There was a lack of unity, as the power of the aggressor forged weak and unsavoury alliances, leaving those seeking genuine peace very isolated and vulnerable. However, it must also be remembered that Hitler had many admirers of his policies, and those of dubious intent could see opportunities to solve their ethnic and financial problems. When Hitler's power was in the ascendancy, groups with unethical motives followed the conqueror, sometimes splitting allegiances within countries and causing great civil unrest. Although Greece was reasonably united, it could not be said that other Balkan states were exempt from those failings.

~~~~~~~~~

Big raid on Plymouth.. Damage & casualties heavy.
No warning here.

The inhabitants of Plymouth and Devonport must have been praying for the carnage to end, as 162 bombers continued to cause havoc. By now there were many homeless citizens, and the supply system was beginning to break down. More than 20,000 houses and many industrial premises were destroyed in the previous three attacks, and it was only by some good fortune that the Luftwaffe finally turned to other targets and eased the horrendous burden on the inhabitants in the town, and the Royal Navy.

Note: Throughout all air raids around Britain, the guns of the armed forces were trained on any enemy bombers who dared to violate our shores. However, they still needed to practice their craft as results were not satisfactory, and their efforts would not improve until radar-predicting components became available. Therefore, in a *'Message Form'* sent *'From Police Headquarters to Essex County Control'* on this day, the *'Text of the message'* read: *'Local Machine Gun Firing will take place from 07-00 to 08-00hrs tomorrow 30-4-41 from the Convent area Marine Parade, Dovercourt.'*

This type of exercise was occurring all around our coastline: in our cities, towns as well as in the countryside, and when inevitably the raiders approached, the guns fought to protect targets most likely to be attacked by German bombers. All these defenders made a major contribution to the conflict, and it must have been terrifying for the invaders as they crossed the coast through a wall of bullets, shells, shrapnel and concussion - intensified and more frightening by night with coloured tracers hosing up at them, and further dramatised by the flash of exploding shells.

Wednesday 30
3/4 of our armies in Greece have been safely evacuated to their new bases. (45,000 men)
Many more may be able to get away.
Our known casualties were 3,000 while the Germans were probably over 100,000.

The German casualty figure could only have been a rather wayward estimate by my father or the press to engender the support of the British public and to make them feel that we had severely damaged the German fighting machine. However, the Italians suffered great casualties during the conflict as reported earlier.

Our air force is getting really powerful. We will soon have great superiority in the air.

That comment may have been encouraged by press statements and was certainly premature. The quantity of aircraft going on raids continued to rise, but the quality of the bombing showed that the results were far from satisfactory. That would not change until the spring of 1942, when the formation of the Pathfinder force, with target marking by flares and new electronic aids, led to a gradual but growing improvement in accuracy.

Little news of Battle of the Atlantic.

In the month of February, Rear Admiral Donitz had only 21 U-boats at his disposal for operations - the lowest recorded in the war. However, during the spring the submarines ranged further out into the Atlantic where there were very few or no escorts protecting the convoys.

Quiet night.

A few bombs were again reported during small night raids, with East Anglia again being targeted.

MAY 1941

Although the threat of invasion had receded, in May the Ministry of Information in co-operation with the War Office and the Ministry of Home Security produced a leaflet for distribution to every household. It was introduced with a message from the Prime Minister.

WINSTON CHURCHILL, MAY 1941

'If invasion comes, everyone – young or old, men and women - will be eager to play their part worthily. By far the greater part of the country will not be immediately involved. Even along our coasts, the greater part will remain unaffected. But where the enemy lands, or tries to land, there will be most violent fighting. Not only will there be the battles when the enemy tries to come ashore, but afterwards there will fall upon his lodgements very heavy British counter-attacks, and all the time the lodgements will be under the heaviest attack by British bombers, The fewer civilians or non-combatants in these areas, the better - apart from essential workers who must remain. So if you are advised by the authorities to leave the place where you live, it is your duty to go elsewhere when you are told to leave. When the attack begins, it will be too late to go; and, unless you receive definite instructions to move, your duty then will be to stay where you are. You will have to get into the safest place you can find, and stay there until the battle is over. For all of you then the order and the duty will be: 'Stand Firm'.

This also applies to people inland if any considerable number of parachutists or airborne troops are landed in their neighbourhood. Above all, they must not cumber the roads. Like their fellow-countrymen on the coasts, they must 'Stand Firm'. The Home Guard, supported by strong mobile columns wherever the enemy's numbers require it, will immediately come to grips with the invaders, and there is little doubt will soon destroy them.

Throughout the rest of the country where there is no fighting going on and no close cannon fire or rifle fire can be heard, everyone will govern his conduct by the second great order and duty, namely, 'Carry on'. It may easily be some weeks before the invader has been totally destroyed, that is to say, killed or captured to the last man who has landed on our shores. Meanwhile, all work must be continued to the utmost, and no time lost.

The following notes have been prepared to tell everyone in rather more detail what to do, and they should be carefully studied. Each man and woman should think out a clear plan of personal action in accordance with the general scheme.'

The notes:

What do I do if fighting breaks out in my neighbourhood?

Keep indoors or in your shelter until the battle is over. If you can have a trench ready in your garden or field, so much the better. You may want to use it for protection if your house is damaged. But if you are at work, or if you have special orders, carry on as long as possible and only take cover when danger approaches. If you are on your way to work, finish your journey if you can.

If you see an enemy tank, or a few enemy soldiers, do not assume that the enemy are in control of the area. What you may have seen may be a party sent on in advance, or stragglers from the main body, who can easily be rounded up.

What do I do in areas which are some way from the fighting?

Stay in your district and carry on. Go to work whether in shop, field, factory or office. Do your shopping, send your children to school until you are told not to. Do not try to go and live somewhere else. Do not use the roads for any unnecessary journey; they must be left free for troop movements even a long way from the district where actual fighting is taking place.

Will certain roads and railways be reserved for the use of the Military, even in areas far from the scene of action?

Yes, certain roads will have to be reserved for important troop movements; but such reservations should be only temporary....

Whom shall I ask for advice?

The Police and A.R.P. wardens.

From whom shall I take orders?

In most cases from police and A.R.P. wardens. But there may be times when you will have to take orders from the military and the Home Guard in uniform.

Is there any means by which I can tell that an order is a true order and not faked?

You will generally know your policeman and your A.R.P. wardens by sight, and can trust them. With a bit of common sense you can tell if a soldier is really British or only pretending to be so. If in doubt ask a policeman, or ask a soldier whom you know personally.

What does it mean when the church bells are rung?

It is a warning to the local garrison that troops have been seen landing from the air in the neighbourhood of the church in question. Church bells will not be rung all over the country as a general warning that invasion has taken place. The ringing of church bells in one place will not be taken up in neighbouring churches.

Will instructions be given over the wireless?

Yes; so far as possible. But remember that the enemy can overhear any wireless message, so that the wireless cannot be used for instructions which might give him valuable information.

In what other ways will instructions be given?

Through the Press; by loudspeaker vans; and perhaps by leaflets and posters. But remember that genuine Government leaflets will be given to you only by the policeman, your A.R.P. warden or your postman; while genuine posters and instructions will be put up only on Ministry of Information notice boards and official sites, such as police stations, post offices, A.R.P. posts, town halls and schools.

Should I try to lay in extra food?

No. If you have already laid in a stock of food, keep it for a real emergency; but do not add to it. The Government has made arrangements for food supplies.

Will normal services continue?

Yes. Careful plans have been made to enable newspapers and wireless broadcasts to carry on, and in case of need there are emergency measures which will bring you the news. But if there should be some temporary breakdown in news supply, it is very important that you should not listen to rumours nor pass them on, but should wait till real news comes through again. Do not use the telephones or send telegrams if you can possibly avoid it.

Should I put my car, lorry, or motor-bicycle out of action?

Yes, when you are told to do so by the police, A.R.P. wardens or military; or when it is obvious there is an immediate risk of its being seized by the enemy - then disable and hide your bicycle and destroy your maps.

Should I defend myself against the enemy?

The enemy is not likely to turn aside to attack separate houses. If small parties are going about threatening persons and properties in an area not under enemy control and come your way, you have the right of every man and woman to do what you can to protect yourself, your family and your home.

Give all the help you can to our troops.

Do not tell the enemy anything. Do not give him anything. Do not help him in any way.

Thursday 1
The battle of the Atlantic – or our struggle to get food & arms into this country from America, is the main problem.
Food – oranges, cheese, meat, onions, sugar, cattle food, are all difficult to obtain now.

In 1940, when food rationing commenced, some of the items initially to be rationed were butter, bacon and sugar. Later during March, meat, preservatives and other similar ingredients fell under the same requirement, and in July 1940, tea, margarine and items such as cooking fats were covered by Government restrictions. Cheese was rationed in 1941 together with many other food commodities, and the limiting process went on through the war as supplies of produce became desperately short. However, there were exceptions. Expectant mothers and children together with the elderly were able to obtain vital foods, which included fresh milk. When the shortage of that wholesome sustenance became acute, dried milk powder became the substitute for many.

It soon transpired that certain foodstuffs that were considered essential as a staple diet before the war quickly became very difficult to obtain and were almost certainly rationed. Inevitably, as the war progressed and food supplies diminished, items previously available became luxuries. Consequently, many 'creative' people were able to substitute items of shortage for items of relative plenty, and the population were to taste culinary delicacies such as corned beef, sausages (with more offal than meat) and substitute mashed potato!

But, most vitally, the nation was being fed. For each individual it was important to have enough calories to survive, and the Government Ministries were very forthcoming regarding what could be obtained, and offered plenty of information on how to produce your own food to stock in the larder. During war years, and for some time after, refrigerators and freezers, so common today for preserving food for extended periods, were not available to the vast majority of the population. They were much too expensive and considered a great luxury, so the larder was the great preserve for providing food for the family table.

The Battle of the Atlantic during 1941 brought home to the Nation that there had to be a limit to many of the essential items once freely obtainable, and it was quite a few years after the war before most of those became readily available again - if they could be afforded.

Hitler's mines, U-Boats, & planes, have been taking heavy toll of our merchant shipping, but we are fast sinking his U-Boats.

Between March and June German U-boats sunk 203 ships, which constituted over 1,120,000 tons of shipping. This was a frightening number of ships lost - a devastating loss of food and supplies, and a terrible loss of life of the brave crews. However, British naval ships sunk 5 U-boats in March, including those of a few top 'ace' Captains; the infamous Gunther Prien being one, and although the German Navy lost a further 30 U-boats by the end of the year, the first month of 1942 saw their numbers rise to 91 boats seeking Allied vessels in a more prolonged and deadly game of cat and mouse.

Untersee-boot, U2 - ocean killer. On 8/4/44, sailing under Oblt. Wolfgang Schwarzkopf, U-2 was in collision with a German trawler and sank. Raised the next day, there were 18 survivors, but 17 had died: the only lives claimed by this submarine during the War.
(Source: David Page, navyphotos)

Quiet night here.
Raids on various towns but very few planes seem to be coming our way.

There were continued attacks on Merseyside, carried out by 43 bombers. It had been the centre of the City of Liverpool that suffered the greatest damage, with fatalities being reported in and around Liverpool and Birkenhead. Bombs were also scattered among other towns and cities across the country.

Friday 2
Evacuation from Greece complete. About 45,000 out of 55,000 troops sent to Greece are now safe.

Even in defeat, the Allied forces had managed to extricate themselves from the jaws of the German military machine. However, as at the Allied evacuation at Dunkirk in 1940, there had been a terrible loss of military equipment and aircraft, which was hard to replace at that stage of the war, and desperately needed by the forces as they prepared to defend Crete.

Note: In researching the figures of casualties and evacuated troops in the Greek campaign, the reference sources consulted vary in several instances. Therefore it was deemed prudent to 'approximate' the numbers quoted in the added text rather than give the conflicting figures. The statistics that my father has quoted must have been taken from media sources of the day.

~~~~~~~~~~

I went up to London for the firm today, to make arrangements re galvanising for Ewarts of Camden Town.

This is another company who do not appear to exist today. Father had progressed as a technical salesman as well as a galvanising technician. With his knowledge of the process and production issues, he would be well prepared for this task. It is also very likely that demands for war work would have been the catalyst for the visit by him as he was now seeking work for the galvanising plant.

~~~~~~~~~~

Trouble in Iraq. Troops are resisting the passage of our men thro' Iraq as in accordance with our treaty.

In the years leading up to WWII, Iraq had been a hotbed of intrigue, coup and counter-coup, assassination, treachery and anti-Semitism. With this in mind, an evaluation of the situation could only be fully comprehended by those who were deeply enmeshed with the political and 'tribal' problems that constantly plagued this regency protected by the British Government. However, I will endeavour to give a brief explanation.

In March 1940, an anti-British, pro-German group took over governmental power, with Rashid Ali Al Keilani as their Prime Minister. In February 1941, when forced to resign from that post, Rashid, then plotted the downfall and elimination of the new Prime Minister, Taha Pasha, and the regent Abdul Ilah, who were both supported by the British.

To compound the intrigue, it was known that the initiative for the coup was promoted by Haj Amin El Husseini, who was known by the elevated title of Grand Mufti of Jerusalem in Palestine. He was intensely anti-Jewish, and had high contacts in the Nazi party, including the notorious Adolf Eichmann. The Mufti wished to hasten the elimination of all Jews in Palestine, and to that end he had Hitler's approval to carry out the 'Final Solution' in that country. Following the outbreak of WWII, and the assassination of the British Commissioner in Galilee, the Mufti fled to Baghdad and was supported financially by the Iraq government. Being pro-Axis, and plotting with those of similar persuasion, the aim was to support the Axis against Britain and France.

On the 1st April 1941 a further coup occurred and yet another government was formed, again with Rashid as Prime Minister. Concerned with the possibility of British reprisals, he decided to honour the Anglo-Iraqi Treaty, and allowed British troops passage through Iraq. However, the British stayed, and Rashid requested assistance from the Axis powers. Hitler sanctioned arms and aircraft to Iraq, but before they could arrive, more British troops had disembarked in Basra, and as a reprisal on the 29th April, several thousand Iraqi troops surrounded the RAF base at Habanniyeh. However, they could not stop the rather antiquated and war-torn RAF aircraft from successfully attacking them on Friday the 2nd May.

Heavy raid on Liverpool.

Repeating previous raids, Liverpool and Birkenhead were targeted by the Luftwaffe, and the dock areas were the enemy aiming points. Regretfully, over 100 fatalities occurred. Of 65 enemy aircraft sent on this raid, Fighter Command claimed 3 German aircraft destroyed.

Saturday 3
Worked all day.
Clocks to be put forward an extra hour tonight. We have been on summer time all thro' the winter – the subject being to squeeze as much daylight as we can out of days which are much too short as far as production goes.

Officially called 'British Double Summertime', this was introduced in 1940 as a means of saving energy resources. It was also due in part to the number of road deaths caused by the 'black-outs', and, for those reasons, it was introduced together with a 20 mph speed limit during 'black-out' periods at night. During winter the time was advanced by one hour over GMT, but in the summer and until the end of the war in 1945, 'British Double Summertime' was in operation, which was two hours advanced on GMT.

Shipping losses last month averaged over 120,000 tons per week. Greek affair caused a lot of this.

The Allied shipping losses throughout the oceans of the world continued to mount.

The German heavy-cruiser 'Admiral Scheer' returned to the port of Kiel on the 1st April after six months at sea, having hunted Allied merchant shipping in the Atlantic and the Indian Ocean. As a solitary raider during that period, the cruiser had accounted for 17 ships totalling over 100,000 tons. It was indeed fortuitous on this date that the ship was laid up in the shipyard at Kiel for an overhaul and therefore not at sea harassing convoys.

On completion of the overhaul and sailing with a task force, the 'Admiral Scheer' then operated in the Baltic in the abortive search for convoys to Russia, remaining for a period in the hostile waters of the Arctic close to Bear Island off the northern coast of Norway. Following the role of support for German troops retreating from the advancing Red Army, the ship returned to Kiel for a refit. It was there, on the 9th April 1945 that the 'Admiral Scheer' was finally attacked and sunk by Allied bombers.

Another big raid on Liverpool. We brought down 16 Gerries which is a record for night defence.
There is a half-moon to help our fighters.

A major attack by over 450 bombers was repeated on Liverpool and Birkenhead, with numerous other locations experiencing raids. Nearly 300 enemy aircraft attacked Merseyside with the docks again being the main target. Massive fires and explosions were reported, resulting in over 450 fatalities and many injured.

Closer to home, Harwich again received bombs. Fighter Command, showing a certain amount of over-claiming and probably supported by press reports after the event, shot down 10 aircraft.

Nothing had been reported locally.

Sunday 4
Usual Sunday. Gardening in the morning and tea at Griggs in the afternoon.

Quisling leader in Iraq has started trouble with our troops – fostered by Germany.

I presume that my father is referring to Rashid Ali Al Keilani.

Small scale hostilities taking place. Hitler is after the oil.

By this date, it is likely that the siege of the RAF base at Habanniyeh was being broadcast to the world.

Prince Regent is calling the nation to his side to oust the Quisling from his position.

During this period, the Germans with their support staff were established in Iraq and were waiting for the arms ordered from Hitler to arrive. They were also paying large sums of money to Rashid and the Mufti for the betrayal of their country.

~~~~~~~~~~

Raid on Belfast. We had warning from 10-30 – 4-30am.
7 Germans down.

Belfast was definitely the main target with Merseyside and Barrow-in-Furness also receiving heavy attacks. Dockyards continued to take a pounding with extensive fires and explosions causing many casualties in these three key locations. East Anglia had taken more punishment at the village of Finchingfield; and Ipswich again suffered.

It is clear that, having failed to wipe out the RAF in the Battle of Britain, Germany was endeavouring to destroy our ability to provide ships for convoys, and was therefore pursuing the ultimate end game - to starve Britain.

Altogether this day, the Luftwaffe lost 5 aircraft.

Monday 5
Busy day at work.
My prospects in my present job appear promising.

Father's ability to control galvanising operations was beginning to give him confidence to progress within Crittall's. He was obviously becoming a valuable asset.

~~~~~~~~~~

Ena seems a little braver during raids. Our little Jane simply ignores them.
We have very anxious nights however, - the end seeming no nearer.

~~~~~~~~~~

Our Air force is now very powerful and Germany is beginning to feel its weight.

During the night of the 4th/5th May, Bomber Command continued to seek out the German 'pocket' battleships by sending 97 aircraft to attack the 'Scharnhorst' and 'Gneisenau' anchored at Brest. Hits were recorded, and to support the perceived success, no RAF bombers were lost - a rare occurrence, as these capital ships were heavily defended.

~~~~~~~~~~

Raid 9-30 – 2-30am. I was on fire watching.
9 Gerries down.

There were heavy raids in Scotland and the North, where enemy bombers continued to target dock areas. Severe damage was recorded, but casualties were remarkably light in comparison with previous raids. However, by this time the war materials situation had become very critical with valuable goods in short supply, and the constant pounding of dock areas had been destroying thousands of tons of desperately needed commodities.

Locally, Eight Ash Green and Clacton received the undesired attention of German bombers.

Despite the continuous and extensive night-fighter sorties (245 aircraft this night) only 3 German aircraft were destroyed.

Tuesday 6

We are wading into Iraq. This affair should not last too long.

Having managed to fly in reinforcements from Basra, the British were able to defeat the Iraqi forces and relieve Habanniyeh. Displaying great initiative and bravery against Iraqi gunfire, the RAF eliminated the Iraqi air force on the ground during this period.

~~~~~~~~~~

Our night fighters are bringing more down now the moon is out.
We are gradually getting more down as the weeks progress.

Once again it is possible that over-claiming and optimism may have enhanced the figures of destroyed aircraft. However, the situation was slowly improving and the 'new devices' installed in more advanced aircraft, together with improved pilot experience, would begin to show much needed progress.

~~~~~~~~~~

America is rising very speedily and may be in the war any time now.

This comment by my father was a reflection of world events as reported by the media of the time, but no-one could have foreseen what was soon to happen to trigger the forthcoming and devastating blow to the United States Navy and Air Force at Pearl Harbour and the Philippines in December.

~~~~~~~~~~

Raid 11-15 – 5-0am.

This was a repeat of the previous night raids, with again Glasgow, Clydeside and Liverpool being targeted together with other towns and cities.

With ruthless efficiency, over 230 bombers carried out the raids in Scotland and large fires and explosions were recorded around shipyards, power stations and armament factories. As a sad consequence, 306 people lost their lives.

In East Anglia, both Ipswich and Clacton had again been particular targets marked out for attack by the Luftwaffe. There had also been an enemy raider reported at Fingringhoe near Colchester.

Although Fighter Command claimed 12 enemy aircraft destroyed, only 4 were subsequently shown as lost by German records during these raids.

We went to bed at 9-15 and stayed there.

Wednesday 7
8 Gerries down last night

As reported on the 6th May, only 4 enemy aircraft were reported destroyed during the extensive raids during the night.

House of commons passed a vote of confidence in the government by a huge majority. Mr Churchill, our great leader, promises further toil, blood, & hardship, but, most certain of all, final victory.

Liverpool, Birkenhead and Hull were the main destinations for the Luftwaffe who despatched 360 aircraft during the night. Docks and industrial installations had again been the targets, which resulted in severe damage to property and more loss of life for inhabitants during that extended battle of attrition. A total of 66,000 houses were destroyed and 70,000 people made homeless - a massive crisis for the areas concerned.

Ipswich continued to be the objective for bombers as were many other towns and cities throughout the country who were playing host to small numbers of raiders.

We brought down 24 Gerries last night.
Great performance.

I am convinced that this is a reporting error by my father - probably with all the enemy bombing activity around, this diary entry may have been written retrospectively (perhaps two days at a time) as this entry should refer to the 7th/8th May, as recorded factually on the following day.

This is a record for night fighters, or 'cats eyes' as we call them.

Flying a Bristol Beaufighter, the names of John 'Cats Eyes' Cunningham, together with his navigator/radar operator, Sgt. Rawnsley, crop up as victors regularly during these air battles. When questioned about their ability to find enemy aircraft during the blackest of nights, rumour has it that they 'suggested' that eating carrots improved their eyesight! This story was put out to the media to cover the fact that radar was the real advantage when intercepting enemy aircraft.

During my younger years, my parents always told me to 'eat up your carrots' to enhance my own eyesight. Now of mature years, I can still spot a 'wee dram of whiskey' at 50 yards, so it must have worked!

On the night of the 6th/7th May, Bomber Command had sent 115 aircraft to bomb Hamburg in difficult weather conditions, which resulted in little success. Strangely, no aircraft were recorded lost if this is the raid referred to by my father in his entry on the 8th May. It is possible that these returning bombers were diverted to other airfields and not reported safe until later.

Thursday 8
We are raiding Germany heavily nowadays. She is getting a touch of what she will get very soon.
We lose few planes in these raids – for example we lost 2 last night against Gerries loss of 24.

As mentioned in yesterday's report, I believe that this is the same entry as that on the night of the 7th/8th May. Although Fighter Command claimed 21 destroyed, the Luftwaffe only lost 13 aircraft. It was a case of mistaken over-claiming and genuine error yet again. This could easily happen if two or more fighters attacked an enemy bomber simultaneously; one not knowing or seeing the other firing on the enemy in the night skies, and both claiming the destruction of the aircraft.

10 Gerries down today in raids over this country.
We lost 1 fighter but the pilot is safe.

Records show that only 4 aircraft - a Ju88 and 3 Bf109's were shot down during daylight raids on this day. However, the following narrative records more destroyed during the night raids.

Raid 12-20 – 5-0am.
13 Gerries down.

Although Nottingham was the main target for the night, part of the main force of over 200 aircraft had been diverted to Hull, with both locations suffering considerable damage. Furthermore, to add more pain to the region, other Midland towns, especially Sheffield, also suffered from attacks by a further 200 plus bombers. During those raids, numerous fires and explosions occurred, and significant damage had been recorded.

Although my father reported 13 aircraft claimed as 'downed' by the RAF this night, the records show only 5 were lost. Therefore, in these rather confusing entries, a total of only 9 enemy aircraft were lost - 4 during the day, and 5 at night.

The one RAF aircraft shot down was a Boulton Paul Defiant, with both airmen reported as being safe. This type of aircraft was crewed by a pilot and radar operator/gunner, and although initially designed as a day fighter it eventually suffered considerable losses against the greatly respected Bf109 during the Battle of Britain, and was then consigned to the role of night-fighter. It was only mildly successful in this role.

Boulton Paul Defiant II, AA370 - pugnacious night-fighter.
(Source: Ken Delve Collection)

On the North Essex coast, Clacton had again claimed unwanted attention from German raiders - in fact, apart from the port of Harwich, the inhabitants of this peacetime seaside resort came under the bombsights of more German aircraft than most other coastal towns in the area. It was not a happy time for those poor folk in the north Essex port.

Friday 9
We gave Germany her biggest raid yet. Hamburg & Brest took most of it tho' bombs were dropped on several other targets.

The battle-cruisers in Brest continued to be the target for a further 89 aircraft on the night of the 7th/8th May, but no hits were confirmed.

With good weather conditions assisting bombing accuracy on the night of the 8th/9th May, the shipbuilding yards in Hamburg had been the main target for 188 aircraft of Bomber Command - a large force for the RAF at that time - and significant destruction was inflicted over a large area causing great fires and loss of life.

A small number of our bombers were sent 'gardening' with some success.

Little news of Battle of Atlantic.

On Friday the 9th May, unknown to the world at large and having been kept an exceptionally close secret by British intelligence, an incident occurred, which concerned the capture of the German submarine U-110 by the British destroyer HMS 'Bulldog'. Located and damaged by British gunfire, and with crewmembers having abandoned ship, the submarine was helpless and slowly settling in the water. Royal Navy crewmen quickly boarded the boat hoping that the encoding machine used to convey radio messages to German bases was still intact. It was - and it was complete, as the operator had no time to destroy the machine in his haste to leave the vessel, probably thinking the submarine was on the point of sinking! The operational 'Enigma' cypher machine was one of the biggest and most important 'catches' of the war. The German High Command knew nothing of that incident, so consequently, British Intelligence were successful in breaking the German communication code by August of 1941 and were then able to plot U-boat positions and thus allow route planners to avoid the deadly 'Wolf Packs'. It had been a major breakthrough, which enabled many ships to be saved and a great amount of food and supplies to be delivered safely to their destinations. Needless to say, it also helped to save lives. The benefit of reading German coded messages allowed convoys to be enlarged and extended across the Atlantic, which was a great bonus for the convoy system, but a bitter blow for the Germans who were unaware at that time that their codes had been compromised.

Little action in Libya – Germans still held.

Rommel's forces had launched an attack on Tobruk on the 1st May. The Australian 9th Division, carefully deployed in their excellent strategic defensive positions, were not overawed by the reputation of the German General or the strength of his army. Doing what they did best, the Australians proceeded to repel and severely maul the attackers by showing extreme tenacity and initiative under intense pressure. It was Rommel who received the 'the bloody nose' and his force had sustained heavy losses in men and tanks.

We are gradually taking control in Iraq.

German aircraft and their crews were being sent to Iraq, and duly arrived at Mosul on the 13th/14th May.

~~~~~~~~~~

Raid 10-40 – 1-30am.
Not so heavy.
3 Gerries down.

The Marconi radio factory at Chelmsford had been the main target for German raiders during the early morning of the 9th May.

The first *'Message Form'* had been written at 03-50hrs by the *'ARP Warden, Marconis, Chelmsford'*. It stated in the *'Message Text – Time of occurrence 02-25hrs – Electricity off, Gas off, Water off, Damage to Plant and machinery unknown. Temporary stoppage of some shops. Approximate number of casualties 12 known and probably 30 in all'*. The next report came in from the Central Report Centre updating the first notification at 04-13hrs. It stated: *'Marconi's and Ridleys mill fire under control. 11 casualties taken to hospital. Search continuing. 7 Marconi'*. This was followed rapidly at 04-45hrs by another, which stated: *'One fatal casualty in MARCONI Road. 4 rescued. Homeless people provided'*. The *'Supplementary Damage Report'* then recorded: *'Marconi works damage in central machine shop stop Fire under control 05-00hrs stop. 12 hospital cases (serious) 14 minor 2 fatal.'*

It must have been most difficult for the rescue and reporting services to grasp the enormity of the incident as the facts emerged. At 10-05hrs, and now with daylight painting a grim picture of the destruction, the tragedy began to unfold, *'Regional Control Cambridge'* reporting: *'Further to my situation report of 06-30 stop Additional damage at Marconi's 2 houses destroyed 4 to be demolished and 250 damaged.'* Apparently caused by a high explosive bomb, the rescue services had to cope with the aftermath of the raid. During the hours of rescue operations, they had at their disposal: *'...5 ambulances, 2 'sitting' cars, 2 stretcher parties, and 2 rescue parties.'* They were all very busy.

As the day wore on it became apparent that there were more casualties than originally expected. A report at 16-16hrs put the casualty figures at: *'Fatal 16. In hospital 24,'* however, that appeared to be changed by the Casualty Officer at 17-25hrs who reported: *'...18 killed and 31 injured at Marconi Works and Marconi Road incident so far as at present ascertained.'*

The final *'Message Form'* had been to *'Regional Control Cambridge, from Essex County Control.'* which recorded the all too frequent problem of weapons yet to be dealt with as an aftermath of the raid. Those tasked to clear the area of danger were informed that: *'Number of UXB's still to be dealt with 77 x small yellows, 1 x paramine, 2 x AA shells, 88 x numbers reported in 24 hours ended noon today 2 HE message ends.'*

The early morning of the 9th May had been a disaster for Marconi's, and it had not been a good day for Chelmsford. But for other towns and cities the tragedy would be multiplied many times over. The next day it would be London that would suffer terribly.

~~~~~~~~~~

There were further isolated incursions during the day, which had been caused by enemy fighter sweeps.

During the night the raids were small, but widespread and destructive all over the country with airfields appearing to be the main targets, although Colchester had received some attention as bombs were reported as having fallen around the town.

2 Luftwaffe aircraft failed to return.

Saturday 10
Went to hospital to check up on my wrist. Now OK.

~~~~~~~~~~

Went to work until 4-30pm.
Tea at Griggs

I am unaware of what my father ate for tea at Griggs, but I am sure that he would have had at least three cups of tea. He was an inveterate tea drinker, and a cigarette would be smoked with each cup! Those were the only times when he would really relax and drift off into deep thought…..

~~~~~~~~~~

Big raid on London at night. 10-40 – 6am.
Much damage & very heavy casualties.
33 Gerries down.
Ena & I saw one Gerry crash in flames.
Our night fighters are getting better results each month.

This was the most devastating raid on London so far. It was a full moon and the Thames tide was at its lowest, making availability of water to damp the fires extremely difficult, if not impossible. Every place within reach of the hoses was explored for water, including swimming pools, canals and ponds. The fire crews searched furiously, and anywhere capable of being reached by those manning the ever-stretching hose lines - some over a mile long - had been investigated. Even though the fires were terrifying and over-whelming the firemen stuck to their task, however, very unfortunately in the course of duty, falling bombs killed many of those very brave men. Although the bombers' concentration point had been in the proximity of Tower Bridge, there was widespread and major destruction in many areas of the City and Dockland areas. Over 1,500 lost their lives during that horrific night.

Apparently, when broadcast by the press, Fighter Command claimed 33 bombers, but in the confusion of battle, over-claiming was again in evidence as the Luftwaffe only lost 11 aircraft.

Certainly, for London, it was a terrible night to remember.

~~~~~~~~~~

Yet again, the raiders targeted the coastal towns of Clacton and Frinton.

Sunday 11

We heavily raided Hamburg, Bremen, Berlin & other objectives in Germany last night.

Our real Blitz has now really started and will get heavier week by week.

Continuing good visibility enabled 119 RAF aircraft to carry out successful attacks in the Hamburg area where many fires were started in the city centre, resulting in several fatalities and severe damage.

A smaller force of 23 aircraft also attacked Berlin, where bombing was reported on targets in the city. There were other minor operations, and bombs were dropped on Emden and mine laying was carried out in the Frisians. 7 of our aircraft failed to return. However, one bomber claimed 2 German night-fighters shot down, which was an unusual event and a small retaliation for the losses inflicted on Bomber Command by the German night-fighters.

~~~~~~~~~~

London had a bad time last night.

~~~~~~~~~~

Marconi's (Chelmsford) was bombed on Friday night. 17 killed.

As previously reported on 9th May, several people had lost their lives during that raid.

Marconi's would have been a legitimate target for German raiders, as the Company was very much involved in 'wireless' communications. Together with Hoffman's, renowned as manufacturers of precision ball-bearings; Crompton's, well known manufacturers of electrical equipment; and Christy's engineering works, the Luftwaffe would certainly have noted Chelmsford as a target of priority in Essex.

~~~~~~~~~~

On this day, an early morning raider in the Chelmsford area had not been so lucky. In a *'Message Form'* timed at 01-32hrs to *'Essex County Control'* it stated: *'Crashed Aircraft Report'*

1. *Behind Strathcote Cottage Beehive Lane Galleywood approx. 1 mile* NE *Church.*
2. *Completely burnt out.*
3. *00-30.*
4. *Unknown but 1 parachutist reported near Forest Lodge Stock.*
5. *Heinkel.*
    Wardens on the spot and crash verified'.

The next report was timed at 04-31hrs, and the text of the message read: *'Reference crashed aircraft report at 01-32. 4 members of crew captured and taken to Chelmsford Police Station.'*

The final report timed at 11-34hrs stated: *'Re Heinkel plane down at Galleywood reported at 00-34 two parachutists came down in field adjoining Mr. Scott's house and gave themselves up to police. A third came down on Mr. Selby's house on Stock-Chelmsford road near 'Ship Inn' and taken prisoner and fourth parachute came down at Crondon Hall. Margaretting Tye.'*

It had certainly been an eventful night for that part of Essex, and at least the defences had something to show for their efforts. Four Germans would be spending the duration of the war, held at 'His Majesty's Pleasure'. However, it was poor exchange for the lives lost in the Marconi incident, which had severely shaken the inhabitants of Chelmsford.

Raids widespread.
10-20 – 2-45am.

Nearly 300 enemy bombers and night fighters were despatched on scattered raids throughout the country during the night. Airfields appeared to be the main targets for the majority of the raiding aircraft, and in addition many towns received attention from the enemy force, with several casualties resulting and much damage inflicted.

East Anglia again suffered, with Ipswich, Elmsett, Great Yarmouth, Felixstowe and Lowestoft receiving attacks.

Closer to home, the following *'Situation Report'* recorded that for the *'Period 09-00hrs 11/5/41 to 09-00hrs 12/5/41'* an incident occurred near Coggeshall: *'At 00-15hrs 4HE and 100 IB fell in fields at Feering.'* Altogether that night, an overwhelming number of incidents occurred in the region - 19 being reported by the Civil Defence and Police. But, was there an error in reporting similar to that on the 26th/27th February?

Coincidentally, the *'Message Report'* from *'Braintree Reporting Centre to Essex County Control'* stated that: *'About 4 HE and 100 IB's fell at Witch Wood 2 miles from Coggeshall along B1024 to Earls Colne at 00-15hrs. 15 IB's and 1 HE all unexploded have been removed to Kelvedon Police Station. No damage was caused beyond fire in the wood which has been extinguished.'* One can only surmise that they had been successfully defused, however, the coincidence of time and weapons dropped does indicate an error by the authorities in the original *'Situation Report.'*

It also appears that enemy night-fighters were targeting RAF planes returning to their bases from the raids on Germany. Fighter Command and AA fire accounted for 7 of these deadly intruders.

Monday 12

America are getting closer to war each day.
The question of convoying their own supplies to England is being discussed. This will ease our shipping problems.
America is all out now aiding Britain.
Altho' dark days may be ahead we are getting more & more confident in our hopes of victory.

Having signed the Lend-Lease bill on the 11th March, President Roosevelt followed this by requesting an appropriation of $7 billion to accomplish the objectives of the Act. Congress approved the request on the 27th March. The preparations were now mounting for America to go on the offensive, and naval strength was expanding to support and protect convoys across the Atlantic.

~~~~~~~~~

Short quietish raid.
11-0 – 1-30am.

The reason for the length of the alert must have been raiders passing to and from their targets in various parts of the country.

There were only 66 enemy aircraft operating over Britain during the day and night, with bombs falling on London, Plymouth, Lowestoft and Falmouth, causing several casualties.

Only 1 German plane was lost during the night raids.

Tuesday 13

The bumps heard on Sunday night were bombs near Purley Farm.
Nearly shook us out of bed.

Purley Farm was situated about two miles from Coggeshall just off the B1024 road to Earls Colne, and is close to Witch Wood. It does seem to reinforce the view that the *'Situation Report'* of this incident may be at fault and the *'Message Report'* may have been correct.

~~~~~~~~~

Rudolf Hess, Hitler's deputy flies from Germany in a plane & bales out over Scotland. He was taken into custody.
Germany said he was insane or else his plane had crashed.
Doctors here say he is sane. Very odd & mystifying.

At just after 11-00pm on the night of the 10th May 1941, Rudolf Hess, the Deputy Führer, and once the closest confidant in pre-war years to Hitler, parachuted into Scotland.

Since the start of the war in Europe, Hess had been slowly falling out of favour with Hitler. By just a matter of degrees, he was probably the least objectionable of the inner circle of Hitler's cronies. He was less anti-Semitic, less unscrupulous, and appeared to want peace with Britain - although his motive for the flight to Britain was to raise his own profile with Hitler. He could see his power diminishing, and wanted to bring himself back into favour. To do this he had secretly decided to make contact with someone he thought could influence those in Britain who might be persuaded to sue for peace with Germany. The man he chose was the Duke of Hamilton, who Hess mistakenly thought was opposed to the policies of the British Government, but who could, he thought, have the ear of the King. However, the Duke was unaware of the plan, and was the rather unwilling recipient of one of the greatest prizes of the war - Hitler's deputy.

Attending a rally in Germany, the 'Nazi Hierarchy': From left to right: Hitler, Goering, Goebbels, Hess.
(Courtesy of the Franklin D. Roosevelt Library Archives)

Having been a soldier fighting in the early years of the First World War, Hess was reassigned at the end of the war to become a fighter pilot, but was too late to see action. However, he was a pilot of renown in the years between the wars, and using skills obtained during air racing, he secretly began to learn to fly the twin-engine Bf110 fighter.

To carry out this inconceivable, yet remarkable journey, he could tell no one, although his senior adjutant learned of his plan just prior to the flight, but kept silent. So it was, after great preparation, and leaving his wife and son without any knowledge of his intent, he set course for Scotland on the evening of the 10th May.

While Hess was in flight, Reichsmarschall Goering had learned of his plan, and announcing that the Deputy Führer had gone mad, he ordered Luftwaffe fighters to have the plane shot down. However, it was too late, as Hess was well on his way to the planned rendezvous.

It was while he was approaching the coast of Scotland that he had two narrow escapes, for as soon as British radar tracked him coming in they sent a Spitfire to intercept. The pilot failed to find the intruder, but shortly after this incident, yet another British aircraft, this time a Defiant night fighter, chased the 'bogey', but to no avail - the cloudy weather and darkening skies had protected him from being shot down by the RAF fighters. However, the weather had also inhibited Hess from finding the Duke's residence at Dungavel House, about 20 miles from the west coast of Scotland. Not being able to find Dungavel, and running low on fuel, he baled out, landing about 10 miles from his intended destination.

Quiet night.

Only Wales and the South coast had scattered raids. It was indeed a quiet night.

Note: There were many unsung operations that were vital to the safety of Britain. Co-ordinating with the guns along our coastline were the searchlight units. Although it could be expected that they experienced plenty of action, it was imperative that they should also practice. Consequently, on a *'Message Form'* sent *'From 'Police Headquarters to Essex County Control'* on the 13th June, the text of the message read: *'Fire Command, Landguard, Suffolk, with permission of Naval Authorities, Harwich, will carry out Searchlight practice commencing 04-00hrs for half an hour on 16th,5th 41. They are also using a launch with target.'*

Wednesday 14
Rudolf Hess's arrival is main topic of the moment.
Strangest thing ever happened. Hitler's closest friend. Seems that things may not be so good in Germany.

People even say it may be the beginning of the end.
No official news has yet been issued.

Having been slightly injured in his fall, Hess was found by a local farm worker, and within a very short period, was taken away by the authorities. He was claiming a false name, but was soon identified as the Deputy Führer. During that period, the Duke of Hamilton had been informed that Hess wished to speak with him. He duly arrived, and Hess told the Duke that he had made the flight to discuss peace terms. Naturally, the Duke stated that Britain was not in the position to adhere to his wishes, and terminated the discussion.

After flying south to meet with Prime Minister Winston Churchill, Hamilton flew back to Scotland with a senior government official, who was an expert on German affairs, so that Hess' identity could be officially verified. Meanwhile, in Germany, the news had been released about the defection of Hess, which was simply put down to the fact that he suffered from mental disturbance and hallucinations. Naturally back in Germany, Hitler was not amused, and promptly arrested those who were involved with assisting Hess, even though they were unaware (except his senior adjutant) of his intentions. However, there was no doubt that the German High Command was not in disarray, and apart from the perceived embarrassment, the whole incident was played down and explained to the German people as an unfortunate episode involving a very sick man.

~~~~~~~~~

Very little air activity.
No night warnings.

Very small raids recorded, with only 2 enemy aircraft destroyed by RAF night-fighters.

Thursday 15
No news re Hess except that he came over to see Lord Hamilton.
In all probability to try & bring about peace.

During this period, Hess had been subjected to a thorough medical examination; initially due to the slight injuries he had suffered during the bale-out and then to assess his mental state. It was deduced that he was basically fit and well, but rather mentally confused and obsessive.

~~~~~~~~~

We are successfully holding Gerry in Libya & are now clearing up in Iraq & Abyssinia.

In Libya, being overstretched and having failed in the attempt to crack the defences at Tobruk, Rommel's forces were in a weakened state. General

Wavell sensed an opportunity to advance a force to retrieve some lost ground; perhaps even to push on to Tobruk, but at least to halt the advance of the Axis forces and push the defensive line further west. Although light on armour, the attack was launched on the 15th May.

~~~~~~~~~~

By this date German aircraft had arrived in Iraq, and on the 13th May proceeded to attack the RAF at Habanniyeh causing a great deal of damage. However, support operations were in hand. The British and Arab Legion force was tasked to relieve Habanniyeh, and troops began to arrive between the 14th and 18th May - this despite constant bombing and strafing by the Luftwaffe and fierce resistance from Iraqi forces. After a desperate battle, and with the aid of Imperial troops and other allies in Iraq, the pro-British forces were able to reduce the hostile action of the pro-Axis Iraqi forces despite German support from the air.

~~~~~~~~~~

Escorted by Major General Orde Wingate, Emperor Haile Selassie returned to Abyssinia and Addis Ababa on the 5th May, where he and the British contingent received a victorious welcome.

~~~~~~~~~~

Raids on small scale 11-15 – 4-0am.
Small scale activity both during the day and at night. Long-range night-fighters were operating over the east of England causing the extended alert.

Friday 16
Vichy government have agreed to new German terms.
Pétain, an old man with an old mans' weakness is giving in to Admiral Darlan anti British French traitor.
90% of the French are with Britain but are fettered.
New terms concern air bases in Syria for Axis drive against Egypt.

The situation regarding the actions and leadership of Vichy France was beginning to cause deep concern amongst the Allies, and it had been evident to Britain for some time that something was brewing in Syria. Together with Lebanon, also under French rule prior to the war, it had fallen under the control of the pro-German Vichy French and evolved as a so-called 'neutral' when Germany invaded France.

However, reports had been filtering through to Britain that, for several weeks, Germans were being landed by ship at Beirut with fake war wounds; others dressed as sportsmen, and still more as 'tourists'. These 'interlopers' were then reported to have taken over airfields from the Vichy French.

It became obvious that German activity in Syria had increased, and it was perceived by the Allies to be a serious potential threat to their forces in North Africa, and also a direct threat to the British bases in Egypt. Any German presence in Syria would also have put at risk British oil supplies from Iraq, so it was imperative that Britain had to protect those vital interests.

Gradually the pressure increased as German planes began using the bases in Syria to refuel on their way to fight the Allied forces in Iraq, and it became very clear that the Vichy French were actively supporting the Axis forces. A decision by the British Government was imminent, and it would mean invading Syria as soon as possible. Churchill certainly had a legitimate cause for concern, and consequently ordered the invasion.

Raid 12-15 – 3-30am.

Carried out by 111 enemy aircraft, the major attack targeted Birmingham during the night, although the raid hit Nuneaton in error. Factories and armament works in Birmingham appeared to be the concentration point for the Germans, but because the bombs dropped had been off the aiming point, fires caused much damage to industrial sectors in Nuneaton.

The enemy lost 2 aircraft, destroyed by Beaufighters.

Note: It must be pointed out that during the previous months, and up to this date, Germany had carried out many raids with small loss of aircraft. This raid on Birmingham was the last of the larger raids for some time. For the millions who had endured constant fear and danger from German attacks, there was to be a lull in the fighting over home territory.

During this 'quieter' period, most raids would be by small numbers of aircraft, and whilst annoying, and causing some damage and casualties, the smaller raids would bring slight relief to the people of Britain. However, it was only temporary.

The reason for the forthcoming reduction in raids was that German High Command started moving forces in preparation for the invasion of Russia.

Saturday 17
We re-capture Sollum from the Germans in Egypt.
Take 500 German prisoners.
Germany, all successes so far, should now begin to taste defeat.
They are up against real armies now.

Wavell's offensive initially met with success as his lightly armoured tanks forced their way first through Halfaya Pass, and then captured Sollum and finally the fort at Capuzzo. However, on the 16th May, Rommel advanced his own heavily armoured force and the attackers were compelled to retire. Their retreat was temporarily halted at Halfaya Pass, where they remained until being removed by German Panzers that had climbed the 200ft escarpment and swept the defenders back into retreat once more. Rommel then 'dug in' his forces to fortify and consolidate the position.

Our raids on Germany are now getting heavier each day. Already we are getting their squeals.

Cologne was the target for 93 Bomber Command aircraft during the night of the 16th/17th May. However, bad weather, good ground defences, and the subsequent inaccuracy of weapons dropped had been very poor and little damage was reported. For this unsuccessful raid, the RAF lost 2 aircraft.

Raid 11-15 – 4-20am.

No activity recorded. The probable cause of the warning could well have been night-fighters roaming the area looking for targets of opportunity.

Sunday 18
America all but in the war. Her stuff is coming over in increasing quantities.
Roosevelt says he will see it gets here.
Little Britain, fighting alone till now, is now getting real assistance.

American naval warships had begun to escort convoys in the western Atlantic as far as Iceland, and it was during those periods that several skirmishes were recorded with German U-boats. America was now beginning to take an active participation in ensuring that supplies were being conveyed to Britain. It was far from safe, but a marked improvement from the days when protection was limited. It would be in the month of June when the British decided to escort convoys for the complete Atlantic route. They organised that the Royal Canadian Navy would cover convoys in the western areas through to a rendezvous south of Iceland, where the British Royal Navy would then escort the ships to Britain. With new technologies and weapons, the scene was set for an improved offensive against the German U-boats.

America, however, had yet to experience the devastating blows that would be inflicted on their own doorstep, when in 1942, having finally entered the war, German submarines appeared around their coastlines picking off ships as they departed for the journey across the Atlantic. As a result of the great distances travelled to reach the coast of America the U-boats had supply submarines supporting the raids, and it was this support that enabled the U-boats to obtain their 'kills'. Aided by the lights along the American coast, which had exposed the ships as they left harbour, the U-boats had been able to close in on their unsuspected prey and consign them to the deep. It was a few months before the US Navy could redress the balance and reduce those attacks that were causing loss of ships and men.

Our air force is great. Our navy greater, but with a big job of work in hand.

It was evident that the British public were acutely aware that Allied forces were struggling to overcome German aggression under very difficult and dangerous circumstances in all areas of conflict. It was also clear that the patriotic emotions stirred during the reporting by the press, cinema and media had been raising hope for the future throughout Britain. However, in reality the situation on this date was far from encouraging.

2 Raids during the night. Not much about. 2 mines fairly close.

Shipping and ports were the main targets around the country, with the Luftwaffe losing 2 aircraft from the raids.

As for the mines, they were probably dropped a considerable distance from Coggeshall, as the explosions could be heard from many miles away.

Monday 19

Hess business still a mystery, but it looks like a split in the axis.

Hess had begun to write letters regarding the purpose of his 'visit'. He naturally tried first to contact the Duke of Hamilton, but being in custody, and unable to communicate openly with anyone in authority, the letter did not reach the Duke - it was now beyond his brief.

51 planes (Gerries) shot down in Syria – at least 20 more damaged on the Ground.

On the 18th June, and as a prelude to an invasion, the 'softening-up' process of the Syrian Air Force began when RAF bombers attacked the airfield at Rayak. However, the raid was not a success. At the same time, bombers destroyed several unidentified aircraft at Palmyra airfield, and they were able to report that at least one of them looked like a He111 of the Luftwaffe, thus indicating Vichy French complicity with the Germans in Syria.

The Royal Air Force and Royal Australian Air Force fighter pilots were also very much in evidence during the initial assault; the 'Pommies' flying Hurricanes and the 'Aussies' flying Tomahawks. Over the period of the campaign the fighters shot down or destroyed on the ground many Axis planes, with the RAAF in particular showing excellent results for their efforts.

Duke of Aosta, last commander in Abyssinia, has surrendered. The war in Abyssinia is ended.

The Duke, resisting to the end, finally surrendered his forces to the British on the 16th May. All that was left was to clear out isolated Italian forces from areas around the country. The hostilities were officially over.

Raid 11-15 – 1-45am. I was on firewatching.
Heavy bomber a few miles off.

It was reported that Lexden and Langenhoe, both situated near Colchester, had received enemy bombs.

Reports state that a variety of enemy aircraft had been lost during the day, but only 1 at night.

Tuesday 20
Bombs dropped last night at Danbury and Chelmsford.

There had been three incidents reported during the night. The first had been at Broomfield, where it was reported that '*4 or 5 HE*' bombs had been dropped at 23-58hrs. The second incident had occurred at Danbury at 02-20hrs when 1 HE was reported, and the final incident at Springfield where it was reported that 1 HE had been dropped.

The Broomfield incident had initially been recorded at 01-12 hrs on a '*Message Form to Regional Control Cambridge,*' and it stated: '*Damage Report - 1 HE near Broomfield Church 2 miles N Chelmsford at 23-58 stop One slight casualty and some damage to telephone lines stop 4 HE in Mill Lane Broomfield at 23-58 caused damage to houses but no casualties.*' The final information regarding the incident was recorded on a '*Situation Report Form*' timed at 05-15hrs. It stated: '*Concise information re damage to house property at Broomfield not yet available report of 1 IB in Pleshey area stop Other information makes it doubtful if IB or flare.*'

Reports of the Danbury incident were first to appear on a '*Message Form*' timed at 02-40hrs. It recorded: '*Damage Report - 1 HE Danbury Church at 02-20. Church on fire - help called for from Chelmsford Fire Brigade - no casualties reported.*' This message was followed at 03-42hrs by a '*Special Report*' that stated: '*Reference message 02-40 Fire DANBURY church now reported as small fire and now extinguished.*' At 03-53, this report was again updated as: '*Supplementary to 02-58. Fire at Danbury church extinguished. Blast damage to houses nearby. Some damage to overhead cables and telephone lines.*' The final report for this incident came in at 04-24hrs and stated: '*Damage Report - Supplementary to message of 02-*

40. Further HE at BUNGALOWS below BELL INN Danbury at 02-20. Damage to houses etc, 6 slight casualties (only 2 reported through correct channels).'

The last incident of the series was recorded in a *'Damage Report'* that recorded: *'1 HE at or near SEWAGE FARM BROOK END SPRINGFIELD at 02-15 Blast damage to surrounding property. Overhead cables and telephone lines damaged.'*

Very cloudy but no day raids.

We still take the offensive in Africa.

Rommel's forces continued to try and push the outer defences of Tobruk, but the besieged garrison still held the line and by July had established a reasonably operational and defensive outer perimeter. However, countless aerial combats took place over the battlefield as the German and Italian fighters struggled to overcome the RAF and RAAF defenders. Many aircraft were destroyed on both sides during these battles, and it was not only the soldiers on the ground that died, as the combatants fought for control of the air above.

Fighting still going on in Iraq.

The British and their Allied forces were getting stronger, and with the German aircraft lacking support and replacement materials, the conflict was swinging in favour of the Allies - they were now heading towards Baghdad.

Germans sending planes to Syria which we have bombed.

It was reported that RAF bombers repeated an attack against Palmyra airfield, and Hurricanes machine-gunned the airfield at Damascus, leaving Axis aircraft badly damaging and burning.

Vichy falling more into German net. France is being sold to Germany.

With French interests spread throughout the world, and as a result of the German invasion and the consequent 'take-over' by the French Vichy government led by Pétain, the gulf between the pro-German and anti-German factions, whether 'free' or in occupied territory, had been wide and acrimonious. Although the majority of French citizens in occupied territory were in that position against their will, the stigma of being controlled by a 'puppet' government would take many years before it could be consigned to history. However, to many a true patriot fighting with the resistance, his or her conscience would be clear. They could not, and would not accept occupation of their beloved France.

The Vichy government would cease to exist the moment France was liberated, but until that day they officially ruled the 'free' south of France, and also in actuality, German Army occupied France in the north, therefore extending their authority to encompass the whole country - with full German approval.

~~~~~~~~~~

Quiet night.

Wednesday 21
Bombs dropped by lone raider on Chelmsford last night. 6 killed. Dropped on flats.

The incident that my father reported had been serious. Early indications came at 01-50hrs in a *'Preliminary Bombing Report,'* which stated: *'HE at Coval Lane Chelmsford 00-50 hours today. Two blocks of flats reported destroyed and damage to other buildings. Six persons reported trapped.'* This was followed rapidly by another stating: *'Chief Warden has asked for Military Assistance to be sent to assist in Rescue Work in Coval Lane.'* There had then been a delay, presumably while the rescue parties gathered themselves and had begun to clear rubble and check the premises for casualties. It was at 05-33 hrs that the next message was sent from *'Central Report Centre'*, that sadly reported: *'Casualties at Coval Lane at present reported are 3 dead, 3 still trapped and 13 rescued.'* The serious nature of the incident had obviously set the authorities quite a task, although at 05-36hrs, a message was sent saying: *'The borough engineer at Coval Lane incident reports that the Brentwood relieving parties will not be required.'* At the scene had been *'...4 ambulances, 1 car for sitting cases, 5 rescue parties.'* At 06-16hrs Essex County Control sent an update to Regional Control Cambridge. It stated: *'Part I. Simple incident at Chelmsford only. Part II. Further to my 01-50 HE at Coval Lane. 3 fatal casualties at present reported no further information yet available. Services used 3 stretcher parties 4 ambulances 5 rescue parties 1 mobile canteen. Extensive damage to house property and damage also to gas water and electricity services. Morale unaffected.'*

Note: The morale issue had been noticeable on the 'Situation Report Form' as a heading that requested the opinion of the writer regarding *'(I) Morale.'* It is evident that the authorities were most keen to know if the bombing raids had begun to demoralise those who were under great stress, and although the incident had produced fatalities, there appears to have been no adverse reaction. The British stiff upper lip had prevailed.

Two more updates came in, one at 06-35hrs and one at 06-45hrs. Both reported: *'Latest casualty return – 5 dead 1 still trapped 10 rescued these are alive.'* The final reports were a sober reminder that the rescue parties could not produce miracles from the devastation. At 09-25hrs and 09-40hrs they stated: *'Casualties – 6 killed 5 seriously injured 3 lightly injured. Damage - 10 flats destroyed, 19 seriously damaged 160 slightly damaged. All residents accounted for.'*

It had been yet another night of distress for the city of Chelmsford. More would follow.

~~~~~~~~~~

Gerry paratroops dressed as Anzacs dropped on Crete, Greek stronghold.
All of them killed or captured.

To capture Crete, Germany launched a massive airborne invasion on the morning of the 20th May.

After the evacuation of a large number of the British, Australian, New Zealand and Greek forces to Crete during the previous month, Hitler considered it vital that he capture this valuable strategic island. He had reasoned that, if he could hold the airfields, then the Allied air forces could not use them as a base and interfere with his supply of oil that he desperately required from the Rumanian oil fields for his planned invasion of Russia. It was therefore imperative that Hitler had to force the Allies out of Crete at the earliest possible opportunity.

The unholy alliance with Russia had been one of convenience to Hitler and Germany. With the original knowledge that Stalin had violently purged his military forces of their top officers, Hitler felt secure that Germany was not in any danger from military action from the Soviets, and therefore forged the 'friendly' agreement with Stalin. However, Russia had been training more 'acceptable' officer material, and thus Hitler became afraid that Russia might once again be a potential force for concern. He therefore decided that it was time to invade before the Russian military had a chance to fully recover, but the Greek intervention has delayed his plans. That decision would lead to disastrous consequences, for when the invasion did eventually occur, the fierce Russian winter turned out to be the German invaders greatest enemy.

The Allied forces numbered about 40,000 active troops, together with very limited support from a few RAF aircraft that remained from the Greek campaign, and a few Royal Navy warships patrolling the coastal waters. The major problem for the force was a serious lack of weapons required to fight any invader, as most had been left behind as the forces withdrew from Greece. Thus, with very depleted resources, the British, Greek, Australian and New Zealand combined forces had to hold the island.

The Germans, however, had their own problems. The aircraft required to airlift the parachute troops were worn and damaged from the Greek campaign, and it was with no little difficulty and an initial shortage of fuel that sufficient Junkers Ju52 transport planes were made available for the impending drop on the 20th May.

The initial outcome of the drop was a severe blow to the Germans, as the resistance was devastating as the troops fell from the skies. As a result of secret code-breaking interception, the Allies had been warned that an invasion was pending, and they were certain that the German forces would be targeting the aerodromes. Therefore, the defending forces were prepared when the first 'chutes blossomed out of the German transport planes and covered the sky like falling leaves. But, they were dropping into an inferno of fire from the defenders, and many of the German troops were killed as they drifted over the target, and many were killed as they landed.

The airfield at Maleme was the dropping zone and the main target for the invaders, and particularly the capture of Hill 107, which was strategically situated to provide an excellent field of defending fire to cover the airfield. It was slaughter on a mass scale. German troops in other locations fared no better as the defenders took a tremendous toll on the airborne enemy troops, with brutal hand-to-hand combats taking place in several locations.

As a result of poor communications, and assuming that all was well with the landing, the Germans sent more parachute troops in a further drop in the afternoon, and similar results occurred. By the evening no airfields were in enemy hands, and with only partial communications amongst the invaders scattered forces, the airborne assault was in disarray and in desperate trouble.

~~~~~~~~~~

No news of Hess.

~~~~~~~~~~

Quiet night.

Underlining a quiet night, as also seen recorded on following nights, must have provided great relief - and sleep.

Thursday 22
Thousands of Parachute troops being landed in Crete. Germans have taken Maleme and its aerodrome, but elsewhere thousands are being 'dealt with' by our troops.
Our airforce cannot operate from Crete and the Germans can therefore attack by bombers & fighters without hindrance.

During the previous night of the 20th/21st May, a task force of German ground troops had been preparing to be shipped to Crete, but the presence of Royal Navy ships had been reported and the force had to withdraw. However, when the German ships finally set sail later on the 21st May, they unexpectedly encountered a large force of British warships. Many of the enemy transports were sunk, and the loss of life taken from the German mountain troops was a devastating blow. The convoy was forced to return and instructed to stay in harbour until the situation on Crete had stabilised.

Meanwhile, a further drop of airborne troops managed to make some progress at Maleme, and eventually cleared a path on the airfield for the first troop carrier to land, coming under intense fire as it did so. However, as the day progressed, more aircraft bringing mountain troops and supplies began to arrive, and having established the bridgehead, they progressed to other areas in Crete to eliminate the brave but inadequately armed Allied forces. For the defenders, this was the beginning of the end as the German troops consolidated their hold on the island.

~~~~~~~~~~

Quiet night.

Friday 23
Little news of Crete.

The German forces were now well established on Crete, however, the Allies were creating pockets of ferocious defence, and the German invaders were still pinned down in many areas. German mountain troops had also been scaling the difficult and mountainous countryside through the day as they fought and stumbled over the rugged terrain to join up with other groups. Throughout all the days' fighting, the Allied force had made it very difficult and extremely dangerous for the German troops, and the enemy casualties were a testament to the fierce resistance in response to the invasion.

~~~~~~~~~~

Our Mediterranean fleet are being badly handled by the German airforce but they are doing wonders in preventing German reinforcements from reaching Crete by water.

The Luftwaffe exacted revenge for the loss of their convoy ships attempting to reach Crete, as several British warships were sunk by bombers and dive-bombers, including the destroyer HMS 'Kelly'. The captain of the 'Kelly', Louis Mountbatten (later Lord Mountbatten of Burma), was one of those rescued.

The Navy was fighting for its life. Having control of the air, the Germans were causing acute distress to the British naval force whose thoughts and actions began to turn to the evacuation of the British and Commonwealth troops.

~~~~~~~~~~

Quiet night.

Saturday 24   Empire Day
Raids on Britain have been few & far between for the last few nights. It may be the weather, but it may also be that the German airforce, altho' large, has been over rated.
There always seems to be a quiet period when Hitler is making an attack elsewhere.
Meanwhile we carry on raiding Germany.

   It was becoming noticeable to the British public that the air raid situation had been easing, as Hitler was indeed looking to make a major attack elsewhere. It would be Russia!

Quiet night.

Sunday 25
Bad news.
HMS Hood, battle cruiser, sunk with all hands. Over 1,300. Unlucky hit in magazine. Bismark was the boat which did it, but it was damaged in the action and is now on the run with several other German warships. The navy will make her pay for this.

   On the 18th May, accompanied by the heavy cruiser 'Prinz Eugen', the battleship 'Bismark' left port with the intention of breaking through the

HMS 'Hood' at anchor.
(Source: David Page, navyphotos)

cordon of British warships and heading for the northern waters of the Atlantic. Their primary mission was that of commerce raiders, with the sole purpose of sinking great numbers of supply ships heading for Britain. They were formidable weapons of war, designed for speed and endurance and possessing devastating fire power, which posed a massive threat to the convoys.

As a result of intelligence gathered from various sources, the Admiralty had anticipated the breakout and had sent the Royal Navy battle-cruiser, HMS 'Hood' and the battleship HMS 'Prince of Wales', to intercept the raiders. The 'Hood' was an old ship that had been launched in 1918, whereas the 'Prince of Wales' had only been recently commissioned. This was to have a critical bearing on the outcome of the battle of the Denmark Strait.

On the 24th May, in the straits between Iceland and Greenland, the 'Hood', sailing under the flag of Admiral Holland, made straight for the 'Bismark' and was the first to open fire at a range of over 10 miles. The 'Prince of Wales' also opened fire striking the 'Bismark', which caused a damaging fuel leak. However, the vulnerable and aged 'Hood' was then dealt a fatal blow as a shell from the 'Bismark' struck home. Witnesses later stated there was an immediate upward surge of flames, followed by a catastrophic explosion. The weakness of the design had somehow allowed a shell to penetrate into an ammunition magazine, which quite literally blew the ship apart. Of the crew of 1,418 men, only three survived that terrible tragedy.

In an effort to avoid the wreckage of the 'Hood', the 'Prince of Wales' itself became vulnerable to the fire of both the 'Bismark' and the 'Prinz Eugen', and had taken several hits. Although not mortally wounded, the 'Prince of Wales' started laying smoke and under cover of that manoeuvre, withdrew from the battle. However, the 'Bismark', was slowed down by leaking fuel and was damaged, so the commander of the operation, Admiral Lutjens, decided to make for the French dry dock at St Nazaire. Leaving the 'Prinz Eugen' to seek safety away from the battle area, the 'Bismark', now on reduced power, was alone - but the Royal Navy was shadowing at a distance. The 'Hood' was soon to be avenged.

~~~~~~~~~~~
Quiet night.

Monday 26
Germans not scattering their parachutists so widely in Crete, but are concentrating more on reinforcing their hold on Maleme.

As usual, Hitler gives no respect for the lives of his soldiers, & just pours them in to almost certain death hoping to tire the defenders.
He has lost thousands of men already in Crete.
The Aussies are going great guns.

German transport aircraft were soon able to supply men and materials by air with relative impunity, and the scale of the operation strongly indicated that all was lost for the Allies. There was no doubt that the Allied forces, although fragmented and ill equipped, were fighting tenaciously to hold their ground in many areas, but the German invasion was irreversible, and the outcome would eventually be conclusive.

Quiet night.

Tuesday 27
We are still chasing the German battleships. The Bismark got another torpedo hit which has slowed her up.
A little bit of luck & we should get her.

'Bismark' at sea.
(Source: David Page, navyphotos)

* *The Hood has been avenged. The navy have sunk the Bismark after a 1,750 mile chase.*
The Bismark was a 35,000 tons battleship and has only been in commission about 4 weeks. Great news.

All British forces were committed to sinking the 'Bismark'. Many ships were now gathering, and during the evening of the 24th May, a small group of Swordfish torpedo planes executed an attack. The damage was superficial as the torpedoes struck the side of the ship, and the massive strength of the armoured belt, constructed to withstand such attacks, did not yield. The Royal Navy force temporarily lost contact with the 'Bismark', but on the 26th May contact was resumed, and during the late evening a further strike by torpedo armed Swordfish was launched from the aircraft carrier 'Ark Royal'. Only one torpedo caused damage. By good fortune it struck the rudder and steering gear, rendering the ship virtually uncontrollable. The only manoeuvre the ship was capable of executing was a large circle, leaving the 'Bismark' damaged and extremely vulnerable as the crew fought to release the jammed gear - but to no avail. During this period the ship was under constant attack, but not fatally damaged. However, on the morning of the 27th May, with HMS 'Rodney' and HMS 'King George V' leading the attack, the 'Bismark' began to take deadly blows. With other Royal Navy ships closing, and many more hits being taken, the final strikes were fatal, as one devastating salvo destroyed the bridge, leaving the ship helpless and without command. As a result of that critical blow, an order was issued to abandon ship and scuttle the 'Bismark'. Many of the crew went over the side, but many were trapped in lower decks as she went down.

In a humanitarian act of compassion for the enemy, when the Navy closed in to take on survivors an alarm was raised indicating the presence of a U-boat, and that situation resulted in the rapid departure and abandonment of the rescue. Eventually, just over 100 sailors were rescued, but over 2,000 perished.

The 'Bismark' had put up a tremendous fight, but in the end had succumbed to a 'lucky' hit by a torpedo, and from then on was virtually helpless and unable to survive. The battle of the Denmark Strait was over. The 'Hood' had been avenged.

~~~~~~~~~~

Several short raids at night. Few planes.

Not many enemy aircraft ventured over our shores, and consequently the only loss was one aircraft destroyed by Spitfires that evening.

Wednesday 28
Bismark sinking is the main topic at the moment.
She was a modern, very powerfully armed, ship, and was claimed by the Germans to be unsinkable.

It was a claim soon disproved.

~~~~~~~~~~

Roosevelt speaks – declares state of emergency in U.S.A.

In a patriotic and protracted speech to the American people, Franklin D.

Roosevelt spoke to the nation on the 27th May 1941. The context of the speech was one of national unity, of being aware of the dangers of Nazism, and the direct threat to the people of the world. There were many key issues raised, and he commenced by stressing that 'Hitlerism' would develop into world domination, and America must not let that happen.

Roosevelt continued by stating that America was currently commencing a massive armament program and increasing naval resources and building a new Army; all this to aid democracies in maintaining their liberty. He related the sad events that led to all those countries losing their freedom to Nazism - in Europe particularly, and announced that $7 billion dollars would be provided in Lend-Lease for those still able to fight for their right to freedom from oppression. He made the point that by providing that aid it would help to defend America.

His praise for Britain in her 'gallant' battle against Germany was profound, but it was the threat of the swastika over 'vast territories' that the free world must defend, and that Hitler's 'honeyed words' for peace would never be trusted.

Roosevelt appealed to the people of America as he explained that industry, farming, religion, and the American way of life was at severe risk, and he painted the desperate picture of those many parts of the world then under Nazi control. The American people had to have a total understanding that it would be America's fate if the country did not rise to the challenge.

However, he was very clear about the state of the war at sea, and stressed that if the Axis could not control the seas, then defeat for them was certain. But, he warned, in the current Battle of the Atlantic, there was the on-going and acute danger of U-boats sinking ships bound for Britain. He revealed for the first time that, at the present rate of sinking, it was '…more than three times as high as the capacity of British shipyards to replace them: it is more than twice the combined British and American output of merchant ships today'. That was a most profound and worrying statement, and he continued by stressing the difficulty of keeping the ocean routes open. 'America cannot'…, he explained, '…wait for Germany to come…' to them, and they must take the fight to the Axis, but, they must be <u>willing</u> to fight. Roosevelt was exhorting all American people to take part in the common defence of the Nation, whatever their views and persuasions, and that they must choose freedom and must not waver from that course.

The speech was factually disturbing for the citizens of America, it was patriotic and in a sense, stimulating, as he encouraged the fight in defence of freedom. He finished his long oratory by confirming the policies he had outlined and finally proclaimed an 'Unlimited National Emergency' existed from that day - Proclamation No. 2487 - 27th May 1941.

Essentially, it was the great 'wake-up' call for America and all its people. The Nation was about to go into top gear, but it would be the events at Pearl Harbour that would put America into overdrive!

They will see our goods over. America are in this as much as we are.

The speech had said it all, and Britain now had the greatest potential ally supporting our country in the fight for survival. Very soon the two great nations would be fighting side by side, but at that moment in time, the battle was desperate and Britain had to look to America for increasing aid from across the Atlantic. However, that task would become more bloody and desperate in the coming year as the Kriegsmarine built up its strength of U-boats in the Atlantic.

Terrific fighting in Crete.
Germans have gained foothold at terrific cost.

The RAF had recently tried to reinforce the sparse numbers of aircraft on the island in an endeavour to counter the vastly superior force of the Luftwaffe. They still had tenuous hold of the unoccupied airfield at Iraclion, but this was soon to be lost as German airborne troops were dropped in the vicinity. They quickly had control of the airfield, as the position was not defended. The Royal Navy had evacuated the British force the previous night.

Night raids. Several bumps.

Bombs were dropped on Jaywick on the Essex coast during the night.

Thursday 29

Germans still raining troops on Crete. They have gained some ground at terrific cost.
Maleme, Canea, & Suda Bay is in their hands, but fighting is still going on.

Despite the confusion of German forces regrouping to eliminate pockets of resistance, the German attackers had nearly reached the southern coast of Crete. The fight for the island was virtually over.

The battle of the Atlantic is still being fiercely fought.
We are losing many thousands of tons of merchant shipping but Germany are also losing U-Boats & shipping at a fast rate. Roosevelt will assist us greatly when he brings his own material over.

During the first six months of 1941, shipping losses were 263 ships (1,451,595 tons) but the German Navy had lost 12 U-boats. The situation would improve in the last 6 months of the year, thus providing a temporary respite, but German industry was building many new and improved U-boats to ravage the convoys in the following year.

Quiet night.

Friday 30
Very little news of fighting in Crete. Situation is serious, tho' we are giving Gerry hordes hell.

Having received orders, and amid the confusion, the defending troops made their way to the nearest pickup points, and if they were lucky, sought out a Royal Navy ship that would take them on board. However, they were still not safe, as the ships had to run the gauntlet of potential attacks by the Luftwaffe, even though much of the evacuation was carried out at night.

Our naval losses must be heavy for they are operating under continued dive bombing by the Germans, but here again we are giving more than we are taking.

Carried out by the Royal Navy under desperate and dangerous conditions, the evacuation was now well advanced, with those capable of evacuation sailing to Egypt. The Navy had taken a terrible pounding, and had lost several ships and hundreds of sailors in the air attacks by the Luftwaffe. There was no doubt that the German control of the air had given a great advantage to their bombers, as they were able to approach the ships with relative impunity. However, the Navy was not toothless, and it also inflicted losses to aircraft of the Luftwaffe.

At sea, and in the air, it had almost been a fight to a standstill. The Royal Navy had been virtually neutralised, and the Luftwaffe received a bloody nose losing many aircraft and troops in the airborne invasion. Whatever cost was incurred upon opposing forces during the closing stages of that sea and air battle, the fight for Crete was lost. It just left a matter of how many of the British and Commonwealth forces could be rescued?

The situation in Iraq is now almost cleared up.
The rebel chief has fled.

Having arrived on the outskirts Baghdad on the 28th May, and as a result of a rumour that many tanks were approaching the city, Prime Minister Rashid and the Mufti Haj Amin El Husseini, together with their associates, fled to Berlin. The insurrection had been quelled.

~~~~~~~~~~

Quiet night.

Saturday 31
Still no news of Crete.

The evacuation was nearly complete. Enduring a constant bombardment from the air, the British Navy had carried out a remarkable but costly evacuation of troops against the most incredible and devastating odds. A large number of troops would be free to fight again, but many lay at rest in the crumbling ruins of the Crete battlefield.

~~~~~~~~~~

Battle of the Atlantic still raging. Roosevelt states that Britain is losing shipping 3 times faster than she can replace them.
America will see to it that this situation is altered.
America is doing a lot of talking (an American privilege). Action is starting but not so fast as the talking.

The United States certainly was gearing itself for action! Built to a standardised design capable of mass production, the first Liberty ship was under construction in America. This would revolutionise the concept of shipping cargo. Eventually launched in September of 1941, and named the SS 'Patrick Henry' it was the first of over 2,750 of its type, destined to provide the requirement of rapidly produced ships for the Allied merchant fleets, both in the Atlantic and around the world as the war progressed.

~~~~~~~~~~

Quiet night.

JUNE 1941

Sunday 1 Whit Sunday
More bad news.
We have evacuated Crete. Approx. 15,000 of our troops got away to
Egypt.
Our losses heavy but Gerry losses heavier.
Hitler expected to take Crete in 2 days. It took him 12 days.
We lost Crete because we could not defend our troops from dive
bombing.

In the final analysis, approximately 15,000 troops were evacuated, leaving nearly 12,000 British and Commonwealth troops and over 5,000 Greek troops to be taken prisoner, some of whom were able to 'disappear' into the fields and mountains to carry on a war of resistance against the fascists. Although it is difficult to verify the final figures, about 3,500 Allied fighting men died, against the German casualties of nearly 4,000 killed. The Royal Navy had also suffered a terrible loss of valuable ships, and with them the irreplaceable lives of over 2,000 sailors.

~~~~~~~~~~~

Quiet night.

It may have been locally, but there were 31 fatalities when over 100 enemy aircraft raided Manchester and Merseyside and also other targets throughout the Midlands. The Luftwaffe lost only 1 aircraft.

Monday 2 Whit Monday
Holiday. Spent the day at Grigglands as usual.
Jane out for first time for a week. She has had a bad chill.

~~~~~~~~~~~

Everybody depressed about Crete. We certainly have done all the
retreating against Gerry so far, - on land anyway.

The previous months for the British and Commonwealth forces had been disastrous, but the tide would begin to turn in North Africa the following year, and the long haul on the road to freedom for the free world would then commence. However, 1941 would bring more reversals in fortune; some more devastating than others. It was not a good year in the war for the Allies.

~~~~~~~~~~~

Our airforce & navy will lick him.
Another day of optimism!

~~~~~~~~~~~

Short raid 3-30 – 4am.

Berwick-on-Tweed and Hull were the main targets for the night, and 15 fatalities were recorded.

Tuesday 3

Vichy Govt. are a slimy lot. Darlan is betraying his country. It will be due to him if France take arms on the side of Germany.
All senses of decency, self respect, & honour, have been ignored in the present war. Even, our Ally, France, is being slowly corrupted.
We will win this war. What sort of slimy excuses will these traitors invent then?

This situation must have severely aggravated and annoyed the British, who probably had a poor impression of the French at that time. Certainly the media of the day must have given a scathing resume of the situation, as it definitely seemed to upset my father! However, there were many brave patriots, and their fight continued under cover in France right through until the end of the war. It must also be remembered that a considerable number of the French Army had been evacuated at Dunkirk, and under General de Gaulle who was then resident in England, they continued their fight when the Allies invaded Europe on the 6th June 1944. Those who did not join with the Vichy, and were not captured by the Germans, fought on with the Free French Army and Navy, together with French Air Force pilots who escaped and joined the RAF when Germany invaded France. All true citizens who were willing and able joined in combat to beat the enemy.

Short raid.

Bombs fell in Essex, and further incidents were recorded in other locations in East Anglia.

Wednesday 4

Syria appears to be Hitler's next move. Syria is French & altho' Germans are oozing in now, France says she will defend Syria alone against any attack by England.
Traitorous words.
If we attacked Syria it would be only to be a step ahead of Germany. – and we are supposed to be fighting for freedom – for France, among other invaded countries.
Does she want to be freed?

With German activity in Syria increasing, the 'softening-up' process by the Allied air component had been efficient and tactically successful. It mattered not that the German Air Force was supporting the Vichy French, as the swift and aggressive Allied air pre-invasion attack had paved the way for the ground assault to commence. Yes, France did want to be freed - of the Vichy French and the Germans.

A free France <u>was</u> worth fighting for.

Wide scale raids.

About 100 aircraft bombed Birmingham and the Medway, and isolated incidents were recorded in other areas, including Langham in Essex.

The Germans lost 3 aircraft to RAF fighters.

Thursday 5

It appears that the Vichy Govt. is not having all its own way in France.
The French people do not want to fight against their old allies, less still do they want to be under German domination.

Father, like many others, had thought that France was an ally regardless of the German invasion, and it was difficult to comprehend that although most of the French preferred an allegiance to Britain, there were others who did not.

German raids are again on a small scale over this country, which makes it appear that they are short of something.

Odd planes about.

With little recorded enemy activity, it is possible that these aircraft were our own night-fighters.

Friday 6

General Weygand, C.O.C. French Forces, pays a visit to Quisling Darlan & Grandad Pétain.
Weygand has been with French forces in Africa since the collapse of France.
He is no quisling, & should not be surprised if he says 'no' to several things to the Vichy Govt.

In the year of 1941, the profile of General Maxime Weygand showed him to be an unbending and self-centred character. He was anti-Semitic and treated Jews with contempt. He was also against the Protocols of Paris, which, having been signed on behalf of the Vichy Government by Admiral Darlan, granted bases to the Axis to allow defence against the Allies.

However, although Weygand disagreed with this policy of giving Hitler French territory, and in his position as Delegate-General to the North African territories, he assisted Rommel by gifting him French war materials against the Allies. The reasoning for this co-operation was that he wanted France to retain the Empire and authority that it controlled before the war. Although a partial collaborator, he was a man who ran his own agenda, and was so distrusted by Hitler, he was recalled from North Africa at the end of 1941 and confined for the rest of the war.

It is with hindsight that our knowledge today of Weygand differs from that which had been insinuated in the media reports of 1941. He did not wish to collaborate with the Allies, and could therefore be termed as an Axis collaborator with his own nationalistic agenda.

~~~~~~~~~~

Quite a lot of discussion here over the ineffectiveness of our resistance in Crete.

There had been no doubt that the loss of Crete was a bitter blow, felt very deeply in both political and military circles, and it could not fail to be felt by the British and Commonwealth public at large. The debate would soon come in the House of Commons, when certain aggressive politicians attempted to put Winston Churchill 'on the mat', but it would take a very intelligent and erudite orator to get the better of him in a contentious debate!

~~~~~~~~~~

Quietish night.

There had been considerable damage evident at Brentford, but no raids were reported locally.

~~~~~~~~~~

Strange Occurrence: In a *'Situation Report'* for the *'Period 09-00hrs 5/6/41 to 09-00hrs 9/6/41'* it was reported that: *'At 20-40hrs 7/6/41, Rifleman 6853654 Edwin Dacy of 7ᵗʰ Battalion K.R.R. was slightly wounded in the left hand when he accidentally fired a revolver in the lavatory of a cinema at Saffron Walden. Dacy received treatment at Saffron Walden General Hospital.'*

Saturday 7
Signed off Colchester Hospital today. My wrist was broken early in November.

This must have been a considerable relief, for although the plaster had been removed, it was important that the healing had been progressing according to plan. This day for my father seemed to be the end of the 'broken wrist' saga - a painful and annoying injury to carry around in time of need.

~~~~~~~~~~

Very little news from anywhere.
Fighting still going on in Abyssinia tho' it is just a case of mopping up the rats.

There were still Italians who refused to surrender. Annoying as it must have been to keep British and Allied troops in the country unnecessarily, it was important that all resistance should be eliminated.

~~~~~~~~~~

Position in Iraq now fairly secure

The result for the Allied troops and the RAF was very satisfying. That they were able to reinforce their airfield in Habanniyeh with troops at short notice and under constant attack by Iraqi forces and German aircraft; they still succeeded in winning the conflict. It was also a very satisfying bonus to the British Government, especially as the initial cause of poor political management together with a corrupt Iraqi government might well have initiated the problem in the first place.

But for the Jews in Palestine, the Mufti and his Nazi 'friends' would continue to threaten their existence for years to come.

~~~~~~~~~~

Quiet night.

Sunday 8
Reported disagreement between Weygand and Darlan. Weygand will not work against his former allies.

Second only in authority to Marshal Pétain in Vichy France, Darlan was perceived as a rather enigmatic character. In his position in June 1941, he virtually ran the Pétain Vichy government, as he had responsibilities in most vital policies. He was, like Weygand, a fervent nationalist, and had favoured the route of collaborating with Germany, but on terms that favoured France. He was not successful in this aim for Hitler was not one to negotiate with defeated parties, although he did agree with Darlan's request to keep Vichy naval ships under his command. Darlan was also seen as anti-British, reinforced by Churchill's decision to instruct the Royal Navy to sink the Vichy warships at Mers El Kebir in 1940 to avoid them being requisitioned by Germany. In fact, Admiral Darlan was not prepared to let anyone have French ships as his dislike for Britain, Germany, and Italy was profound, and it was suspected that he was about to issue orders to scuttle his fleet rather than submit it to the Allies or the Axis. If that was so, he had been too late, as the Royal Navy carried out the task for him.

Darlan was eventually forced to hand over his political powers during 1942, but remained in charge of the French armed forces. However, whilst in Algiers during that November, a 'putsch' carried out by the French resistance and other disaffected parties rendered him impotent, and having been put under pressure by the Allies he was forced to change his allegiance and support the Free French. He did not live long enough to see the result of that decision, for on Christmas Eve 1942, a member of the French resistance shot him to death.

We in Britain can only imagine what it must have been like to live under the Axis jackboot, and the difficulties those in limited power would encounter. There must have been great disputes regarding Axis infected policy, but it can only be conjecture as to why my father made the comment that Weygand and Darlan were in disagreement.

It appears that, in the final analysis, both Weygand and Darlan were architects of their own agenda, and their own downfall.

Roosevelt warns Vichy Govt. against co-operation with Germany. Darlan hesitating.

Whilst mindful of the warning, and soon to be stripped of responsibility in the Vichy government, Darlan would become isolated and vulnerable to Allied manoeuvring in his position in North Africa.

Quiet night.

Although a few bombs were recorded in Essex, with one notable incident at Stisted, it appears bad weather may have hampered the raiders.

Monday 9
The 'Hess' business still remains a mystery, tho' it appears pretty certain that he was a fugitive.

Revealed after the war was a reported attempt by German agents to assassinate Hess. While difficult to verify this claim, some agents had apparently parachuted in to England. However, they were caught but their motive was never proven, although the intelligence agencies were reasonably sure that an attempt had been made

There were one or two episodes of note concerning his captivity. On one occasion he slipped his captors and attempted to commit suicide by leaping over a balcony. He was injured in the fall and spent many weeks incapacitated with his injuries. He was also allowed to write a series of letters to his family, as well as one to Adolf Hitler - whether or not Hitler received it was not known, but if he did, he reaction was not recorded!

Eventually, as the war progressed and finally ended, Hess was sentenced at the Nuremberg war crime trials to life imprisonment at Spandau prison in Germany. The terms of confinement were that he would be guarded for the rest of his life by the war powers; Britain, France, Russia and USA. As the years progressed there were attempts to release him, but the Russians always vetoed the appeals.

On the 17th August 1987, aged 93, Hess committed suicide by hanging himself, but the mystery surrounding the whole episode of his flight to Scotland together with his motives and the surrounding secrecy never went away. The details and facts still remain clouded with conjecture now, many years after his death. However, it certainly was a strange and mysterious affair, and only when final details are released by the relevant MI6 records, will the truth be told - or will it?

It is hinted that we are gaining ground in the battle of the Atlantic, tho' it is by no means won yet.

By this date U-boats were encountering increased difficulty in finding and attacking the convoys. The Allies increased their anti-submarine forces around the ships with growing numbers of escort vessels, and combined with the strength of the improved and consolidated convoy system, it became inevitable that the U-boats were less potent as an aggressive force during this period of the Battle. The Royal Navy had at last begun to successfully fight back with counter measures designed to reduce shipping casualties.

It is estimated that we have lost about 2,000,000 tons of shipping since the battle began about 5 months ago.

Having previously mentioned that shipping losses to U-boats had been recorded at less than 1,500,000 tons, the figures stated in this entry may well have been losses by all causes world-wide.

Scattered raids.

Tuesday 10
Crete debate opens in the House of Commons.
Winston explains matter by saying that we sent all the material we could possibly spare to Crete, without weakening more important positions in Egypt and at home.

It was realized that the defence of the island would be hazardous, but the task was taken on and the result was more satisfactory than if we had let Gerry walk in.

During the debate, Churchill said: 'We provided in Crete a deterrent to enemy attack sufficient to require a major effort on his part, but to attempt to be safe everywhere is to make sure of being strong nowhere. . . Suppose we had never gone to Greece. And suppose we had never defended Crete. Where would the Germans be now? Suppose we had simply resigned territory and strategic points to them without a fight, might they not . . . already be masters of Syria and Iraq and preparing themselves for an advance into Persia?'

The House may not have been truly satisfied, but the truth was that, like our fighting forces, he was fighting politically from a defensive position and could do no more than parry the voices of discontent for that moment.

~~~~~~~~~~

Quiet night

Nothing of significance had been reported locally.

Wednesday 11

We started to walk into Syria on Monday.
We are meeting slight opposition from the French, but we are advancing satisfactorily.
German 'tourists' had started to arrive in Syria, so we got going before Gerry did.
Gerry is after oil.

On the 7th/8th June, British, Indian, Australian and Free French forces under the command of General Sir Henry Maitland, struck north from Palestine into Syria and Lebanon. It was reported that, preceding the attack, several hundred Palestinian Jewish patriots carried out acts of sabotage to pave the way for the Allies. Maitland sent one part of his force to capture the vital port of Beirut; another force was sent through the mountainous terrain of Druse intent on capturing Damascus, and the final attacking group headed for the Vichy French garrison at Deir-ez-Zor.

~~~~~~~~~~

Raids widespread & slightly heavier. Bombs dropped in Witham (in allotments).
No damage.

Perhaps the Germans were trying their own form of 'Gardening' in the allotments? Whatever the motive, the *'Situation Report'* had two items of interest for the *'Period 09-00hrs 9/6/41 to 09-00hrs 12/6/41,'* but especially for the 11ᵗʰ June. The first item of interest recorded in the *'Situation Report'* was of a flying incident. It was reported that: *'At 10-20hrs 11/6/41 a British Hurricane aircraft, No 6677, crashed and burnt out in a field at Thaxted. Pilot safe. Military guard RAF.'*

The second was one of 5 air raid incidents reported locally, and one report stated that: *'At 03-50hrs 3 HE fell at Witham, causing damage to 11 houses. No casualties.'*

There had been increased activity on this night with small scale but damaging raids widespread through the southern parts of England. Sadly, 56 people were reported killed during these incursions.

Thursday 12
Headlines in papers read:-
German troops mass on Soviet frontier! *Gerry is after oil.*
The point is, what will Stalin do – resist or give way to pressure?

For some considerable period it had become very evident to those within Allied intelligence services that it was Hitler's intention is to renege on his 'pact' with Stalin. The Soviet leader was receiving warnings of German military movements towards Russia's borders from his own intelligence services and also from Britain (but he was suspicious of their intent), and was being placated by the German government who stated that German forces were being relocated due to Allied bombing! It appeared Stalin did not wish to believe that an invasion was being planned, and it appeared that he did not put his forces on high alert to counter German movements. Russia was unprepared for the coming invasion.

We are still forging ahead in Syria, in spite of a certain amount of resistance.

The invasion was supported throughout by the RAF, the Royal Australian Air Force, and Allied warships, but the 'Armée du Levant' Vichy defenders under their leader General Henri Levant fiercely resisted the invasion and made it very tough for the Allied troops on the ground.

In Lebanon the fighting was desperate. Attack and counter-attack had been exchanged, with Vichy forces fiercely resisting British and Australian troops.

Raid at night.
Several planes overhead but heard no bombs.

Some slight bomb damage was reported in Lowestoft, but very little else was recorded.

Friday 13
It seems that we can look forward to less night raiding, as several government officials are dropping hints to that effect.

This observation was most likely the result of the rising tension between Hitler and Stalin, clearly indicating confrontation. It was also very likely that British Government intelligence agencies and code-breakers were pointing to this fact, and that it was evident to them that the reduction in raids had been attributed to the probability that Germany was going to invade Russia.

Gerry pocket battleship hit by aerial torpedo.
Trying to limp home.

Originally launched in July 1939 as a pocket battleship *(Panzerschiff)*, 'Deutschland' had been re-classified as a heavy cruiser in 1940 and re-named 'Lützow'. It had been sailing to Drontheim Fjord to carry out torpedo practise on the 12th May, but later that day, the ship had more practice than expected. The 'Lützow' was attacked in the Eger Sound by a British bomber, which successfully dropped a torpedo and severely damaged the ship. Consequently, the mission was terminated, the ship returned to port for repairs, and as a result of the damage spent a considerable time being restored to full operational order.

We raided the Ruhr last night on the biggest scale of the war.
Tremendous damage by our 'beautiful' bombs.

On this night, 91 aircraft attacked the target of Soest, but conditions did not assist accurate bombing. A further 82 aircraft bombed Hamm, 80 more bombed Schwerte and 61 bombed Osnabrück with very little damage recorded.

Other, smaller raids occurred with Bomber Command reporting 4 aircraft missing from all the attacks.

Quietish raid at night.

The main targets for about 100 Luftwaffe bombers and night-fighters had been the South-East and South Coast. It was a better time for the RAF night-fighters as 6 enemy aircraft were destroyed.

Saturday 14
At work all day.

Still going forward in Syria. Damascus surrounded & asked to surrender.

The advance of the Free French, Indian, Australian and the British force had been thrusting towards Damascus under difficult conditions. Resistance had begun to take a heavy toll on defenders, and also on the Allies.

~~~~~~~~~~

Bremen reported sunk & Europa hit.
That's the stuff.

Originally built and launched in 1928 by the Germans to challenge for the Blue Riband, the 50,000 ton 'Bremen' became the fastest liner to cross the Atlantic, taking the prize from the old British liner, the 'Mauretania'. Due for completion at the same time as 'Bremen', her sister ship 'Europa' was seriously damaged by fire and had sunk during fitting out; was then raised and completed and joined the 'Bremen' on the Atlantic run. She briefly held the record until the 'Bremen' regained the prestigious title of fastest ship in the world back again in 1933.

In 1939, having sailed the Atlantic for several years and with the war imminent, the 'Bremen' was in New York Harbour. The British, not wanting the ship to return to Germany, tried to stop her sailing, but 'Bremen' outran the British cruiser tasked to stop the crossing, and disappeared into the Atlantic; the crew somehow managing to repaint the ships structures camouflage grey 'en route'! Temporarily berthing at Murmansk, the ship finally arrived in Germany in December 1939.

Plans were made for 'Bremen' to become an armed troop transport, but when this had been considered unsatisfactory, the ship languished at Bremerhaven where in March 1941 a massive fire gutted the ship causing it to be totally destroyed. It was subsequently determined that it had been sabotaged by a disgruntled crewman.

Also considered as an armed troop transport, the 'Europa', survived the war and was given to France as war reparations, where it was refitted for passenger carrying once again. The ship's name was changed, with great significance, to 'Liberté'. Sunk once more in a storm whilst being refitted, the 'Liberté' was raised yet again and finally operated as a liner until it was laid up and scrapped in 1962.

~~~~~~~~~~

Quietish night.
We had a short raid but heard nothing.

This was probably a lone raider as there is no outstanding occurrence highlighted in my records.

~~~~~~~~~~

We raided Germany heavily last night again. They are now getting a taste of war.

In a repeat of previous raids on Brest, the targets were the 3 large ships, the 'Scharnhorst', 'Gneisenau' and the recently arrived 'Prince Eugen', but bad weather combined with smoke-screens prevented accurate bombing by 110 RAF bombers, all of which returned safely. There was a further raid on Schwerte, with other minor operations being recorded elsewhere on the continent.

Sunday 15
Spent morning in garden.

Father at last had time for more gardening. After a rather hectic period at work, and now with a fully healed wrist, he was able to enjoy some time in cultivation and tending some of the vegetables that would soon be ready for eating or processing for storage.

Tennis at Griggs after dinner, then went for ride around the country side. First pleasure ride since the war started.

It is evident that this was a quieter period in the war at home, where peacetime activities were once more being enjoyed, albeit for a short period. Obviously, with petrol rationed, it could only have been a short trip around the locality, and may well have been with 'Pop', who, being a farmer, was able to visit his two other small farms in the locality. Whatever it was, he did three things that gave him pleasure and satisfaction on that day - gardening, tennis, and an enjoyable ride around the beautiful English countryside in summer. It was also very likely that my mother and Jane went with him on that pleasurable excursion. However, it was an unusual day.

Hitler is again very quiet lately. Preparing for his next 'blitz' we expect.
It might be anywhere at any time.

Hitler was saving the majority of his resources for the assault on Russia. He would continue bombing raids on Britain, but they would be on a reduced scale as a result of his commitment on the Eastern Front.

No night raids.

Monday 16
Germany is getting very heavy raids each night now.
Our new bombs are creating terrific chaos especially in the Ruhr.

The targets for the night of the 15th/16th June were 91 aircraft to Cologne and 58 aircraft to Düsseldorf, but the raids were not successful with 1 aircraft failing to return from the Cologne raid, and 2 more were reported missing from other minor raids.

Beautiful weather, but still no German air activity, other than a few small scale night raids.

Short night raid.

Nothing of significance had been recorded in Essex or East Anglia.

Tuesday 17

Another heavy raid over Germany. Our raids are now heavier than anything we have had, since last Sept.
Wonder how they like their medicine?

Cologne, Düsseldorf and Duisburg were the major targets for 209 aircraft during the night of the 16th/17th June. Although there were a few casualties, bombing was scattered and very little damage was reported. The RAF recorded 1 aircraft lost on these raids, and 1 on another of the minor raids that night.

Short raid.

Probably single raiders again.

Wednesday 18

Topic of the moment – what is Russia going to do?
Germany is massing men & material on the Russian frontier, & Russia appear to be doing the same.

Having carefully prepared and carried out deception operations prior to the intended invasion, Hitler and his commanders eventually conceived a plan to attack with a three-pronged offensive. Consisting of over 3 million men and vast quantities of armour, aircraft, guns and support materials, Hitler's invasion force of fighting men from several Axis countries gathered at the Russian borders. The danger was now becoming evident.

For the Soviets, the pre-war economy had become more biased towards military production, and their resources had increased significantly. However, Stalin was still not convinced that Germany would invade. His intelligence sources continued to give him clear signs that it would occur, even the date of the invasion, but he did not wish to believe those signs. He therefore took the miscalculated risk that Germany would not invade. It was a disastrous decision. With widely dispersed and unprepared forces, together with young and inexperienced leaders placed in command after the notorious officer 'purge', the Red Army was extremely vulnerable and just not ready for a confrontation with Germany. Stalin had at his disposal far greater numbers of superior T34 tanks, guns and more aircraft than the German invaders, but the lack of organisation, training, communication, and most importantly, the lack of quality aircraft and the men to fly them, made it almost inevitable that any initial thrust by Germany would devastate Red Army forces stretched inadequately along the frontiers.

Little change in the situation in Africa but we are now much stronger in these regions.

2 short raids. Fire bombs (about 4) fell in West Street.

The *'Situation Report'* by the Essex Constabulary for the *'Period 09-00hrs 16/6/41 to 09-00hrs 19/6/41'* recorded that: *'At 00-39hrs 19/6/41, 6 incendiary bombs fell harmlessly in a field at Coggeshall.'* This isolated violation was only one of two that occurred locally during the temporary lull in enemy activity.

The *'Message Report'* for the same incident is *'From Essex County Control to Regional Control, Cambridge'* which states: *'Minor bombing report. IB's dropped at Coggeshall 6 miles east Braintree 00-37. No damage or casualties stop.'* There is also a further report. *'IB's dropped near Isinglass Factory, West Street, Coggeshall at 00-37 on 19-6-41. No damage, Police and Warden on spot.'* This was very close to home - for the Pudsey family at least, as their house, 'Grigglands', was just 100yds away from the factory. In post-war years, my father and mother, Jane and I moved next door to my grandparents, and we lived but 75yds from the factory. However, at the time of the incident, my father and mother and Jane (I wasn't even a twinkle in the eye!), lived in St. Peters Road on the north side of Coggeshall.

Incendiary bomb - dropped on Coggeshall circa 1940/1.
(Source: Coggeshall Museum)

Also on this day a very unfortunate accident occurred. It was recorded that: *'At 19-30hrs 18/6/41, a schoolboy was killed at Great Wakering when a landmine exploded in a fenced in field at the side of an unmade road. It is thought that the boy either threw stones on to the minefield or pushed a stick through the fence. Two other boys who were present are missing.'*

There were many accidents similar to this throughout the war, as the exuberance and inquisitiveness of youth toyed with weapons and explosives that looked interesting or harmless. Although constantly warned, it did not stop the young being killed or seriously maimed by this type of ghastly occurrence.

Thursday 19
Great war secret out.
Radio location – or a means of detecting planes miles away and directing our fighters to them.
This will go a long way to beating the night raids.

In 1935, under a cloak of secrecy, Robert Watson-Watt and his team had successfully proved that a plane could be detected at a range of nearly ten miles by sending radio waves from the BBC Daventry transmitter. The aircraft reflected the waves, which had then registered on receiving equipment. The race was on to provide a working solution for the defences of Britain. Encouraged by Air Chief Marshal Hugh Dowding, soon to be the saviour of the country as he strategically marshalled his 'fighter boys' during the Battle of Britain, the radar progressed through the phase of being ground based to one of being airborne. The key to the equipment was the radar transmitter, an advanced piece of equipment incorporating the resonant cavity magnetron. Although Germany was at least as knowledgeable as Britain in the race to perfect radar, it was this small but vital piece of equipment that put Britain ahead, and provided a workable operating radar system; initially for defence, and later for attack. It was the ground based 'Chain Home' radar systems along the East and South coasts of England that were to provide the valuable defence system so essential in obtaining early warnings of incoming German aircraft.

It was a significant move for the authorities to release such information. The reason could only have been that it had become obvious to the Germans, who were already aware of the 'devices', and had begun to use similar technology themselves.

The early radar sets installed in aircraft were rather crude - they required endless patience to operate and understand, and performed erratically. However, as the war progressed, improvement in clarity, range and accuracy enabled the night-fighter crews to benefit from those advances. It was during 1941 that great strides were made and the results began to show in the number of victories scored at night by the RAF. The problem was that the Germans had also made advances, and as the Allies took the fight further into occupied territory, so the Luftwaffe night-fighters took a heavy and destructive toll of our bombers - the most potent of their weapons being the upward firing cannons (schräge musik or 'jazz' music - the word schräge in strict German terms meaning upward) installed in the Bf110. New technologies, new weapons and new tactics made the sky an ever more dangerous place for all protagonists.

Turkey sign pact with Germany, but refuse to sever friendly relations with Britain.

On the 18th June, Germany and Turkey signed a Non-Aggression Pact. It served two purposes; (1) it kept Turkey out of the war for the duration, and (2) it allowed Germany to protect its position for the invasion planned against Russia. Therefore, both parties were tied in yet another alliance of fear and convenience.

Quiet night.

Friday 20
Visited Aldous Ltd, Shipbuilders of Brightlingsea re Galvanising.

Aldous Ltd had been an old well-established shipbuilding company. The most popular boats built by them at the turn of the last century were oyster-fishing smacks. Quite a number were built to be operated by local 'oystermen' and the shipyards were kept busy with these designs for several years. When the requirement slowed down, other types of boats were built, and various repair and maintenance work had been carried out at their premises in Brightlingsea. During WWII contracts for repairs were quite regular as a result of damage to boats from enemy action, and also refit requisitions to suit operational and design upgrading. There would naturally be a requirement for items to be galvanised; hence the visit by father.

There is no record that the company exists today.

Germany getting hit very hard by our Air Force.

This entry could be referring to the raid on the 18th/19th June on Bremen by 100 bombers, when low cloud made accuracy difficult and resulted in the loss of three of our aircraft. There had been further attacks on the warships at Brest, where smoke screens yet again hindered the bombers, making identification of targets almost impossible.

There were repeated attacks on Cologne and Düsseldorf by a small force of bombers on the night of the 19th/20th June, but very little damage was reported.

Reports (unconfirmed) of skirmishes on German – Russian frontier.
Troops massing on both sides.

As with Hitler's invasion of Poland in 1939, it was likely that the opposing forces were probably being provoked into making the first hostile move using devious and dastardly methods, so that the claim would be that 'they started it first'. It was the prelude to the invasion, with Germany looking for reasons to do so, but wanting to be accepted as the offended party. The rest of the world was not fooled. Hitler was clearly and openly going to be the invader.

~~~~~~~~~~

Short raid.
Little about.

Incidents were reported in several parts of the country, with some activity being noted in Norfolk.

Saturday 21

Looks as if Germany & Russia will be at each other very shortly.

By this time, it had become obvious to the anti-Axis world media that something was about to happen. The conjecture would not last long. The German forces were ready to pounce on the Russian Bear, which was initially quite tame, but was soon to turn very grizzly!

~~~~~~~~~~

We are hitting occupied France every day now.
Our bombers, escorted by Spitfires & Hurricanes, found their targets,
& our fighters shot down 28 Gerry fighters who tried to stop them.
Our losses 4 fighters & 1 bomber 2 pilots O.K.

The Battle of Britain was over at the end of October 1940, and by early 1941 the RAF had used the time and resources to rest exhausted pilots and repair and replace war-torn aircraft. It was now ready to 'Lean into Europe' by taking the initiative and the fight to the enemy with our fighter and bomber squadrons operating together.

As early as January 1941, a Wing of Spitfires and Hurricanes escorted 6 Blenheims to attack Luftwaffe installations in the Forêt de Guênes. Also, at the turn of the year, the offensive had commenced by flying operations coded 'Rhubarbs'. These were carried out by small numbers of fighters, mostly at low level using overcast conditions to keep their entry over the enemy coast undetected. The operations were fraught with danger, and several aircraft and pilots were lost carrying out these 'hit and run' raids. However, the large sweeps were now in ascendancy.

One of the Hurricanes lost on this day had been flown by a very well

Cannon armed and tucked up close. Hawker Hurricane IIc based at Tangmere.
(Source: Ken Delve Collection)

known Battle of Britain pilot. In a *'Message Form'* to *'Essex County Control'*, it was reported that: *'At 19-30hrs approx. 21/6/41, the pilot of a British Hurricane aircraft landed at Brightlingsea following an explosion which took place about 2 miles off Clacton. The pilot, Flight Lieut. Stanford Puck , DSO, DFC, was suffering from facial abrasions.'* I can only guess that the reporting officer may well have misunderstood the name of the pilot, as he had sustained facial injuries that may have caused the officer to write down the wrong name. In fact it was the legendary 'Bob' Stanford <u>Tuck</u> who had risen to prominence through the Battle of Britain, and who, by January 1942 when he was shot down over France and made a prisoner of war, had claimed at least 27 enemy aircraft destroyed.

On this occasion, Tuck had been shot down in the Channel after destroying two Bf109 fighters, and had spent two hours in his dinghy before being gratefully picked up by a coal barge outward bound from Gravesend.

Note: Tuck's luck deserted him one evening when, with no other aircraft in the air as a result of heavy low cloud cover and extremely poor visibility, he was scrambled and vectored onto a German raider. He chased it for many miles in and out of cloud, until eventually, more out of frustration than expectation he was able to take a quick squirt at it before it disappeared for the last time into an impenetrable dark haze. At that point, he had calculated that he had been over the Brecon hills in Wales.

Unknown to Tuck, he had sufficiently scared the German raider into jettisoning his bombs, and they struck the only building for miles around, high up in the hills. The bombs had destroyed a small radio hut, killing the one occupant on duty at the time.

It was a few days later that he was informed that his sister's husband had been killed while on active service in Wales. It was the bombs from the raider that had killed his brother-in-law, and it was Tuck's actions that had unknowingly caused the tragedy. It had been a remarkable and tragic twist of fate, and it would take a very long time before he was able to recount the terrible coincidence to his sister.

Tuck's combat luck eventually ran out on the 28th January 1942 while he was on a strafing mission over France. He was shot down by flak and captured, spending most of the remainder of the war in prison camps. However, as the war drew to a close, he made his escape after narrowly avoiding being shot by the advancing Russians and was repatriated back to England. He was a remarkable man, an excellent pilot, and luck - both good and bad - had played a great part in his life.

~~~~~~~~~~

Short raid.

There were several 'in-coming' enemy raiders totalling about 60 aircraft over the south of England during the night. The Southampton area received the brunt of the attack, and there were 28 fatalities. For some, there would be no relaxation of vigilance, for others a swift and deadly end from the blast of an exploding bomb. To say that there had been little activity was purely proportionate to the massive raids earlier in the year.

~~~~~~~~~~

Another incident was recorded on a *'Message Form'* to *'Essex County Control'* on this day, which graphically described the terrible risks our merchant sailors were taking as they endeavoured to carry valuable supplies around our coasts. It was reported that: *'At 15-00hrs 21/6/41, 18 survivors and one deceased member of the crew of SS'Kenneth Hawkfield', were landed at Harwich, after their vessel had been sunk by a mine in the North Sea. The survivors consisted of 17 British subjects (including 2 Naval gunners) and 1 Japanese. Crew left for the North on 22-6-41.'*

It must be recognised that the brave sailors epitomised those who were so committed to saving Britain from starvation, by enduring bombs, mines, torpedoes and not least hostile and turbulent seas to bring food and essential supplies to our shores. Without the merchant fleet, Britain would surely have been starved into submission. It was they, and the Battle of Britain pilots who saved the Nation in those early desperate years.

Sunday 22
* *Germany marched against Russia at 4 AM this morning, without warning.*
Hitler must have food & oil, & hopes to get it from the Ukraine.
Russia should cause him a lot of trouble, if only she can organise her massive army & mechanised forces to meet Hitler's first onslaught.
Germany were driven to take their action by our tightening blockade.

Operation 'Barbarossa', German invasion of Russia showing deployment of the attacking forces.
(Source: J. Pipe, feldgrau)

168

In the early morning of the 22nd June, German forces attacked Soviet positions as they blasted their way forward over the frontier. Although it is hard to imagine, it was calculated that over 3 million men were involved in this pre-emptive strike by the Axis invaders. Opposing them, the Soviet defenders numbered slightly less, but in terms of tanks and guns, they possessed a greater number than the Axis. However, superior strategies and tactics gave the Axis the initial advantage as they swiftly rolled deep into Soviet occupied territory.

Hitler had decided upon a three-pronged attack along the Soviet frontier, although during the planning stages his generals had recommended a single drive to Moscow. However, the Hitler plan was carried, with Generalfeldmarshal von Rundstedt's Southern Group *(Heeresgruppe Sud)* with Panzergruppe 1 *(von Kleist)* driving for the Ukraine and the Caucasus, Generalfeldmarshal von Bock's Middle Group *(Heeresgruppe Mitte)* with Panzergruppen 2 *(Guderian)* and 3 *(Hoth)* driving through to threaten Minsk and Smolesk from their bases in Poland, and Feldmarshal von Leeb's Northern Group *(Heeresgruppe Nord)* with Panzergruppe 4 *(Hoepner)* targeting Leningrad and the Baltic States.

The Soviet-German Non-Aggression Pact was dead.

Heavier raids at night.

Raiders were active in eastern England, with bombs having been recorded falling in Essex. Home security suggested that the German/Russian situation would keep our raids by the Luftwaffe at their present level.

Monday 23
Russia fighting back hard. This is no easy task for Germany.

The German, Rumanian and Finnish forces totalled 183 Divisions, with weapons consisting of over 3,300 tanks, 7,000 guns, and nearly 2,000 aircraft. Opposing them were 132 Russian Divisions with 20,000 tanks, considerably more guns, and over 7,000 aircraft. As previously stated, it was the target of the Northern Group to drive on and capture Leningrad, with the added task of supporting a further group codenamed 'Silberfuchs' *(Silver Fox)* who were to capture the vital port of Murmansk. The Middle Group would ultimately drive on to Moscow, and the Southern Group had been tasked to capture the vital industrial and mineral resources in the Ukraine.

Although superior in firepower and aircraft, the relative surprise and intensity of the attack was devastating for the Russian forces, and the attacking Axis invaders had driven deep into Russian territory by the end of the first day. Once again, the German 'Blitzkrieg' tactics had been successful.

~~~~~~~~~

When informed of the invasion, which had secretly been expected for quite some time by Allied high command, Prime Minister Winston Churchill immediately announced that Britain would provide aid to their new Allies in the East. Although the reputation of Stalin had been well known and reviled by Churchill, it was deemed vital that Russia should be supported against the Axis powers.

~~~~~~~~~

2 Raids at night on smallish scale but 8 planes dropped around & in Witham. No bombs.

It was reported that Cressing, near Braintree, had received the attention of the Luftwaffe during the night. However, I am unaware whether 'dropped' means shot down as I can find no record, or just dropped down to low level. If there were no bombs, it would be unusual for the raiders to strafe at low level in darkness, so I am a bit mystified by my father's observations.

Tuesday 24
Russia claim to be holding the Huns after Germany had advanced 7-8 miles into Russian occupied Poland at one point.

By the end of the 23rd June, Southern Group forces had crossed the River Bug in Poland and captured Brest-Litovsk.

This day also saw the capture of Kaunus and Vilna in Lithuania by the German Northern Group as they headed east. The German forces were rapidly advancing in all sectors of the front.

Germany losing large number of planes.

The Russian propaganda 'machine' was performing considerably better than its own defences! At the end of the first day of fighting on the 22nd June, the inadequacy and lack of preparation of the Soviet forces had become very apparent. It was the Luftwaffe's task to destroy the Russian air defences to allow the German armies to roll through their Soviet counterparts and drive deep into Russian territory. At the day's end, the Russians had lost over 1,800 aircraft - over 300 shot down in the air, and nearly 1,500 destroyed on the ground during raids on 66 Russian airfields. Although most of the Russian aircraft were deemed as obsolete, some were their latest fighters, but most were annihilated when caught on the ground by the Luftwaffe on that first disastrous day for the Russians. Contrary to the comment made by my father, and probably reported by the media, only 35 German aircraft were lost on that first day.

In America, President Roosevelt announced that his country would provide military aid to Russia.

Every day now we are carrying out offensive sweeps over German occupied France – bombers escorted by fighters. All very successful & with very little losses to ourselves. Average of 20 Gerries shot down per day in these sweeps.

As Fighter Command became more aggressive, other types of raids were initiated with different tactics to suit varying situations. For example, in an operation specified as a 'Circus', the aim was to draw up enemy fighters into combat, and, with a small number of Blenheim bombers acting as bait, they would be escorted by dozens of RAF fighters eager to do battle with the Luftwaffe. If several squadrons of fighters went over without bombers to 'mix it' with German fighters, this was called a 'Rodeo', and 'Ramrods' were carried out by small numbers of fighters against ground targets. During these types of operations, losses could be quite heavy on both sides if the enemy could be enticed into battle.

Wednesday 25
No German advance anywhere, so far.
Massive tank battle now in progress, with Russians doing great damage to Hun war machine.

Contrary to the report, the German armies were making significant advances supported by the formidable Luftwaffe air offensive. In most regions the Russians were defending with great courage, but their defences and armies were weak and their attempts to stem the incoming tide of German invaders had been, in many instances, futile.

The Panzergruppe 1 captured Dubno, in eastern Poland, which had been part of Russian territory.

We are to forget all past differences with Russia, & will fight together in a common cause.
Downfall of Germany.

As history would tell, the Russians joined the Allies for the duration of the war only. It could not be termed as an 'unholy' alliance between Russia and the Allies, but more an alliance with the dictator, Stalin. It was of primary importance to rid the world of Hitler and fascism, by leaving the potentially great threat of communist domination until later.

Communism was not an important priority in 1941.

~~~~~~~~~~~~

Quiet night.

However, our bombers were continuing their battle by taking the fight into occupied Europe, and still suffering. On a *'Message Form'* compiled on this day *'From Divisional Control, Colchester to Essex County Control'* the following text highlights their trauma, as damaged planes and desperate and weary crews struggled to return to their bases in England. Having cleared the enemy coast, the dark and dangerous waters of the Channel beckoned: *'Reference aircraft report of 04-59hrs 25/6/41, Polish navigator picked up by Clacton Lifeboat and now in Clacton Hospital. Name Idzikowski Zbigniew. Sergeant Gunner Franckowski made safe parachute descent at Holland-on-Sea. Total saved at present 2.'* It is interesting to note that the writer of the report had taken pains to clearly and concisely separate the letters of the Polish names so that the medical authorities were in no doubt as to his identity. Many brave Europeans were fighting with our forces to help liberate their countries, and thousands died as a result. This incident was typical of many during all phases of the war, but the marine rescue services, scouring the Channel for survivors, were not as well prepared as later in the conflict. Sadly, a heavy toll was exacted of aircrew trying to cross that last stretch of water before 'home', and for many it would be the final journey to eternity.

Thursday 26
Our daylight sweeps continue satisfactorily.
So far, we have shot down 137 fighters & have lost only 36 of our own in the last ten days.

There were periods when several squadrons flying as Wings would draw up enemy fighters into combat and massive aerial battles would commence. They were dangerous, confusing and costly for both sides. Naturally, in the grand mêlée of whirling, spitting and screaming aircraft, over-claiming came to be expected. In effect, it had been the reverse of the Battle of Britain, as it was the turn of the RAF to fight over enemy territory. The ability of an unfortunate pilot to get home when shot down over occupied Europe was greatly diminished. Many lost their lives or were incarcerated in prison camps for the duration of the war, but a few were able to evade and escape via diverse and protracted routes and make it safely back to England.

~~~~~~~~~~~~

Russians still holding, & in places, repulsing the Huns.

In the east, the German Northern Group forces had advanced and captured the Latvian town of Dünaburg.
Hundreds of German planes are being shot down.

The Luftwaffe carried out its first devastating attack on Leningrad. This was the commencement of a catastrophic and extended period of assault on the city and inhabitants. However, the Northern Group forces would not have it all their own way, as the Germans had estimated that they were opposed by over 1,000 Russian aircraft in that region. On the 25th June the Russian air force attacked airfields in Finland and Norway in a partially successful attempt to nullify Luftwaffe air offensives in their region, and to delay Northern Group forces from reaching their objectives.

We should be getting peace feelers shortly if I'm not mistaken. They will be ignored, of course.

I really feel that my father was being extremely optimistic with this statement. Were the media creating this and were the propagandists winning the media war? I think, with hindsight being the main assessor, those assumptions are now very evident.

Meanwhile, Finland & Hungary declared war on Russia.

Raid 12-30 – 3-15am.

It appears from records that the Luftwaffe had been concentrating on shipping strikes and mine laying in the Channel during June, and it is quite likely that isolated raiders may have encroached inland to carry out sporadic attacks, thus alerting the defences. However, there did not appear to be any incidents locally.

Friday 27

Russia still fighting back hard. Altho' the Germans have advanced they are being held on all fronts now.

Continuing its advance in the east, the Middle Group surrounded Soviet army divisions near Minsk, and also captured Riga, Bobruisk and Przemysl.

Now is the time for us to hit Germany hard – while they have their hands full.

In 1941, that could only be achieved by the RAF. It was Russia who had their hands full as the German military machine rolled inexorably through Soviet territory.

We are advancing in Syria. Damascus is now in our hands.

The capital fell to the Allies on the 21st June. However, the Vichy forces in Lebanon would continue fighting.

Short raid at night.

Raiders were reported as having unloaded their bombs in East Anglia, but no damage or casualties were evident.

Saturday 28
Worked in morning till 12-30 & then on firewatching from 12-30 to 6-30 at the works.

~~~~~~~~~~

Jane, now 2½ years old, is beginning to feel that something is going on which is not quite right. She is very nervous when she hears a plane even in the day time.
Ena is very fit nowadays & not quite so nervous now the raids are not so heavy.

Mother, however, could not fail to have passed on her fears to and for Jane. For many years after the war my mother would sit in the cupboard under the stairs whenever there was a thunderstorm. I guess it was a natural thing to do having been so used to taking shelter during air raids. Now, sadly, she is somewhat deaf, and is very rarely aware that the skies are rumbling and flashing. As for myself, born in 1943, I find storms disconcerting as a result of their massive natural power, but whether or not it's for the same reason, I don't know.

~~~~~~~~~~

Small scale raids.

There were a few minor incidents over East Anglia, but nothing of significance was reported locally.

Sunday 29
Germany losing great amount of material & men, but is forging ahead at one or two points.
Russians are resisting strongly all along the line.

It was reported that German forces captured Grodno, Brest-Litovsk and Vilna on this day, and that near Bialystok several divisions of the Russian army were surrounded.

From northern Finland, German and Finnish forces launched 'Operation Silver Fox' on the 29th June in an endeavour to capture the port of Murmansk.

~~~~~~~~~~

Can Russia hold them?
Everybody is asking this question.
They are fighting well so far – better than Germany expected.

It had yet to become evident to the British public that the Russians were retreating in all sectors, and had still to organise their forces into an effective defensive (let alone offensive) force. If they had any strategy for the battle, it was, at that time, simply to survive.

~~~~~~~~~~

Quiet night.

Monday 30
Hun troops threatening Minsk on Polish – Russian border.
Hard fighting in progress.

German Middle Group forces captured the city of Minsk on the 28th June, followed by the capture of Lemberg *(Lvov)* on the 30th June.

East of Minsk, German fighters destroyed 100 Soviet bombers that had been attacking German forces.

During the rapid north-west progress of the Panzers near captured bridges over the Dvina river, Luftwaffe fighters flying in support of the North Group destroyed 65 Soviet bombers as they unsuccessfully attempted to halt the advance.

~~~~~~~~~~

It was announced that the Vichy-French government had severed contacts with Russia on the 30th June. Former Axis allies were rapidly reacting to the invasion, and were now rejecting Russia as a 'friend'.

~~~~~~~~~~

We continue our very heavy night raids over Germany & daylight sweeps over occupied territory.
We lost about 50 fighters in these sweeps but shot down over 150 Hun fighters.
Good going.

This was not yet the day of the long-range fighter, as the earlier variants of the Mustang would not commence operations with the RAF until July 1942. Therefore short-range interdictions were the only option. With limited range and endurance, many RAF fighters would find themselves short of fuel, possibly shot up and damaged, and with no option for the pilots but to bale out and be guests of the Third Reich for the duration of the war. Many, not so lucky, would rest forever in graves in France and the Lowlands, whilst others would be 'missing, believed killed', with their only epitaph being their name on the Runnymede Memorial. As mentioned previously, just a lucky few were able to evade and find their way home, helped in nearly every case by the emerging underground movements in the occupied countries.

~~~~~~~~~~

Quiet night.

It is fair to say that during this month there were many small raids with losses to the Luftwaffe of one or two aircraft on some nights. However, although the raids had been an aggravation and had caused damage and casualties throughout the country, the effects had not been catastrophic, thus providing Britain with a breathing space and the RAF an opportunity to take the battle further into German occupied territory.

JULY 1941

Tuesday 1
Germany still being hotly resisted on all fronts.

There was no doubt that Germany was being contested on all fronts. It had failed to invade England and Rommel was being held in North Africa. With the issues in Iraq and Abyssinia concluded and the invasion of Syria and Lebanon nearly complete, the chess-board of warfare throughout Europe and the Middle East was beginning to stabilise.

It is true that the Allies had suffered a reverse in Greece and Crete, but the small bastion of defiance in Malta would eventually help to provide the springboard for the Allies to take the fight to the Axis, and eventual victory in North Africa. Yes, maybe my father was right, Hitler <u>had</u> bitten off more than he could chew, for Russia would stick in his throat until the end.

Position in Libya has not changed for weeks.
We still hold Tobruk.

There had, however, been a further attempt to relieve the siege at Tobruk when Wavell had initiated 'Operation Battleaxe' on the 15ᵗʰ June. Lieutenant-General Beresford-Peirse was placed in charge of the two Divisions allocated to the operation, but although initially successful, the British tanks crumbled under the potent 88mm guns of the German Panzers at Halfaya Pass and Hafid Ridge, and were virtually annihilated, with over 150 tanks being destroyed. Accepting defeat, General Wavell ordered the remnants of his forces to retreat. 'Operation Battleaxe' had been a failure, but Tobruk still remained in Allied hands.

As a result of the situation in North Africa, General Sir Claude Auchinleck had replaced General Wavell on the 21ˢᵗ June. Although Wavell was held partially responsible for the reverses in fortune, circumstances had not favoured him. His resources were thin and in many situations his equipment was not comparable to the Axis weapons. Regardless, Churchill and his advisors had thought that a change of commander would bring new initiatives to the conflict.

Quiet night, tho' we had a short warning.

There had been no report of any incidents in Essex and East Anglia.

Wednesday 2
Very confusing reports of German-Russian battle.

Apparently there is a chaotic mass of men and material hammering away at each other and both sides deep in each others territory.
Germany are held in places, but have penetrated Russian territory at a number of points, tho' they admit that their advance is not going according to expectations.

Although Hitler had planned the subjugation of Russia to be completed in six weeks, the facts show that the German advance into Russian territory had probably exceeded his Commanders' expectations, and although the strategy was playing out as planned, there had been less resistance than expected. The quality of the opposition at that stage of the battle had been poor as previously explained; the Russian forces were missing the experienced tactical ability of the military leaders so cruelly eliminated by the Stalin purges. One can only imagine the terrible death and destruction as the major battles were being fought, both in the air and on the ground, but the almost total superiority of the Panzer tank divisions supported by the 'blitzkrieg' component of the Luftwaffe had been the primary reason for the massive success of 'Operation Barbarossa' to that point. Command of the air had allowed control of the land battles. That success would continue for a considerable period until the Red Army were able to resist in force and hold the German advances in vital sectors - but the new leaders had to learn fast.

On the previous day, the armoured forces of Panzergruppe 4 of the Northern Group under von Leeb crossed the Dvina and captured Riga in the East, whilst Panzer units of the Middle Group had reached the Bereina after taking Minsk.

On the 2nd July, on the extreme southern front in the East, German and Rumanian armies began their offensive from Moldavia towards Vinnitsa and the Black Sea port of Odessa.

Short raid.
There had been no report of any incidents in Essex and East Anglia.

Thursday 3
Our bombing of Germany continues on ever increasing scale, by day & night.

On the previous day there was a 'Circus' operation by 12 Blenheims on Lille power station, and 2 aircraft failed to return.

Bremen, Cologne and Duisburg were the targets for the RAF on the night of the 2nd/3rd July by a force of 139 aircraft. Bomber Command reported mixed results in hazy conditions, with a further 4 aircraft failing to return.

Very little definite news from Russia, except a report saying they are strongly resisting at all sectors.
Can they hold back the Huns while they call up & organise on war basis?
They have fought well so far.

On this day, Stalin was heard for the first time since the invasion. In a wireless broadcast he demanded that the Russian people powerfully resist '…in our patriotic war against German Fascism'. He further demanded a scorched earth policy if the Red Army was forced to yield ground, and also the summary execution of those who did not carry out the policy or were seen to be cowards in the face of the enemy.

~~~~~~~~~~

Quiet night.

There were no reports of any incidents in Essex and East Anglia.

Friday 4
Germans gradually creeping into Russia, but at terrific cost. Russia are very confident, or at least, appear to be, and are certainly giving Gerry his biggest shock since the air battle of Britain.

It was reported that the Middle Group *(von Bock)* had captured Ostrov.

~~~~~~~~~~

Our day & night raids are now unceasing.
I wonder how they can take it.

It was evident that Bomber Command was still suffering from lack of accuracy in bombing techniques, and although weather, night-fighters and other issues continued to conspire against them, it was clear that new technology was desperately needed. Sadly, many bombs were wasted and many young lives were lost over the fields and towns of occupied Europe from the outset of the war, and the tragic losses continued during that phase of increased activity by Bomber Command. However, no one, but no one, could ever fault the bravery and endeavour of the cream of British, Commonwealth and Allied youth in the RAF, and in all other sectors of our fighting forces.

~~~~~~~~~~

Short raid.

The East Coast, Midlands and South-West were raided by 75 enemy aircraft. Slight damage and a few casualties resulted.

Saturday 5
Russians still fighting back hard.

Fighting very confused over a large area, with no definite fighting line.

Russia are not falling, as France did, to any wedge movement by the Gerry's. They open up to let the heavy tanks thro' then close up to meet the infantry & motorised units. This is upsetting the Germans.

If that was indeed occurring, the Red Army was learning fast. The tactic was certainly capable of stalling and confusing the German advance as it split their attacking forces and confused the supporting German air component. As the Soviets separated and isolated the tanks from the infantry and other units, Luftwaffe targeting would become uncertain and dangerous to both sides, as the lines of battle became less defined and ground targets less positive to identify.

Quiet night.

There were no reports of any incidents in Essex and East Anglia.

Sunday 6

As far as we can gather, the Huns have not yet come up against the main Russian defences, or the Stalin line as it is called. When he does, there should be wholesale slaughter.

It was reported on the 5th July that units of the 6th Army had broken through the 'Stalin Line' East of Lvov. Meanwhile, Panzers of the South Group advanced towards Zhitomir and Berdichev in the Ukraine.

On this day, the 6th July, the North Group continued its advance, and was in the vicinity of the Gulf of Riga.

The slaughter my father had alluded to was occurring. However, there had been a different and darker element at work as the German armies advanced. Following behind their regular forces had been the notorious and deadly 'liquidation squads'. As Stalin was requiring a 'scorched earth' policy when his forces withdrew, so it was that the German liquidators left nothing in their wake as their regular army units advanced. Men, women and children were slaughtered at random, and property destroyed. This policy of murder, torture and deportation of civilians useful as forced labour was to have a serious revenge factor for any unlucky German airman shot down over Russian territory. No mercy was shown, and very few airmen returned to their units. Almost none if captured.

We are advancing a little thro' Syria.

Although the conflict was virtually over in Syria, the bitter fighting continued in Lebanon until the Allies eventually captured the important port of Damour, which fell on the 9th July. Consequently, the Vichy commander, General Dentz, finally conceded defeat in Syria and Lebanon and announced an armistice at Acre on the 12th July.

The Allies had consolidated their position in that troublesome area of conflict by reducing the threat of German intervention, securing their vital resources, and insured their strategic position as a base to launch further attacks on the Axis in the future.

Only one more pocket of resistance left in Abyssinia.

That was to carry on for several months before finally being concluded.

Short raid at night.

Bombs fell along the East coast, from Kent up to Yorkshire. Nearer to home, Suffolk and Norfolk received the attention of the Luftwaffe, with the port and town of Great Yarmouth regrettably suffering 12 fatalities.

Monday 7
Russia still doing well.

Meanwhile we are pummelling Germany in the west be by our terrific aerial bombardment.
Day & night our bombers & fighters are hitting Germany, from all accounts, harder than he was raiding us. He never did do much in daytime except for a short raid in dirty weather.

Father, I fear, had again been somewhat over-optimistic regarding the damage the RAF had been inflicting on German occupied territories, and may have temporarily set aside the considerable damage and loss of life that German bombers had caused during their raids on Britain. As previously stated, he could only draw conclusions from the media at the time, and the restrictions that were placed on them by the Government when reporting events was always tempered by the need for security and the necessity of keeping morale as high as possible.

Short raid at night.

Southampton was the main target this night, and 26 people perished. The RAF gained some revenge by shooting down 6 of the raiders - five by Beaufighters, and a rare night victory by a Spitfire. A night 'kill' in a Spitfire was a very difficult operation as there was no on-board radar system, and the pilot had very little to guide him to the enemy aircraft other than general directions given by ground control or bursting flak to indicate the proximity of an enemy bomber. Even if it had been possible to fit a radar system (it was not!) the pilot would have been in over-load in endeavouring to fly the plane <u>and</u> operate the locating system in the cramped cockpit of the Spitfire.

Tuesday 8
Raids over Britain are still on a very small scale.
We do get an occasional warning, but never hear many planes about.
There are now far more of our planes in the sky at night than German,
& they are giving Germany many unhappy moments.

The raids over Britain had reduced as a result of Germany's commitment to the battle on the Russian Front. It was also true that Bomber Command was sending greater numbers of bombers over Europe; but to reinforce my previous observations, the effectiveness had not been satisfactory and bombing techniques and training just had to improve.

Note: Training in RAF Bomber Command could be nearly as dangerous as operations. Many thousands of young men were lost during the war years when going through Operational Training Units and Heavy Conversion Units, until finally being sent to squadrons to prepare for their first operations. If they made it that far their luck had held. There is no doubt that, when passing through that phase of training, there would inevitably be losses. Many came to grief through no fault of their own, as they were usually given clapped out ex-operational aircraft in which they had to learn their skills to survive. Weather, lack of aircraft serviceability, inadequate training and sheer bad luck took the lives of many crews - not just one life of the pilot as in fighters, but sometimes the complete crew. It was a terrible waste of lives, but during war needs must and they had to learn to survive, and learn very quickly, for when on operations the odds of making it through a tour were even less, because the enemy also wanted to kill them.

However, some were lucky and were able to survive one or more tours of duty. One of the lucky ones had been a friend, the late John Nelson. In the earlier years of the war, he was (I recollect) a Radio Operator on Wellington bombers, and he and his crew were on a training exercise. Along the south coast near Brighton they lost power on an engine, and being a rather war weary aircraft, they were losing height fast and had to look for a place to land. All they could find was a small green field, and their only option had been to sit the aircraft down with the wheels up due to the limited size available. This the pilot did with great skill, leaving the old bomber smouldering and groaning whilst they made hasty exits. 'Where did you land?' I asked. 'In heaven…', said John. I was thinking him somewhat irreverent, when he added '…we had landed in Roedean School for girls, but I was a newly married man!'

However, many were never so lucky and many would not survive. Bomber Command had to improve in training, aircraft, tactics and equipment. It would be gradual, and it did happen, but it did not stop the rate of attrition of aircraft and crews.

~~~~~~~~~~

Nowadays, we three go to bed – still downstairs – without a thought of raids.
Jane, 2½years, has just been inoculated against diptheria.

However, sleeping downstairs, they were still ready to make a dash across the garden to the dugout. But on this night my father did not have to worry about my mother bolting through the vegetables!

There was an attack again on Great Yarmouth, but not an alert locally. It was reported that Spitfires shot down 1 raider in the morning, and 5 enemy bombers were destroyed during night raids.

Wednesday 9
Ena is fitter than ever now we are getting some sleep.

~~~~~~~~~~

With the Russians doing much better than everyone, including Hitler, expected, there is a growing wave of optimism spreading thro' the country.
Hitler is still advancing it is true, but at terrific cost.

On the previous day in the East, Panzers of the North Group captured Pskov and advanced towards Novgorod and Leningrad. As previously observed, the defenders of Leningrad had over 1,000 aircraft at their disposal, but they were not equal to the combat aircraft and experienced pilots of the Luftwaffe, who had in excess of 800 front line bombers and fighters available on this date. The Russian fighters, however, were very manoeuvrable, and the German pilots suffered some frustration when trying to get them in their sights for the kill. One-sided it may have been, but the Luftwaffe did not have the air battles all their own way - and the Russians had many more aircraft to lose.

Following the example of the North Group in the East, the Middle Group captured Vitebsk.

~~~~~~~~~~

As an indication of the speed and devastating intensity of the German advance, from the outset of the invasion to this date, the Red Army had lost 2,500 tanks, and 300,000 of their fighting troops were now prisoners of war.

~~~~~~~~~~

Quiet night.

The North received some raids during the night, and 3 German aircraft failed to return. It is believed that these aircraft may have been misled by a British radio device called 'Meacon', and were probably lured off course and subsequently crashed into the hills and cliffs of the Yorkshire coast during fog.

Thursday 10
Started my 2 day holiday today. Took my car to be decoked.

Low quality fuel with no additives caused a build-up of carbon in the engine, which in turn clogged up vital parts and resulted in the engine running inefficiently. The remedy was to strip down the engine and clean the carbon from the valves, the head, and combustion chambers. If this job had been carried out correctly, the engine, and thus the car, would run smoothly. However, it was not a five minute job!

When car engines became more efficient in design and manufacture, decoking was consigned to the past for nearly all modern vehicles. In 1941, and for many years after, it had been necessary to carry out this process.

There appears to be a lull in the fighting between Germany & Russia. Germany says 'to reorganise their forces'.
This is the first time the Gerries have been forced to stop for rest.
Russia appear confident.

As a result of the massive logistical supply problems encountered when the German armies stretched their way into Soviet occupied territory, there were obviously occasions when their forces had to halt and replenish aircraft, armour, personnel, and general supplies. Although they were able in some instances to use captured materials, the edict from Stalin that nothing of use must be left for the advancing Germans would ensure that little would remain of practical value. Also, there was the growing problem of what to do with the prisoners of war.

For the first time, there was a sign that the German army had not been having everything its own way. On this day in the East, the South Group had to repulse a violent Soviet counter-attack in the area west of Kiev.

Around the area of Lake Ladoga, which was north-east of Leningrad, the Finnish Karelian Army fighting with the Nazis began an offensive.

Quiet night.

Hull was the target for raiders during the night. 22 people lost their lives and fires were widespread, with serious damage resulting. Only 1 of the raiders was destroyed.

Friday 11
Lull continues, altho' there is still plenty of air activity on the eastern front.

Panzers of the South Group were now only 10 miles from Kiev.

~~~~~~~~~

In an unprecedented move, Stalin replaced three of his key commanders. He appointed Voroshilov to command the northern front, Timoshenko on the central front, and Budjenny on the southern front. One can only assume that, with the devastating Russian defeats to that point, the Russians needed new blood. There was no doubting the Red Army forces commitment and bravery, and the losses were horrific, but as men (and women) died or were wounded, so they were replaced by a never-ending supply of new troops and equipment. Inadequate they may have been, but at least resistance was still there.

~~~~~~~~~

'Haw-haw' hasn't got so much to shout about lately. This little rat will have plenty to squeal about when British troops can lay hands on him.

William Joyce was born in New York. His father was Irish and his mother English. It was in his youth, and during a brawl that he had his nose broken causing the nasal drawl that had become annoyingly familiar to thousands of British listeners in later years.

As he matured he became fit and athletic, which was to benefit him during the many brawls throughout his life. It was during his upbringing in Ireland that his father's business became the target of the emerging Sinn Fein, which forced the family to move to England, and it was there that he fell under the influence of Sir Oswald Moseley and the British fascist party. He joined that group, rapidly became a recognised speaker, and his views on Jewish issues were extreme, vitriolic, and savagely anti-Semitic. Naturally, there were those who did not agree with these opinions, and the methods of his 'thugs' to suppress the violence were extreme. However, those tactics began to tarnish the fascist cause in Britain, and Joyce left the party.

As a result of his views and tactics, and with the threat of internment, Joyce and his family left for Berlin just prior to the outbreak of the war. Shortly after his arrival, he was introduced to the Private Secretary to Ribbentrop, Germany's Foreign Minister, and a confidant of Hitler. The result of that meeting led Joyce into broadcasting, and he secured the post of 'speaker' for German transmissions to Europe, which could be received in Britain. It was soon established that this 'Englishman', of highbred tone and nasal delivery was a traitor to the cause of freedom and reviled for his irritating, but accurate broadcasts. Fifth columnists, fascist sympathisers, and unwary prisoners of war, provided Joyce with endless material to goad and scare the British population. Although listening to his broadcasts had been forbidden in Britain, many did, but very few were taken in by the rhetoric and evil content of his invective.

Throughout the war Joyce, soon nick-named 'Lord Haw-Haw' due to his nasal delivery, continued to speak to the British people, but when the war finally ended, and in a bid to escape, he was wounded and captured. Naturally, the people and the press were highly charged in their desire to see him hanged for treason, and after his trial, but still defiant, he was taken to the gallows and hung at Wandsworth Prison.

No longer would the words 'Germany calling, Germany calling' be heard. It was a fitting end to a traitor.

Very few planes over.

Saturday 12
Gerry has started his second drive at Russia.
They are now in touch with the 'Stalin' line of defence. This should hold them up for some time, if not altogether.
It is difficult to know which reports to believe. Russian & German claims seem pretty high.
Possibly both are stretching things a bit.
Germany always did.

Regarding claims, there is no doubt that both sides were making overstated (or understated if it served a good purpose) claims for public consumption. Having noted some of the reports recorded by my father, and reviewing his comments based on media information, it appears that the Russians were inflating their figures to a far greater extent than were the Germans.

On this day, Britain and the Soviet Union signed a Mutual Assistance Pact declaring that neither state would make a separate peace with the Axis Powers.

Slightly heavier raid at night. Little damage.
During the night bombs fell in Essex and Norfolk as well as other areas in the Britain. The results were described as 'ineffective'.

Sunday 13

Our day & night raids still continue & are giving Gerry a taste of real bombing.

We are dropping more bombs in every raid than the Huns dropped over here in any one raid.

Quote from Official History.

A directive had arrived at Bomber Command on the 9th July 1941.

'Sir,

I am directed to inform you that a comprehensive review of the enemy's present political, economic and military situation discloses that the weakest points in his armour lie in the morale of the civil population and in his inland transportation system. The wide extension of his military activities is placing an ever-increasing strain on the German transportation system and there are many signs that our recent attacks on industrial towns are having great effect on the morale of the civil population.

...I am to request that you will direct the main force, until further instructions, towards dislocating the German transportation system and to destroying the morale of the civil population as a whole and of the industrial workers in particular'.

That would indicate, and tactics dictated that a renewed effort would have to occur by attacking the cities around the Ruhr area during the nights of full moon, and when there was no moon, the cities in the Rhine area. When the weather was unfavourable, other more distant cities would be targeted.

One can only conclude from the directive that Bomber Command was beginning to be aware that the bomb targeting was poor. As became the case with German raiders, regardless of the industrial and military targets allocated, the lack of bombing accuracy inevitably meant that civilians would suffer. However, with this directive, the key objectives were to be the civilian working population, and the all-out bombing campaign was an uncomfortable step change for the war in the air.

Yet we are told our present raids are child's play compared with what we will drop on Germany by the end of the year.

This situation would not change until May 1942, when the 1,000 bomber raids commenced.

~~~~~~~~~

Quiet night.

Five locations on the East Coast were raided with 4 fatalities reported in Great Yarmouth.

Monday 14
Reported that Hitler & Goering have fallen out.
Goering said the airforce was not prepared for the attack on Russia,
but Hitler took the matter out of his hands. Nothing has been heard of
Goering lately.

It was quite possible that Goering was indeed falling out of favour with Hitler at that time. With Goering's boast in 1940 that he would annihilate the RAF and thus create the potential for the Germans to invade Britain, our fighter pilots during the Battle of Britain proved him wrong. Although the German Air Force continued to be formidable in the skies, their previously successful tactics of 'blitzkrieg' would soon begin to struggle in the ability to gain authority over the improving strategies adopted by the Russian forces. Consequently, even if the rumour was unfounded, it may well have been 'enhanced' by British authorities to cause dissent amongst the German hierarchy.

Russia still holding Gerry back.

During the previous day, troops from the North Group continued their advance from Pskov in the direction of Luga, which was 75 miles from Leningrad.

On this day of the 14th July 1941, having believed that the Russian campaign would be swiftly concluded, Hitler ordered the German war industries to change the emphasis of production from guns and armour to U-boats and aeroplanes. Little did he know what the future would bring to that catastrophic conflict. Little did he know how tough and resilient the Allies would be in their fight against fascism. It was only when the invading Russian hordes were surrounding his last bunker retreat in the ruins of Berlin in April 1945, did he finally realise that all was lost. It was at that fateful moment he took his own life together with Eva Braun, his new wife. That was his future.

Quiet night. Good job – was my night for fire watching.

There had been no report of any incidents in Essex and East Anglia. However, the killing continued as 28 people lost their lives during a short raid on Hull.

Tuesday 15
Doubt about the Hitler Goering story. Probably Hun propaganda.

As suggested previously it may have been our propaganda, but there was no smoke without fire, and certainly later, as the war progressed, the relationship between Hitler and Goering became very strained. Although German pilots were very successful when executing attacks with their fighters and bombers, the Allies also had large air forces, and it was becoming a war of attrition in the air as well as on the ground.

~~~~~~~~~

Russia still doing very well. Terrific losses on both sides. Germany have not got very far ahead since the battle started.

German forces of the Middle Group had surrounded 300,000 Red Army troops in the Smolensk-Orsha pocket.

Around the perimeter of Leningrad, over 300 miles of trenches and fortifications were being constructed by hundreds of thousands of men, women and children, in preparation for the arrival of the German forces.

Russia are now our allies. Agreement has been signed.

As previously noted, they would only be allies for the duration of the war. They would prove to be intransigent, dishonest, and extremely difficult to work with. Later in the war, as their power increased, they were consistently aggressive with their policies that in many instances worked against Allied requirements for the conclusion of the conflict. The war had been the means to an end for Stalin, and as soon as WWII finished, so Russia's power expanded to the detriment of western interests and continued world peace.

~~~~~~~~~

Quiet night.

Wednesday 16
Japanese government resigned 'en bloc'.
No information as to the policy of the new government.

America had handed a note to the Japanese Ambassador requesting the intentions of Japan in respect of a peaceful settlement to the Far East problem. The Japanese Foreign Minister Matsuoka had rejected the note and had not replied. Within the Japanese government, there were factions within the Army and Navy, supported by Premier Konoye, who did not support this stance as they wished to put counter proposals to the American government to suit their future aims. As a result of this disagreement, Konoye consulted Japanese Emperor Hirohito and offered the resignation of the entire cabinet. He then received authority from the Emperor to form a new cabinet, which in essence was exactly the same as the previous, but with Matsuoka excluded.

~~~~~~~~~

Russians still doing well & holding up the German advance.

On the Eastern front, Finnish troops had broken through Red Army positions to the north of Lake Ladoga.

On the centre front, the German Middle Group had Soviet divisions surrounded in the Ulman pocket, and were mercilessly destroying their positions.

If Russia are issuing correct air loss figures she is doing exceptionally well. She is shooting down 3 & 4 to 1 of her own.

The figures provided by the Russian authorities for world consumption were certainly not to be trusted. In the extremely vicious air fighting that had occurred since the invasion commenced, the word 'slaughter' would probably be most apt. Of course, Soviet fighters were able to destroy Luftwaffe planes, but the reverse of the figures claimed would have been more representative of fact. As an example, by the end of the month, Luftwaffe fighters of Jagdgeschwader 54 supporting the North Group had claimed their 1,000th kill. It is possible that the Germans also might be over-claiming, but this figure came from JG54's records, and not the unreliable propaganda agencies of the Soviets.

~~~~~~~~~~

It was reported that Stalin's son, Lt. Jacob Dugashvili, was taken prisoner near the town of Vitebsk. It would have been interesting to know what the Dictator's personal view of his son's capture would be, being aware of his poor respect for human life. It was certain that it did not deflect Stalin from his policies and conduct of the war.

~~~~~~~~~~

Following fierce fighting, it was recorded that Smolensk had fallen to German Middle Group forces.

~~~~~~~~~~

Quiet night.

Great Yarmouth was again bombed, but with minimal damage reported.

Thursday 17

Still very little news from Libya or Abyssinia, altho' situation in Abyssinia is virtually concluded.

The situation in Abyssinia was indeed virtually over. As mentioned earlier, several isolated pockets of Italian resistance still remained, and it would take until late November before the enemy forces were finally routed and the affair brought to a close. It had certainly dragged on.

~~~~~~~~~~

Position in Libya has been static for some weeks now.

The Allied position at Tobruk remained precarious. However, throughout the siege, ships and submarines of the Royal Navy and destroyers of the Australian Navy had continued to supply the beleaguered forces through the port facilities at great cost. They were always under the threat of attack by Axis aircraft, and a large number of ships were damaged or sunk. Due to the failure of 'Operation Battleaxe' there were insufficient supplies to maintain the garrison, and therefore the numbers of troops supporting the siege were reduced to ease the situation. It was presumed that they were evacuated by departing Allied ships.

News about the same from Russia.

In the South, Rumanian army forces captured Kishinev in the lower Dnestr.

In the East, units of the Middle Group advanced across the Dnepr River near Mogilev.

Short raid at night.

Bombs fell again in East Anglia and other regions, but it was Hull that received the undivided attention of an attack by 30 enemy bombers, which caused a great deal of damage both to business premises and residential areas, resulting in 129 fatalities.

Friday 18

Our planes are more active every day. There is hardly a moment day or night when you cannot hear the drone of a fighter or a batch of bombers going out over Germany.

Germany should now know what it feels like to be bombed, but the weight of bombs is likely to increase daily, as our air power grows.

It is unlikely that these comments were taken from the media. There is no doubt that my father, like many others, was very aware that the raids on Germany were increasing - this being experienced by the sight, sound and number of our aircraft passing overhead. East Anglia was the host to many bomber stations, and there was no doubt and obvious to all that the strength of RAF Bomber and Fighter Command had been improving. There were grievous losses, but although painful in the destruction of planes and men, the RAF was slowly getting stronger - the formidable four engine Lancaster and Halifax bombers had yet to see service.

LIE IN THE DARK AND LISTEN

Lie in the dark and listen. It's clear tonight so they're flying high,
Hundreds of them, thousands perhaps, riding the icy, moonlit sky.
Men, machinery, bombs and maps, altimeters and guns and charts,
Coffee, sandwiches, fleece-lined boots, bones and muscles and minds and hearts,
English saplings with English roots deep in the earth they've left below.
Lie in the dark and let them go; Lie in the dark and listen.

Lie in the dark and listen. They're going over in waves and waves
High above villages, hills and streams, country churches and little graves
And little citizen's worried dreams; very soon they'll have reached the sea.
Lie in the dark and let them go, theirs is a world we'll never know.
Lie in the dark and listen. And far below them will lie the bays
And cliffs and sands where they used to be taken for summer holidays.
Lie in the dark and let them go. Theirs is a world we'll never know.
Lie in the dark and listen.

Lie in the dark and listen. City magnates and steel contractors,
Factory workers and politicians, soft hysterical little actors,
Ballet dancers, reserved musicians, safe in your warm civilian beds.
Count your profits and count your sheep, life is passing above your heads,
Just turn over and try to sleep. Lie in the dark and let them go;
There's one debt you'll forever owe,

Lie in the dark and listen.

Noel Coward

~~~~~~~~~~~~~~~

Quiet night.

Saturday 19
Russia resisting strongly on all sectors.

In a major change of operational planning, Hitler issued a directive ordering Panzers and troops of the Middle Group to cease their advance to Moscow and join the South Group. The aim was to destroy the Soviet 5th, 6th and 12th Armies near the Dnepr-Dnestr front. Hitler's reasoning had been to secure the agricultural and mineral resources of the Ukraine in an endeavour to support the war effort. Although his commanders tried to object, they were overruled.

Russia has certainly proved to be far more powerful than most people appreciated. Up till now, she has been rather a dark horse, & still is really, but her present resistance to the Huns is very surprising & satisfying to say the least of it.

By this time, it must be very evident to the reader that the British public and the rest of the world were being fed with grossly inaccurate information regarding the German invasion of Russia. The German aggressors were advancing on all fronts, and although the Soviet forces were ferociously defending their weak positions, and at some points holding and even counter-attacking German forces, at this stage of the campaign there was very little indication that the demands and completion of 'Operation Barbarossa' would be anything other than successful. However, there must have been one thing that must have concerned Hitler - Russia was still fighting and there had been no indication that they would cease to defend their country. It was a fight to the death and Russia was bleeding badly.

~~~~~~~~~~

Short raid at night.

One short raid was reported at Corby.

Sunday 20

We can now see how it is possible for the war to end suddenly & quicker than most people realise.

If Russia can hold the Huns, it would be impossible for Germany to launch a big scale attack elsewhere, & very doubtful whether she could release sufficient men & material to resist an attack from another source – say the British on the continent.

Is this the media daring to suggest an invasion of Europe? Surely not after such a short period since May when Prime Minister Winston Churchill was still urging the public to be prepared to resist an invasion from Germany? I feel sure that it was my father who was feeling more than encouraged, even excited, by the news available at the time. If the real facts were known, I am positive that all the Allies would have been extremely concerned. It was true that the resources required to continue the conflict would ultimately have disastrous consequences for the ability of Germany to continue defending itself on all fronts, but that would be a long way in the future. On the 20th July 1941 it could not and would not be a consideration.

Monday 21

The Victory or 'V' campaign was launched this week end, its object being to brace the spirits of the peoples in occupied territories.
The 'V' is appearing everywhere on the continent – chalked on walls, Nazi soldiers backs, and the morse equivalent played in tunes on the wireless, on motor hooters, etc.
It is proving to be most annoying to the Germans.

A Belgian, Victor de Laveleye, had conceived the original idea for the 'V' campaign. Working for the BBC, he had been broadcasting to his country, and in January of 1941 had proposed to the listeners of his homeland that the letter 'V' should be the emblem to rally his people to 'Victory'; the aim being to dent the morale of the occupying German force. The 'V' was used in every conceivable way; both obvious and subliminal, painted and chalked, scratched and tapped, sung and whistled, just anyway and anywhere to get the message over to the Germans that the inner strength of the people, although cruelly suppressed, would eventually rise up and crush them.

Britain soon took up the rallying cry of the 'V', and the BBC appointed Douglas Ritchie, alias 'Colonel Britton', to broadcast the brilliantly conceived 'psychological weapon' throughout Europe. However, due to the tremendous response and activity it generated, it eventually became rather disruptive to the British secret services and their covert operations. But, Churchill himself fully approved of the concept, and the campaign flourished. It gave the oppressed hope, and damned the occupiers by its simple brilliance.

~~~~~~~~~~

Raid at night.

The most serious incident this night was reported at the port of Lowestoft, where 15 inhabitants were killed.

Tuesday 22

Jane is not too well at the moment. Another tooth I expect.
With quieter nights Ena is more her old self & she is now getting fairly brave when we get small scale night raids.
She has stuck the nightmare nights like a brick, but the roar of enemy bombers overhead night after night in the Winter would get the strongest down in the end.

More so to those people in the towns and cities being constantly battered and annihilated by the massive raids earlier in the year, with more devastation to follow as the war progressed. New and more terrifying weapons would later arrive to convince the British public that the war was far from ending. It was the people in the towns and cities that received the majority of the bombing raids, and it was in those concentrated areas that the greatest fatalities and destruction resulted.

Later in the war, the Germans had their own reply to the 'V' campaign highlighted the previous day. However, there was nothing passive about the new and terrifying weapons of war invented by the Germans when their 'V' *(Vergeltungswaffe)* campaign was launched from France in 1944. The assault that would commence with V1 flying bombs *('Doodlebugs')*, followed shortly after by the unannounced and devastating V2 rockets, created havoc again in and towns and cities in the South East of England. Predominantly targeting London, they were random and lethal; their widespread and destructive effect killed and injured thousands of people, which further added to the great damage inflicted upon the infrastructure of our capital city and surrounding areas.

A minor raid was reported in Great Yarmouth.

Wednesday 23
Matters between the Japs & French Indo-China coming to a head. The Japs are after bases.

It was becoming clear to America and Britain that Japan would be in an advantageous strategic position to threaten Western interests with the impending agreement with Vichy France. The global position had become more precarious.

America has warned Japan that this wanton aggression is getting a habit which must be stopped.

The American State Department had been deeply concerned regarding the so-called 'passive' Japanese aggression in the Far East, and was forced to consider imposing further economic restrictions. Aimed as a warning, it exacerbated the situation by making Japan more determined to gain entry into Indo-China to obtain the oil and other materials that were required for its expansionist plans.

Altho' the Huns are slowly moving forward in Russia, the Russians are confident that Germany will be beaten.

On the 21st July it was reported that the Luftwaffe had launched its first raid on Moscow. Carried out by 127 bombers, the results did not indicate severe damage. A further 73 raids would occur up to the end of the year on the Russian capital.

Panzers of the North Group reached Lake Ilmen as they advanced to Leningrad on the 22nd July.

After a siege lasting one month, Brest-Litovsk was captured by German troops.

Quiet night.
No local incidents reported.

Thursday 24
Russia definitely slowing up the 2nd Hun attack.
They completely wiped out a German infantry division which had just arrived at the front in the Smolensk area.

Although the Red Army may have inflicted some damage on the advancing German armour, the 'wiped out' statement does not appear to confirm the records, as Smolensk was about to be encircled by the German Middle Group army.

We carried out the biggest daylight air raid of the war today. Our main objectives being the Gneisenau & the Scharnhorst, the only remaining Hun Battleships.

It had been evident from the number of raids sent to Brest that the German warships were still considered to be a very dangerous threat; even when still in harbour. Their destruction was deemed vital to save our own shipping.

As a result of the departure of the 'Scharnhorst' to La Pallice at the last minute, the original raid of 150 bombers was reduced to 100, and in good visibility, hits were reported on the 'Gneisenau'. However, those were not confirmed, and to make matters worse, German fighters got among the bombers and 12 Bomber Command aircraft were destroyed. It was a sad conclusion to a plan that had been in preparation for quite some time. At the same time as the raid on Brest, 15 RAF bombers attacked the 'Scharnhorst' at La Pallice. Several hits were registered, and although the damage was light, the ship was holed, took on several thousands of gallons of water, and sailed that night for Brest to initiate repairs. For that reason, the raid was considered successful as it forced the Germans to keep the ship in harbour for another lengthy period. However, the bombers did not have fighter protection and 5 were lost to fierce fighter opposition.

There was a diversionary raid by 36 Blenheim bombers escorted by Spitfires. The raid achieved good bombing results, but not the main objective, which was to draw away German fighter cover to allow the other two raids to operate unhindered.

'Scharnhorst' berthed and firing salute from port guns.
(Source: David Page, navyphotos)

Quiet night.

No local incidents were reported.

Friday 25
Russia holding the line everywhere.

Japs. sending boats to Indo-China. This move appears to be the first step to a move towards Singapore.

Regardless of the American stance, the 'new' Japanese government were able to adhere to their original plans and proceed with their move into Vichy French Indo-China. There was now a potential threat against British interests in the Far East.

The Japs. will be finished off after Gerry is wiped off the map.

That may well have been the attitude conveyed by the media, but the situation was becoming irreversible - Britain and America were on the road to war with Japan.

Short raid at night.

RAF aerodromes in East Anglia were targeted, but because of poor weather conditions the results were not successful for the German raiders.

We raided Berlin.

The raid on Berlin had been carried out by only 9 bombers, and out of that small force, 3 were shot down. The main raids were on Hannover and Hamburg, with the latter suffering fires in the shipyards and city. 7 RAF aircraft were reported missing from these raids.

Saturday 26
Horrible day – simply teemed with rain after lunch for several hours, when I was firewatching at the works (12-30 – 6-30).

Russian affair still satisfactory.

The situation for the Red Army was far from satisfactory, for on this day three Soviet armies were surrounded and destroyed in the Mogilev area. This appears to be the result of the battle recorded on the 15th July when it had been reported that 300,000 Soviet troops were trapped in the Smolensk-Orsha pocket.

Raid on London. Not too bad. Drone of planes for about 3 hours, but I think a lot of them were our own bombers, & fighters.

A short raid on Lowestoft was reported on this night. However, it is another situation where I think my father was incorrect with the information in this diary entry. As mentioned earlier, it leads me to believe that on certain occasions he made have made entries retrospectively a day or two later. In this one, which I believe should have occurred on the next night of the 27th July. London was indeed raided with the loss of 85 lives - the majority having been killed while in shelters. Other locations in the South-East also reported incidents.

Sunday 27
Agreement between Japs & Fr. Indo-China, settled by Japs. & Vichy Govt.

Japan had immediately gained a strategic advantage, obtaining naval and air bases with which they could now threaten Dutch, American, and British interests in the Far East. For Britain it was ominous as Singapore was now at severe risk.

We are all powerful on the air now and can lick Hitler's airforce in combat any time.
Germany are getting bigger raids than we had to put up with, but as

Churchill said these are childsplay to what we are going to give in a few months.

Raid as described the previous night. 3 German aircraft were destroyed.

Monday 28
Russia are breaking the German offensive & are holding a line all along the front.
Germany can't find excuses fast enough to suit the occasion.

It was on the previous day, the 27th July, that Hitler sent orders to von Bock's Middle Group to turn his Panzers south; to leave the proposed assault on Moscow and revert Axis forces to conquer the vital and valuable economic riches of the Ukraine.

Meanwhile, Axis forces had been entangled in a fierce battle with encircled Soviet troops only 25 miles from Smolensk, and were finally destroying the remnants of the beaten Soviet defenders that had been trapped in the Smolensk pocket.

It was also reported on the previous day that Tallin, the capital of Estonia, had been liberated by German troops of the North Group.

We still keep hearing about a German invasion of this country but he (Hitler) can have faint hopes of success should he dare try.

This source of the information could only originate from the media, and probably resulted from general talk amongst the community, based on stories and reports in the newspapers and on the 'wireless' or cinema. As previously stated, it was highly improbable that with Germany's commitment on several fronts, and with the problems beginning to emerge in Russia, Hitler would have had the ability to invade Britain.

Quiet night.

German raiders dropped bombs on Great Yarmouth and Suffolk, but very little damage resulted.

Tuesday 29
Darlan signs official agreement with Japs re Indo-China.

The Vichy French had finally conceded their valuable resources to the Japanese.

America has sent a force of 40,000 troops to watch American interests in the Phillipines.

Consisting of over 7,000 islands, the Philippines had been in American hands since the Spanish-American War. It was vital for America to protect those islands from any potential threat, especially the harbours and bases that could fall to Japan if war occurred. The largest islands were Luzon, with Manila as the main city, and Mindanao.

We are not idle, and the Japs will get a severe mauling if they overstep the mark.

That was again a note of misplaced optimism, soon to be crushed by events.

Very few neutral country's left now.

However, there were several countries that were in most difficult situations, both politically and strategically, but they had managed to retain their neutrality. For differing reasons, some awaited the outcome of the struggle against the Axis powers - some genuinely were neutral, and others were politically constrained by necessity into neutrality. However, the evil of fascism and Japanese expansionism had placed the majority of the 'free' world on the side of Britain and America. The British Commonwealth had already unreservedly supported the fight against Germany and Italy, but World War II had more horrors yet to unfold for the Allies on the other side of the globe.

Quiet raids at night.

Only minor incidents had been reported in East Anglia. By this time only small 'nuisance' raids were in evidence as the German commitment in Russia continued to drain resources.

Wednesday 30

Russia counter attacking all along the line and have forced Gerry back at certain points.

As previously recorded, there were attempts at counter-attack in isolated areas, but the predominant aggressors were the German armies and the Luftwaffe. The effect of the invasion had been overwhelming and catastrophic for the Soviet forces.

Japan adopting threatening attitude and putting pressure in Thailand.

Continuing with their intransigence and pursuing 'passive' aggression, Japan had begun to put pressure on a country that was considered an ally. During Thailand's fight against the French, when it managed to gain some land concessions, Japan had been very supportive. However, Japan now needed access routes through Thailand to enable them to have the ability to invade Burma and Malaya.

~~~~~~~~~

America & Britain can be just as threatening when the time comes.

Whether or not threats were made, the destructive path to war was inevitable, and it would be the Allies who would initially be overwhelmed as the war in the Far East systematically unfolded.

~~~~~~~~~

Short raid. Little about.

Nothing of significance had been reported locally.

Thursday 31
News as yesterday.
Very few fresh developments.

If ever there had been a 'day of infamy', then this day would probably be significant as the most evil in history, as it demonstrated the worst and most despicable excesses of the human race. It was on this day that Reinhard Heydrich obtained the final signature of Reichmarschall Herman Goering on a document that sealed the fate of millions of Jews throughout Europe. It became known as 'The Final Solution'.

Hitler hated the Jews, and with Himmler, Goering, Heydrich, Eichmann and many others, he conspired to rid the world of the Jewish race. It was the hatred that had manifested itself many years before the war, which escalated to deportation, brutal killings of tens of thousands, and eventually led to the extermination of millions of innocent men, women and children in concentration camps.

It is beyond most rational minds to comprehend the evil that surrounded the suffering of the Jews, and the systematic and calculated extermination in the specially constructed sites of death can only be confirmed by viewing the hell that was Auschwitz, Birkenau, and other sites of mass murder.

The human race must never forget that terrible period of history, of man's inhumanity to man. Father, like millions of others, had been unaware at this time of the horror that was unfolding throughout Europe, and the realisation after the war when the facts were revealed must have seemed incomprehensible. But it did happen. It was mass extermination on a scale as never before.

~~~~~~~~~

Quiet night.

It is now noticeable that August starts an intermittent period of reporting in the diary.

AUGUST 1941

Friday 1
Our troops in Libya carrying out patrol activities which are very harassing to the huns.
Tobruk is now hitting out at the surrounding Germans.

I believe that this is one of those retrospective entries again, as the following report is recorded as happening the next day, the 2nd August.

Always prepared to take the fight to the enemy, Major General Morshead had been searching for weaknesses in Rommel's positions. On the 2nd August, Morshead concluded that the German forces surrounding Tobruk were vulnerable at certain points on the salient. Supported by an artillery barrage, a battalion from the garrison endeavoured to exploit the weak positions in the Germans defence. However, heavy enemy retaliatory fire caused severe losses, and they were forced to withdraw to the town. Thereafter, until relieved, only small incursions into no-man's land were attempted.

~~~~~~~~~~

Quiet night.

Saturday 2
Firewatching at the works after dinner to 6-30pm.

~~~~~~~~~~

Gerry is making other offensives on the Eastern front, but is losing a tremendous amount of men & material.
Russia has proved a nasty shock to Hitler.

It was still most evident that the real facts were not reaching the British public. Maybe Hitler was slightly surprised at the level of sacrifice and defensive resistance shown by the oppressed Russian armies, but that cannot have dissuaded him from ultimately believing in a swift victory.

On the 31st July, the North Group reached Lake Ilmen as it advanced towards Leningrad.

As the Middle Group continued to liquidate Red Army remnants in the Smolensk pocket on the 1st August, Soviet troops displayed fierce resistance near Orsha and Vitebsk west of Smolensk. During the same day, the Russians had also been able to launch a powerful counter-offensive on German positions at Gomel, south of Mogilev and adjacent to the Dnieper River. Although this was a relatively isolated occurrence, it did indicate that Russian forces could gather sufficient resources to mount a rare counter-attack when the opportunity arose. However, it was to be many months before this could be termed as a change in battle trend.

On this day, Britain had severed all ties with Finland as a result of support given to the Axis military forces. It was also reported that the USA had agreed to a Lend-Lease plan for Russia, to support the fight against the Axis powers.

Short raid. Little about.

East Anglia received a few bombs, but little damage was reported.

Sunday 3
We raided Berlin last night. The heaviest Berlin has had yet.
Here we come, Hitler, hold your hat on.

Optimism with attitude, the confidence rising again!

However, the raid, carried out by 53 of our bombers was not a success. The RAF had been more successful on their raid by 80 aircraft to Hamburg, with several conflagrations being reported. Simultaneously, 50 bombers raided shipyards at Kiel, and although damage appeared substantial to the aircrews, it was omitted from their reports. In total, 11 RAF aircraft failed to return.

If Russia hold Germany for a few more weeks, and she will, it can be said that Hitler's end is very close.
May be this year. I still think about early spring will see it cleared up.

With this entry apparently influenced by media reports, my father had been able to hazard a guess as to when it might all end. If the real facts were known, with Russia in an extremely desperate situation and on the brink of defeat, it would have been almost impossible to come to that conclusion.

Following the surrounding of Roslavi, 38,000 Red Army prisoners were taken by the German Middle Group forces.

Quiet night.

It was reported that 25 enemy bombers raided coastal targets from Aberdeen down to Harwich, but little damage resulted.

Monday 4
Russia wipe out another Gerry infantry division. 'Pity'.

With the possible delay in media reporting events, I can only conclude that the above statement may refer to the counter offensive reported to have taken place on the 1st August (recorded in events on the 2nd August), at Gomel, adjacent to the Dnieper River.

Spent the day at Griggs.
Ena, Spud, Olly (Peggy), Ruth, Pop & Myself went bean picking after dinner.

Whilst it was very much a family effort, the reason may have been a shortage of willing labour, as the nation was occupied with many different demands of war. However, there was help at hand. Having originally operated in WWI, the Women's Land Army had been reformed in 1939, and by 1941 nearly 75,000 women between the ages of 19 and 30 registered to join and work the

The RAF lend a hand with home-front cultivation, while an Avro Anson receives attention in the background.
(Courtesy of the Franklin D. Roosevelt Library Archives)

land. Although Grandfather may well have had some assistance from this valuable Army, it was necessary for all 'hands' to be available during harvesting periods. The family may even have been paid for every bag they picked, which would go to the large London markets like Spitalfields for sale and distribution around the country.

Quiet night.

Nothing of significance was reported locally.

Tuesday 5
Dull day. We have had several storms lately & have had quite enough rain.
We want fine weather now for the harvest. It should be a record year.

As always, the weather governs the harvest. Wet and windy weather can 'lay' the corn, and with the machinery available during 1941 it could lead to difficulty for the binders when the time came to cut the crop. It would often mean hand cutting with scythes, gathering and tying the sheaves, and then standing them to dry. Having had personal experience of this in my youth on Grandfather's (Pop's) farm, it was a time consuming and onerous task. In time of war, it was vital to harvest as much of the cereal crops as possible, especially as our convoys were under constant attack by U-boats and German raiders.

Gerry is forcing his way into the Russian Ukraine, but making little headway.

The Middle Group Panzers of von Bock's force had already been ordered to turn south and capture the riches of Ukraine. Meanwhile other Middle Group armies had concluded the encirclement of Smolensk, and had taken 310,000 Soviet Red Army prisoners.

When considering Russian prisoners of war, if they did not die of their wounds, or in transportation to the camps, the treatment by their German captors was callous and brutal. Compared to other Allied prisoners who suffered hardship and near starvation in prisoner of war camps, the Russian prisoners were treated worse than animals - starved, beaten and humiliated. Many tens of thousands died after capture, but it was the retribution suffered when those who survived returned home after the war that had been despicable. Stalin considered them the lowest of the low, and many were punished for the simple reason that they had 'allowed' themselves to be captured by the Germans.

Quiet night.

Nothing of significance was reported locally.

Wednesday 6
Our day sweeps are on again over France & Northern Germany.
Gerry will get no rest from now on.
Day & night he will have to defend himself against our crippling blows.

Typical reported action:

The Hornchurch Station Commander, Group Captain 'Harry' Broadhurst was leading the Wing at the head of 54 Squadron, recently returned to its old station from the north. They were on an escort operation to bombers attacking Hazebrouck aerodrome. The Wing was circling above the target at 14,000ft in pairs and fours whilst the bombers below went into their attack, when suddenly Broadhurst saw a Spitfire below him being chased by a Messerschmitt Bf109. When he saw the Spitfire pilot take to his parachute, Broadhurst decided that it was time to intervene. He dived after the enemy accompanied by his No. 2 and between them they cut off the German fighter and shot it down. As they were collecting themselves after this dive, a second 109 attached itself to the tail of his No. 2 and the two Spitfires hurriedly broke formation outwards to shake off the newcomer. The Group Captain's combat report tells of the confused and strenuous fighting, which then followed:

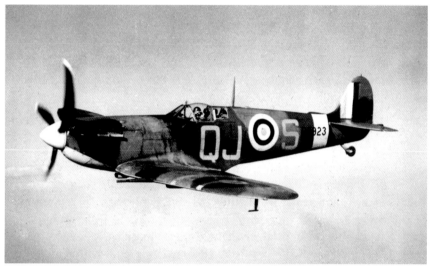

Evocative shot of a cannon armed 92 Squadron Supermarine Spitfire MkV.
(Source: Ken Delve Collection)

'We reformed in line abreast and my No. 2 called that there was an E/A *(enemy aircraft)* diving on my tail. We again broke outwards and my turn was so steep that I partially blacked out. I flew a full circle and next found myself 50yds behind a Me*(Bf)*109 with a yellow nose, which was just opening fire on my No.2 who was flying straight and level 50yds in front of him. Both aircraft were dead in my sights and I was unable to fire until the E/A overshot and pulled up to the left, while Red 2 broke to the right. I was then able to give a short burst from the quarter. I saw strikes on the engine cowling and the airscrew stopped dead. Red 2 again called a warning of more E/A approaching to attack and I was unable to follow up my attack on this E/A, which I consider was probably destroyed.'

News about the same from Russia.

Air raid at night.
Not many Gerries about.

There were scattered raids during the night, and just before midnight a German raider crashed into the sea just a few hundred yards off Clacton Pier.

Thursday 7
The Japs still adopting a threatening attitude, but hesitates to take the final plunge.

Russia resisting everywhere.
They raided Berlin last night. Germans blamed the RAF.
This air raiding from two fronts will need a lot of explaining by Goebbells.

Following the initial German 'softening-up' raids on Moscow by the Luftwaffe, Stalin was determined to take the battle to the heart of the Reich. He subsequently ordered that Russian aircraft must bomb Berlin. On this day, 5 Ilyushin bombers of the Soviet Navy took off for the German capital - allegedly from Estonia. According to reports, two were shot down, two failed to reach Berlin and one was able to drop bombs near the capital.

As if he considered himself anything less, Joseph Stalin appointed himself Generalissimo of the Red Army.

Quiet night.
There were raiders about in East Anglia as bombs were dropped on Great Yarmouth.

Friday 8
Russian airforce raided Berlin again last night.
Germans now admit that Russian aircraft had been over Berlin.

As reported on the previous day, it was a fact that Russia had bombed Berlin. I believe that the immediacy of that report indicates yet again that the diary entries may be retrospective, as there is no record that the Soviets bombed Berlin again the following night. However, my limited research on this raid does indicate that the Russian Air Force did mount a further attack with a small force on or around the 11th August using Pe.8 and Yer-2 bombers. Despite some aircraft being shot down by AA and Finnish fighters en route, it was reported that several of the bomber force had managed to dispose of their loads over Berlin. The results were not documented, although it is likely that the propaganda dished out by Goebbels would have significantly underplayed the incident. But, it must have been concerning for Germany that bombs were targeting their cities from two sources - Britain and Russia. America was yet to follow.

Germany still making childish claims about successes in Russia.
Nobody, not even the German public, put any faith in German claims.
They have proved them wrong so often.

It was recorded on this day that armies of the Middle Group, which had surrounded Red Army forces at Uman, had concluded the battle and had taken a staggering 103,000 prisoners.

Short raid.

Bombs were reported as having fallen in Suffolk, but with no recorded damage.

Saturday 9
Germany pushing into Ukraine but still meeting stubborn resistance everywhere.
Russian airforce are playing havoc with the Luftwaffe.

Unfortunately, the reverse was occurring. However, constant attrition had been affecting both sides, but because of the lack of an adequate aircraft and pilot replacement program the Luftwaffe would soon be under severe pressure. Although Erhard Milch replaced Ernst Udet as State Secretary for aircraft production in November 1941, at this time in August the German aircraft manufacturing industry was barely producing 300 aircraft per month. However, the Soviets appeared to have a better co-ordinated and constant line of replacements. Equipment failure in the coming winter would exacerbate that situation as German lines of supply, having been stretched too far, began to falter and fail. That situation was yet to come, and for several weeks more the German invasion would continue to drive through Russian territory.

Russian winter will soon be here and Gerry will be held up, if he can be resisted until then.
This battle will decide whether the war will last years, or merely months.

It was understandable that the media would have reported the potential difficulties of fighting in the Russian winter. The observation was to eventually prove very true, with terrifying consequences for both sides. It became a battle of attrition with German forces becoming increasingly static in their movement of equipment and troops - frozen to a standstill in the extremely harsh and unforgiving icy Russian environment. Hundreds of thousands were to lose their lives during that horrific winter with neither side giving ground without severe cost. But 1943 was to be the turning point for the German invasion, and from then on it was the Russians who would contest command of the battle, which would continue until the very last days of the Third Reich when Russian troops eventually entered Berlin in the spring of 1945. Yes, the war did have a long while yet to run, and many millions were yet to die.

Short raid.

Lowestoft was again bombed, causing further damage and 6 fatalities. Both Lowestoft and Great Yarmouth had suffered considerably from German raiders during the recent months, as had other important coastal targets, and the impact on the communities and industry had been significant.

Sunday 10

Opinion very varied about Russians position.
Most people confident she can hold & even beat Gerry, but others very doubtful about it.
This fact is certain either Gerry must have been in a bad position for oil & wheat, or else he made an unforgivable miscalculation about the power of Russia.

The battle was almost fatal for Russia during this period, with German forces still pushing the Red Army back further into their homeland. Meanwhile, behind the lines Russian industry was rapidly mobilising to produce more weapons and train more fighting men and women to stem the advance, but all depended on halting the German armies as soon as possible to give them the time to rebuild resources and prepare later in the year for limited offensives. Russia was powerful but severely wounded and needed time to regroup its forces. The dreadful winter weather would provide that valuable respite.

Short raid but few planes about.

Nothing of significance had been reported locally.

Monday 11

Very little news.

Short raid at night.

Again, nothing of significance had been reported locally.

Tuesday 12
News about the same everywhere.

Quiet night.

There were scattered raids conducted by 37 enemy aircraft over the Midlands and Eastern Counties, with damage recorded at several locations. There were 8 casualties reported at Bassingbourn.

Wednesday 13
Germany pushing slowly ahead in the Ukraine.
Russians fighting back strongly.

The Red Army was gradually beginning to show signs of retaliation as another Soviet counter-attack had been reported at Staraja, south of Lake Ilmen, against German North Group forces.

No further move by Japan.
Bluff again?

Japan was determined to carry out its policy of expansion and was certainly not bluffing. It would, of course, have been easier to avoid conflict, but it was not in the character of those in power in Japan to accede to peaceful demands. Their war industries were growing by the day, and their forces were preparing for the inevitable conflict.

Short raid.

Nothing of significance reported locally. Raiders passing through to targets further afield probably caused the raid alert.

Thursday 14
Little news.

Short raid.

Nothing of significance reported locally - yet again! Incidents were certainly less frequent during this period, and although constant alerts were being sounded, the results had no impact on the community.

Friday 15
Winston goes to America to see Roosevelt. They meet aboard the 'Prince of Wales' – our latest battleship & discuss arms problems &

post war actions. They formed a mutual collaboration pact & decided to send all possible aid to Russia.
The meeting was kept dark until it was all over & then the news was broadcast to the world.

Meeting aboard the battleship 'Prince of Wales', the results of the Conference, known as the Atlantic Charter, were issued to the press:-

<u>Joint Statement by President Roosevelt and Prime Minister Churchill, August 14, 1941:</u>

The following statement signed by the President of the United States and the Prime Minister of Great Britain is released for the information of the Press:

The President of the United States and the Prime Minister, Mr. Churchill, representing His Majesty's Government in the United Kingdom, have met at sea.

They have been accompanied by officials of their two Governments, including high ranking officers of the Military, Naval and Air Services

The whole problem of the supply of munitions of war, as provided by the <u>Lease-Lend Act</u>, for the armed forces of the United States and for those countries actively engaged in resisting aggression has been further examined.

Lord Beaverbrook, the Minister of Supply of the British Government, has joined in these conferences. He is going to proceed to Washington to discuss further details with appropriate officials of the United States Government. These conferences will also cover the supply problems of the Soviet Union.

The President and the Prime Minister have had several conferences They have considered the dangers to world civilization arising from the policies of military domination by conquest upon which the Hitlerite government of Germany and other governments associated therewith have embarked, and have made clear the stress which their countries are respectively taking for their safety in the face of these dangers.

They have agreed upon the following joint declaration:

Joint declaration of the President of the United States of America and the Prime Minister, Mr. Churchill, representing His Majesty's Government in the United Kingdom, being met together, deem it right to make known certain common principles in the national policies of their respective countries on which they base their hopes for a better future for the world.

First, their countries seek no aggrandizement, territorial or other;

Second, they desire to see no territorial changes that do not accord with the freely expressed wishes of the peoples concerned;

Third, they respect the right of all peoples to choose the form of government under which they will live; and they wish to see sovereign rights and self government restored to those who have been forcibly deprived of them;

Fourth, they will endeavor, with due respect for their existing obligations, to further the enjoyment by all States, great or small, victor or vanquished, of access, on equal terms, to the trade and to the raw materials of the world which are needed for their economic prosperity;

Fifth, they desire to bring about the fullest collaboration between all nations in the economic field with the object of securing, for all, improved labor standards, economic advancement and social security;

Sixth, after the final destruction of the Nazi tyranny, they hope to see established a peace which will afford to all nations the means of dwelling in safety within their own boundaries, and which will afford assurance that all the men in all the lands may live out their lives in freedom from fear and want;

Seventh, such a peace should enable all men to traverse the high seas and oceans without hindrance;

Eighth, they believe that all of the nations of the world, for realistic as well as spiritual reasons must come to the abandonment of the use of force. Since no future peace can be maintained if land, sea or air armaments continue to be employed by nations which threaten, or may threaten, aggression outside of their frontiers, they believe, pending the establishment of a wider and permanent system of general security, that the disarmament of such nations is essential. They will likewise aid and encourage all other practicable measures which will lighten for peace-loving peoples the crushing burden of armaments

FRANKLIN D. ROOSEVELT

WINSTON S. CHURCHILL

(Source: Samuel Rosenman, ed., Public Papers and Addresses of Franklin D. Roosevelt, vol.10 (1938-1950), 314.)

Note: The reader may have noticed the reference to Lease-Lend in the above statement. It may have also been noticeable that I have consistently referred to the Lend-Lease proposals. There was an office set up in America to deal with these arrangements, and it was officially referred to in Government circles as <u>Lend-Lease</u>...?

Locally, there had been limited Luftwaffe activity, but bombs were dropped on Sudbury.

Saturday 16
The weather has been horrible lately, just when the farmers need a dry spell for harvest.
Very little corn is cut yet owing to the rain.
It must have been concerning for the farming population as the harvest was beginning to be at risk. Pop would have been preparing for this eventuality, but would still have been very concerned. He and Spud would have been discussing the implications and the threat to the yield of the crops.

Germany still pressing into the Ukraine.
Odessa is cut off.
The situation would be resolved when Rumanian forces took Odessa on the 16th October.
Russian troops still fighting as strongly as ever.
Panzers of the German North Group capture Novgorod on the road to Leningrad. Simultaneously, German and Rumanian forces of the South Group capture Nikolaev, which was a very important Soviet naval base on the Black Sea.

Short raid at night.

Lowestoft again recorded bombing, but there were no reports of any damage.

Sunday 17
Russian positions about the same.

No change in Africa or Japan.

Japs do not feel too inclined to start a war in the far east.

Where did my father get that impression? I suppose that hindsight has given us a clearer understanding of the progress to war, but the broadcasting authorities at that time may have sent out confusing signals to the public. It was quite likely that, being unaware and not privy to all the machinations of the opposing governments, and also being subject to restrictions in reporting, even the media were confused.

Went shooting after dinner (2 Bunnies).

Father, I recall, was pretty handy with his 12-bore shotgun, and he would be pretty useful at harvest time when the cutting of the corn was guaranteed to disturb many 'bunnies'!

Plenty of aircraft & convoys about at night, but most, if not all, of the planes were our own.

However, Hull was the main target for 27 enemy bombers during the night resulting in limited damage. 11 fatalities were reported.

A minor incident was reported in Suffolk.

Monday 18
Little news.

Quiet night.

Nothing of significance was reported locally.

Tuesday 19
Germany are having a tough fight. They have given up the push towards Smolensk and appear to be concentrating in the Ukraine & against Leningrad.
They have had terrific losses.

The German North Group had rapidly advanced and captured Narva as it inexorably progressed towards Leningrad.

~~~~~~~~~~

Short scattered raids at night.

Dover was the nearest location recorded as having received bomb damage. Otherwise there was nothing reported locally.

Wednesday 20
Winston arrives back in this country.
He called at Iceland on the way back.

~~~~~~~~~~

His talk with F.D.R. was a subtle move.
He got it in before Germany started their peace offensive.

It appears that my father may have assumed the Russians would force Germany to sue for peace. I am not sure whether or not the media had insinuated that fact, but naturally, in the light of known events and with hindsight, that was a very optimistic view. It certainly did not allude to that assumption in their official Press Release to the world, although it would be entirely natural as many other key issues were discussed, but remained highly confidential as it could have been extremely harmful to the war effort.

~~~~~~~~~~

No move by Japan yet.

~~~~~~~~~~

Quiet night.

Lowestoft again reported a lone raider.

Thursday 21
We have sunk over 600,000 tons of enemy shipping during the past 5 weeks. This is a record.
It is unlikely that we lost a quarter of this figure in the same period.

~~~~~~~~~~

Gerry is pushing hard for Leningrad & Odessa.

It was reported that on the previous day, the 20th August, armies of the South Group had captured Cherson on the Black Sea coast, which was considered the gateway to the Crimea.

Hitler had made another of his strategic changes. He ordered the 'investment', not capture, of Leningrad. He further ordered the transfer of Divisions from the North and Middle Groups to capture the Crimea and the Donets basin, which was an industrial region considered vital to the

Soviets.

Note: Since my father had started recording the German invasion of Russia in 1941, it must have become obvious to the reader that the subject of his observations had commanded both his and the world's attention. When put in the context of importance, it may be argued that many other battles and incidents could have proven pivotal in the defeat of the Axis powers. What was incontrovertible was that it was logistically, materially and destructively by far the largest singular conflict in WWII. Many millions died as Hitler sought to subjugate the Soviets and provide the so-called 'living space' for the expansion and improved wealth of Germany.

It has been no great coincidence, therefore, that so much has been entered into the writings of the diary, as it must be accepted that, with America not in the war at that stage, and with so much resting on the desperate need to defeat Hitler, preceding and subsequent entries should offer a consecutive blow by blow account of the progress of major events during the campaign. That I, as the 'expander' of my father's entries, should endeavour to offer some insight into his observations must only be taken as a token effort to provide guidance to the evolving conflict. Although it may appear somewhat disjointed in content, it can only be a personal and possibly inadequate effort to marginally enlighten the reader struggling to comprehend the enormity of the events as they occurred.

~~~~~~~~~

Short raid.

Lowestoft continued to be targeted by enemy bombers, and sustained some damage from this raid.

Friday 22
Our planes are now hitting occupied territory very hard in our day sweeps.

That may have been so, but at a cost, as those operations were constantly fraught with danger. On the 9th August 1941, Wing Commander Douglas Bader, famous for his return to flying after a terrible accident that cost him his legs, was leading a sweep over France. Although he managed to bail out, he lost one of his artificial legs and was unable to escape. Although Bader did not appreciate it at the time, it had been probable that in the confusion of aerial combat he may well have been shot down by one of his own squadron! Via a neutral intermediary and with German agreement, the RAF parachuted a replacement leg to his captors a few days later. However, it should be noted that the British authorities did not wish to be seen to be co-operating with the enemy, so the RAF insured that the aircraft was on an active operation. The inventory of the bomber that night might have recorded '…bombs, incendiaries and one artificial leg', perhaps?

Bader had many admirers and a few critics, but none could fault his determination to beat Germany, and as a POW he did everything in his power to make life hell for them. He was a remarkable man, a fighter ace, and a victim of the policy of 'leaning into France' - a policy that he readily and aggressively endorsed.

However, those commanding the policy of the costly offensive fighter sweeps were beginning to have doubts. It may well have kept their 'fighter boys' busy, but Fighter Command had been losing too many valuable pilots and too many aircraft.

Our night raids are also getting very heavy again.

RAF bombing did continue on a slightly greater scale on many nights, with over 200 aircraft taking part in the larger raids. But, as previously commented, there was still much to be desired of the accuracy necessary to inflict severe damage on the enemy industrial infrastructure.

Most of Gerry's planes are in the east and only very few come over here.

It had become very evident that in recent weeks the rate and quantity of incursions by the German Air Force had become slight in comparison to the earlier months of 1941. The Luftwaffe was otherwise occupied in the East, and the respite given to Britain was desperately needed to build up reserves, strengthen the relationships with America and other active and potential Allies, and to formulate plans for future operations to win the war. Regrettably, many thousands were yet to lose their lives achieving that aim. It was also evident that Hitler was capable, and prepared, to move more 'Gruppen' of aircraft back to the West to carry on the aerial assault against Britain if he thought it necessary at that time. But as winter approached his options would rapidly diminish…

Saturday August 23 to Friday September 19 - nothing recorded.

There were further enemy incursions during the last few days of August, with unsuccessful raids on airfields in East Anglia during the night of 27th/28th August, and 50 enemy aircraft raiding several areas during the night of 29th/30th when Suffolk and Norfolk received some bombs. On the last night of the month, Hull was again the target and sustained further damage and 38 fatalities. There were isolated incidents elsewhere, including a few in Suffolk.

Germany continued to lose the odd raider or two during most days and nights in this 'quieter' period.

~~~~~~~~~~~

It is worthy of note that on the 29th/30th August, the first flights by Bomber Command in support of resistance groups in Europe commenced, so they could, as Churchill commented '...set Europe ablaze'. The bombers were to carry out many drops of agents and supplies by parachute all over Europe to enable the fight to be taken to the heart of enemy territory. Many of these extremely resourceful and brave patriots were to lose their lives during the war; many were captured and tortured, but few revealed information vital to the Nazis. Their lives could be lonely and dangerous, and several of those who survived were decorated for bravery at the end of the war - others, unsung, were to perish by shooting, torture, or by a solitary death in concentration camps. A significant number of Bomber Command crews who flew them to their locations would also lose their lives, as their task was virtually as dangerous as that on other missions. The job demanded resilience and bravery by all concerned, and all bar none rose to the occasion.

SEPTEMBER 1941

Following the lapse of entries for August (for which my father apologises later) the September raids on Britain by enemy bombers were light and ineffective, with East Anglia reporting incidents on the night of the 2nd/3rd. Although raids, casualties and fatalities were reported in other parts of Britain, Norfolk and Cambridge were the nearest to our area during the night of the 8th/9th. With raids continuing to occur elsewhere, East Anglia recorded ineffective attacks on the 16th/17th, and incidents in Essex on 17th/18th.

~~~~~~~~~~

The Red Army continued to be under severe pressure from all Groups of German armed forces.

The siege of Leningrad had commenced on the 4th September, when North Group forces experienced severe resistance from Red Army defenders as they encircled the city. Hitler, having issued the order for the 'investment' of Leningrad, consigned the defenders and inhabitants to a long and bitter period of degradation and death. Constant battering by the Luftwaffe and ground artillery gave no respite to those incarcerated in that besieged and battered city.

The drive to capture the Lend-Lease port of Murmask was temporarily halted by the Red Army on the 7th September, although mobile units of the South Group made a breakthrough at Konotop to advance further into the Ukraine.

On the 14th September, the German Middle Group completed the encirclement of two Soviet armies at Kiev in the Ukraine.

~~~~~~~~~~

The supply convoys continued to be under attack from U-boat 'Wolfpacks'. One convoy that fared worse than most was designated SC42. Departing from Sydney, Australia, on the 30th August 1941, the convoy was bound for the British port of Liverpool.

The freighters were carrying massive supplies of cargo, consisting of diverse materials such as steel and grain, gas-oil and flour, and many other valuable commodities. The convoy of 65 ships had passed Cape Farewell off the coast of Greenland on the 7th September and was being escorted by a dozen corvettes of the Royal Canadian Navy. However, the British Admiralty were aware that the convoy was being shadowed by German submarines, and orders were sent to instruct the convoy to sail further north closer to the east coast of Greenland. It was at that location during the evening of the 9th September that the first blows were struck. Submarine

U-432 unleashed several torpedoes sinking two of the heavily laden vessels. This action brought a frenzy of activity as 14 more U-boats were attracted to the convoy. By the 11th September, 16 ships had been consigned to the deep, with great loss of life to the heroic merchant sailors, and the loss of much needed materials destined for Britain to continue the fight against the Axis powers. Although against orders, some ships stopped to pick up survivors - a brave, but somewhat foolhardy task, as a static ship was extremely vulnerable. However, some captains could not ignore the humanitarian desire to save lives, and in doing so risked their ship and cargo, but at least some men were saved.

It was reported that two U-boats were sunk during that disastrous encounter for the convoy, whilst the remainder of the ships straggled into Liverpool over a period of several days - battered but not beaten.

Saturday 20
Biggest daylight sweep by RAF so far over occupied territory.
Hundreds of fighters & bombers took part.

The Commander-in-Chief Fighter Command, Air Marshal Sholto Douglas, who had controversially taken over from Dowding in November 1940, now had serious reservations about the policy to 'lean into France', as the 'Father of the RAF', Hugh Trenchard had originally (but unofficially) suggested. The reality of the situation was that RAF losses, and the inflated claims made against the Luftwaffe defenders during those offensive sweeps had not been the most efficient way to take the fight to the enemy. Fighter Command had claimed nearly 450 enemy aircraft destroyed carrying out the policy, but in reality less than 200 had been destroyed, whilst the RAF lost nearly double that claimed, and over 400 pilots had been killed - a severe loss to Fighter Command.

It was also evident that enticing German fighters into combat and drawing them away from the German/Russian Front was really not working, but it was vital that the fighter offensive should continue. With Russia now in the war, and under intense pressure from the German invaders, the fighter sweeps would emphasis Allied support for their cause. Doing nothing was out of the question, and those who may question Fighter Command's policy in 1941, do so with the benefit of hindsight. It was considered to be the correct and only course to take at that time - and the 'fighter boys' wanted action.

Short raid at night.
Nothing of significance was reported locally.

Sunday 21
Very busy at work & in the garden has put me well behind with my records but I will try to pull up from here.

The reason for the lapse in entries is that my father was very busy indeed. With the galvanising operation now up and running; with fire-watching still a necessity; with the harvest that he was helping to gather as well as a garden to tend, and with the family now beginning to get some form of normality, he must have had full and busy days.

~~~~~~~~~~

Germany have advanced deeply into Russia in the Ukraine area, tho' Odessa still fights back. Gerry is miles east of Kiev which is expected to fall at any moment.
Leningrad still fighting hard.

After sustained and aggressive pressure, it was reported that German South Group forces had captured Poltava on the 18th September, and to compound the severe problems of the Soviets, on the 19th the Middle Group captured Kiev.

~~~~~~~~~~

Incidents were reported in East Anglia, but with no recorded damage.

Monday 22
Kiev has been evacuated by the Russians.
Russians are still pushing Gerry back in the Smolensk sector.
Leningrad troops are counter attacking.
Russia needs tanks & planes as fast as USA & we can send them, as we are now doing.

On the 17th September, the USA allocated $100 million to the Soviet Union for the purchase of war materials.

Both Britain and America were preparing to send vast amounts of weapons and aircraft to Russia. Britain had promised many Hurricane fighter planes, and American P39 Airacobra fighters destined for other areas of conflict were diverted to Russia. Neither of these aircraft could be recognised as the best front line fighters at that time, but the Russian pilots were able to gain the maximum benefit from their limited performance. There is no doubt that some of the Soviet pilots were a match for the average Luftwaffe pilot, and the task for the Germans had not been made any easier as the Russian air forces grew in stature and experience.

~~~~~~~~~~

Warnings every night for the last week or so but only scattered attacks. Nothing fallen within 10 miles since last winter.

My initial concern at this last statement was that my father had been at the whiskey bottle! It does appear that the last entry for weapons having been dropped in the immediate vicinity of Coggeshall, or his works in Witham, had occurred in the middle of April - not quite winter, but considerably earlier in the year than my first impression when reading his observation. The constant reference to raids, with the interspersed 'quiet nights' and raiders overhead must have deluded me. Pass the bottle, please Father?

Tuesday 23

Father had not recorded anything for this day.

However, bombing incidents were reported in East Anglia, but with no significant damage evident. There may not have been an entry in the diary, but the raiders continued to come, ships were being sunk, armies were fighting, countries were being invaded and the war progressed with the inevitable result of death and destruction involving many innocent people.

Wednesday 24

Altho' our raids on Germany are heavy, they are not yet as heavy as we should be giving possibly due to the fact that we have been sending some of our planes to Russia.

It was predominantly fighter planes that were being sent to Russia at this stage, and it was unlikely that this would have caused a loss of aircraft for raids on Germany.

~~~~~~~~~~~~

Russia still fighting strongly & counter attacking in places.

It was reported that Middle Group forces began an offensive against the vital land bridge to the Crimea at Perekop.

On the 25th September, Hitler ordered that all attacks by the North Group on Leningrad cease, and that the city should be starved by siege. He instructed that when the city surrendered, it should be razed to the ground. It would take nearly 900 days until the siege ended, a period of inhuman privation, starvation, distress and death - but the city survived, not to be captured by the German forces, but by relief from the Soviet Red Army.

Towards the end of September, the attacks by German South Group to force an entry into the Crimea were thwarted and temporarily halted by Soviet forces. However, the German Middle Group was reported to have launched an attack to capture Orel.

During the last days of September, the South Group prepared to advance towards Kiev in the Ukraine; the North Group surrounded and destroyed Soviet forces at Velikije Luki, and Axis Finnish troops captured Vyborg.

The 28th September was a very significant day for the Soviet Union. It was the first day of the three-power conference held in Moscow to discuss aid to Russia from Britain and America. That the Allies should assist that distrusted and dangerous regime displayed the overwhelming importance of ridding the world of Hitler and fascism, but later would open the gates to communism. At the cessation of hostilities, the 'Red Curtain' would fall on countries throughout Eastern Europe, and it would be many years before those counties experienced freedom once again.

Thursday September 25 – Tuesday October 14 – nothing recorded.

During the last few days in September, bombs fell, but caused little damage in Great Yarmouth in Norfolk and Mayland in Essex during the night of the 26th/27th, and East Anglia again on the night of the 28th/29th. Other regions still continued to attract raiders with both damage and fatalities being recorded, the worst in the North Shields area where 41 perished.

OCTOBER 1941

On October 1st 1941, the First Russian Protocol was signed by the three Allied powers authorising Lend-Lease arrangements for the Soviet war effort. The aid was confirmed in a personal letter sent by President Roosevelt to Stalin on the 8th October.

German forces restarted 'Operation Taufin' on the 2nd October to capture the city of Moscow. The belated commencement had been stalled as a result of other strategic issues, and with the policy indecision by Hitler concerning Leningrad it was deemed vital that Moscow should now be taken as soon as possible.

It was reported that Orel was captured by Middle Group forces on the 3rd October, and on the central and southern fronts, Brjansk, Berdjansk and Mariupol were captured on the 6th, and Vjasma on the 7th, although fighting continued in isolated pockets of resistance.

~~~~~~~~~~

In early October, having expressed his outrage over incidents of German submarines torpedoing American freighters in the Atlantic, President Roosevelt sought the revision of the 1939 Neutrality Act, to enable American merchant ships to be armed. The Senate approved the revision on the 7th November.

~~~~~~~~~~

German bombers continued to cause death and devastation throughout the country during the early part of October. Notably, there were raids closer to home with Leiston receiving bombs on the night of the 10th/11th, and the ports of Ipswich and Great Yarmouth on the night of the 11th/12th. The following night both Tendring and Walton-on-the-Naze received unwelcome visitors as they dropped their loads at random on unsuspected inhabitants.

Wednesday 15
Altho' Russia are still fighting back strongly, the enemy have advanced many miles since my last entry.
They have taken most of the Ukraine, cut off the Caucasus, taken Vyazme and Briansk in a drive to Moscow.
Terrific battle for Moscow has been raging for 14 days.
Germans 70 miles from Moscow but they are being slowed up. Hitler all out for defeat of Russia before winter sets in.

On the 9th October, Hitler confidently announced that, to all intents and purposes, the war in the East had already been concluded in Germany's favour. He was to regret that statement to the end.

In the final battle with surrounded Red Army troops along the Sea of Azov, Axis forces of the South Group had taken 100,000 prisoners on the 10th October. Further Soviet reverses followed when it was reported on the 12th October that units of the Middle Group captured the town of Kaluga, rapidly followed the next day with the capture of both Kalinin and Rshev; just 100 miles to the west of Moscow. As a result of rumours of the impending capture of the capital by the German Army, thousands of inhabitants had been seen to flee in panic. This cannot have been without foundation, for on the 16th October, the Soviet government together with all their diplomatic corps, evacuated Moscow to relocate in the somewhat safer location of Kuibyshev. That situation could only have been exacerbated by the announcement that Rumanian forces had captured the valuable Black Sea port of Odessa on the same day.

Following the final encirclement and capture of both Brjansk and Vjasma, Middle Group forces had taken an incredible 673,000 prisoners. Continuing reverses for Soviet forces were recorded in the Ukraine on the 21st October when the 6th Army of the South Group captured Stalino in the industrial Donets Basin, and further success continued for units of the Middle Group when they captured Kharkov and Belgorod on the 24th. Compounding Soviet losses at the end of October, the offensive by the German Middle Group 11th Army finally made the breakthrough at Perekop on the 27th October, thus opening the gate to the Crimean peninsular.

Finally, in the month of October, the United States of America provided further support for Britain and the beleaguered Soviet Union, when President Roosevelt approved the appropriation by Congress for an additional $6 billion in Lend-Lease aid.

The outlook to that point at the end of October had been dire for the Soviet Union. Resistance to advancing German forces had been broadly uncoordinated, although intensely and bitterly contested. That the Soviet forces had been able to absorb and accept the bitter defeats imposed on them since the start of the invasion was almost unbelievable and extremely costly in weapons and manpower, and the immense loss of life had been catastrophic. However, Soviet resources appeared almost unlimited, and the Russian 'Bear' would fully awaken at the outset of winter. With German forces largely unprepared for battle in the severe conditions rapidly approaching, the Red Army and Air Force would begin to hold and slowly drive back the Axis forces from the brink of, what inevitably appeared, the extinction of the Soviet Union.

~~~~~~~~~

During the night of the 15th October, East Anglia, and particularly Great Yarmouth again sustained light damage from small raids.

On the night of the 22nd/23rd October, minor attacks were recorded in Essex and Suffolk, with other areas also being targeted. A significant number of mines and bombs were dropped by 37 enemy aircraft in 14 different locations during the night of the 25th/26th with a few falling in East Anglia. Of 42 raiders who penetrated our defences on the nights of the 30th/31st and the 31st/1st November, Great Yarmouth and the surrounding area suffered some damage, but fortunately no fatalities were recorded.

On the plus side, nearly 20 enemy aircraft were recorded as destroyed during October, near or over home territory.

~~~~~~~~~

It had been announced in Japan on the 17th October that General Hideki Tojo had replaced Prime Minister Konoye, who had become politically isolated. Tojo, previously the War Minister, was an advocate of war with the West. He would not be disappointed.

~~~~~~~~~

On the 31st October, there was outrage in the United States when the USS 'Reuben James' became the first American warship sunk in WWII. The ship was torpedoed by the submarine U-552, and over 100 sailors perished. It was claimed by Germany to have been an accident.

Thursday October 16 – Monday November 17 – nothing recorded.

NOVEMBER 1941

The month of November commenced in the East with the capture of the town of Simferopol in the Crimea by the German Middle Group 11th Army, who then intensified their aggressive advance by executing the capture of Feodosia on the 4th. Meanwhile, Panzers of the Middle group achieved their objective by capturing Kursk on the 3rd November.

Considering the dominance of the Axis forces as they progressed throughout the Soviet Union, Stalin, in a dramatic speech in Red Square, Moscow, predicted that '…the Fascist German invaders are facing disaster'. On the day of that compelling but optimistic statement (the 7th November), leading elements of the Wehrmacht were no more than 100 miles from the capital. Whether on not he truly believed that prediction, it was remarkable in content and prophetic for the future of the conflict. Yet, on the following day another town, Tichvin, fell to North Group units on the Leningrad front.

However, the optimism shown by the Soviet leader was consequently soon to emerge with consistent and well executed retaliatory action by Red Army forces.

~~~~~~~~~~

On the night of the 7th/8th November, 392 RAF bombers were despatched by Bomber Command for the largest raid yet on Germany. With storms and icing forecast over the Channel, it had been decided to split the raid between Berlin, Cologne and Mannheim, with limited tactical sorties being sent to other locations.

Only half the raiding force managed to bomb outlying areas of Berlin, hitting industrial, utility and domestic premises, causing light damage and a few casualties. A further 60 plus aircraft bombed Cologne, but very little damage was reported, and although about 40 bombers reached Mannheim, subsequent reports indicated that no damage had been evident.

Consequently, as a result of all the raids this night, 37 aircraft were lost, which was a high price to pay in aircrews and aircraft for such little return.

~~~~~~~~~~

While the main preoccupation of the Luftwaffe at that time seemed to be parachute mining of seaways around the British Isles, variations of those highly dangerous weapons caused severe damage due to their massive blast effect when dropped on land. They were included in bomb loads as enemy raids continued throughout Britain with anything up to 50 aircraft operating at any one time, but it was not until the night of the 8th/9th November that incidents were recorded in Essex and other adjoining counties; including an incident noted in Norfolk on the 10th. Nearer to home, Dovercourt, Bradwell-on-Sea and Frinton-on-Sea received the unwanted attention of raiders on the night of the 17th/18th.

~~~~~~~~~

On active service in the Mediterranean, the 22,000 ton aircraft carrier HMS 'Ark Royal', the third ship to carry that name in the Royal Navy, was sunk on the 14th November after sustaining a torpedo strike by U-boat U81 on the previous day. Assisting in the delivery of fighter aircraft to the beleaguered island of Malta, the carrier had been returning to Gibraltar and was struck amidships by a single torpedo.

Initially, the damage could have been repaired sufficiently by crew specialists and the ship towed the 30 short miles to Gibraltar. However, apart from the severe damage, communications systems had been knocked out and a premature order to abandon ship was given. Unfortunately, those who initially may have rescued the stricken Ark Royal had left the ship only to return later in an endeavour to save her - but it was too late. At 0619hrs on the 14th November 1941 she capsized and sank. All but one of the total complement of 1,488 crew had been rescued, but it was a devastating loss of a valuable aircraft carrier for the Royal Navy.

Tuesday 18
Russia make large scale counter attack in the Caucasus & are pushing Gerry back in places.

As if to show further contempt for Stalin's prediction, on the 15th November, German Middle Group Panzer and infantry forces began the second phase of the battle for Moscow. Further Middle group units captured the eastern Crimean port of Kerch on the 17th November, and as if to ridicule Stalin's prediction once more, Panzer units captured Rostov-on-Don.

~~~~~~~~~

Very few air raids lately.
We often get the alarm but do not hear many planes.

Raiders again visited Lowestoft, although no significant damage was reported.

Wednesday November 19 – Thursday November 27 – nothing recorded.

Southend reluctantly received enemy raiders on the 24th/25th November, and parachute mines were dropped in Essex on the 27th/28th with considerable blast damage being reported.

The battleship HMS 'Barham' had been sunk on the 25th November. Together with the battleships HMS 'Queen Elizabeth' and HMS 'Valiant', 'Barham' was tasked with intercepting Italian supply convoys destined for North Africa. Just north of Sidi Barrani, the German submarine U-331 launched three torpedoes that caused the battleship to slowly capsize, then be totally torn apart by a massive explosion. Although quite a number of the crew were saved, over 800 perished in the devastating aftermath of the U-boat attack. It had been another massive blow to the Royal Navy.

By the 21st November, some German forces were positioned no more than 35 miles from Moscow as the offensive continued in that sector, and Panzers captured Klin on a 50 mile front north west of the capital. However, the predicted tide was about to turn, as Rostov, captured in a deep penetration by Panzer forces on the 21st, was evacuated by all German units as the danger of being cut off at the rear became acute. The stretched and weary armoured columns were in a very vulnerable position, and against the explicit orders from Hitler to hold ground, Feldmarschall von Rundstedt rapidly withdrew his forces to avoid a humiliating defeat.

The winter conditions had begun to bite. On the 27th November, German units of 9th Army reached the Volga Canal, which was a mere 60 miles north west of Moscow. Significantly, it was observed that some armed patrols had infiltrated into the western suburbs of the capital, and were even within sight of the Kremlin! But, Hitler's dream would not be fulfilled, as German troops would never achieve the conquest of Moscow, and the ideological centre of communism would remain forever secure from the threat of fascism.

Friday 28
Russia make large scale offensive in the Caucasus under General Timochenko.
Recaptured Rostov and are pushing Gerry back fast.

As if to finally barricade Moscow from German advances, and in extreme weather conditions made worse by temperatures well below zero, the depleted and mauled Middle Group forces led by von Bock suspended all offensive operations following fierce and protracted engagements. They were just 50 miles from Moscow. Immobile, rendered weary and ineffective by severe weather conditions and constant fighting, the German forces had to acknowledge that Moscow would not be taken. To compound their misery, fresh Soviet forces, kitted out with clothing and equipment suitable for the most severe weather conditions, were waiting to pounce on the desperate plight of the Germans. The tremendous tenacity of the Red Army forces was destined to wrest the Soviet Union from the brink of defeat, and Stalin's prediction was about to come true.

Saturday 29
Our Libyan offensive going well but our casualties are heavy.
We are hitting General Rommel's army hard & he is suffering heavily.

Having now replaced Wavell, the new commander in the Middle East, General Claude Auchinleck, had been receiving a growing number of tanks, trucks and guns. It was with these resources that on the 18th November, 'Operation Crusader' was mounted against Rommel and the Italian and German Divisions of the 'Afrika Korps'.

Auchinleck's plan had been to head for Tobruk and join up with the forces that had stubbornly held that position for a considerable period. With over 700 tanks and supporting armour, the strategy had been to attack at three points; directly at Tobruk, and on the left and right flanks. Although numerically outnumbered by the Allied forces, Rommel had a clear advantage in the quality of tanks, but more seriously for the attacking force, he had superior guns - the 88mm being a very formidable and potent weapon.

The tank battles would be far ranging, scattered, confusing and deadly. They would consist of all the elements that mobile mechanised forces would encounter as they fought to gain the advantage. Over the next few days, numerous frenzied and destructive tank and gun battles occurred: many fought around the airfield at Sidi Rezegh, which changed hands several times, but the British armour was outfought and outgunned to such a degree that Rommel had visions of destroying the complete 8th Army! This might have been achieved were it not for Auchinleck who ordered his forces to continue with the offensive, and in doing so stretched Rommel's Panzers and supporting armour, which then allowed the RAF to bomb and strafe their columns mercilessly.

There had been severe casualties on both sides, and the position at the end of November was in the balance; both for Rommel, and for the 8th Army.

~~~~~~~~~~

A local incident occurred on this day and was recorded on a *'Message Form'*. It came from the *'Braintree Report Centre, to Essex County Control'* and was logged as a *'Coggeshall Police report.'* The contents stated: *'Flare container found in LINKY WOOD, Bradwell at 08-45 by Mr A. Ham, Keepers Cottage, Ash*

Lane, Bradwell 29/11/41 - marks stencilled in green LIESERUNG-S4 SHP AUSGESBRER PIGHT.' Previously having contained flares, it would be impossible to determine where or when they were unleashed - but drop they did! One could only hope that their fate had been harmless; wherever they had fallen.

Sunday November 30 – Friday December 5 – nothing recorded.

DECEMBER 1941

The Luftwaffe continued to harass individual ships and convoys by mining and shipping strikes around Britain's coast. However, nothing was recorded for the first few days of the month in local areas.

Saturday 6
Russians still chasing Gerry in the South (Ukraine).

The 5th December saw the Soviet counter-offensive commence north-west of Moscow at Kalinin.

The very next day, three Soviet armies comprising of 18 Divisions released from the Russian Far East borders began a massive and decisive counter-offensive to drive back and destroy von Bock's Middle group forces, now weak, ineffective and static on the approaches to Moscow. The Soviet force had not been without significance, as the Red Army was supported by 1,700 tanks and 1,500 aircraft, and was fresh and better prepared than the German Group it faced. Within two days, the Soviet forces had broken through the German lines at many points, which caused the very ill-prepared troops, frost-bitten and fatigued, to abandon much needed heavy armour and equipment that had been immobilised by the severe winter weather.

Rostov, evacuated by the Germans a few days previously, was once more in Soviet control by the 6th December and by the 9th they had retaken both Klin and Tikvin in their successful counter-offensive.

No incursion of significance by German bombers was reported locally.

Sunday 7
Japs attack Hawaii Islands (U.S.A.) & declare war against U.S.A. & Britain.

The 7th December 1941, a day never to be forgotten in American history, the 'day of infamy' on which the Japanese attacked the mighty US Navy battleships as they lay at anchor in Pearl Harbour, and also attacked US Army airfields in the Philippines. Although aware for some considerable time that Japan would probably attack American interests in the Pacific, the US forces were slow in organising defences and building up resources to deter the attacks. Intercepts of Japanese communications had already indicated to those in command that negotiations relating to Japanese expansionist plans were at an end, and the likelihood of attack was imminent.

The American government had relied on the recent build up of a handful of fighters and bombers based in the Philippines to help to discourage the Japanese from attack, but they were small in number and poorly equipped.

However, their large naval fleet at Pearl Harbour was seen as the greatest significant deterrent to the expansionist plans of Japan, and the US forces had been grossly ill prepared for the pre-emptive strike by 420 aircraft of the Japanese navy carrier force under the command of Vice Admiral Nagumo. Consequently, in a very short period, 5 of the 8 battleships moored at Pearl Harbour were sunk or severely damaged. It was carnage.

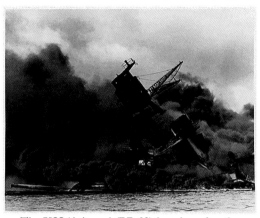

The USS 'Arizona' (BB-39) burning after the Japanese attack on Pearl Harbour, Hawaii.
(Courtesy of the Franklin D. Roosevelt Library Archives)

The Japanese bombers came in waves, led by torpedo carrying planes targeting the battleships. Having exacted great damage on several ships, the following attack was carried out by dive-bombers with armour piercing bombs, and later, in the second major wave, already damaged and burning targets were struck yet again. In two short hours the Japanese naval air attack had decimated the ability to provide an offensive naval weapon for the Allies in the Pacific.

Airfield damage from Japanese attack at Pearl Harbour, Hawaii. Ford Island seaplane base showing USS 'Shaw' exploding in centre background.
(Courtesy of the Franklin D. Roosevelt Library Archives)

The simultaneous raids on the airfields in the Philippines were almost as catastrophic for the unprepared, and inadequate US Army air contingent that had been struggling to build up their resources in the months leading up to the attacks. The handful of US Army aircraft that had been able to get off the ground to engage the large force of enemy aircraft found themselves alone in a hornet's nest, and due to poor communications and lack of adequate training, failed to make an impression on the superior Japanese aerial armada. As a result of poor dispersal and inadequate defence facilities around the airfields, many of the recently arrived B17 bombers and P40

The 'Zeke' or Zero Navy A6M was a variant of the aircraft that attacked Pearl Harbour and the Philippines. The aircraft pictured here has the hint of the US star on the fuselage, with a number on the nose similar to Marine Corps aircraft, probably signifying that it was captured.
(Source: Ken Delve Collection)

fighters, together with the old aircraft they were replacing, had been caught on the ground and mercilessly bombed and strafed to destruction.

Having taken a dreadful toll on the ships, aircraft and military facilities, the loss of life was horrific. Over 2,400 Americans died that day at Pearl Harbour and in the Philippines, and the shock of the attack on American territory was devastating for the nation.

There was, however, one vital component of the American naval fleet missing from Pearl Harbour that day. All the American aircraft carriers were at sea. As the war progressed, it would be they who would provide the means for the US Navy to fight back with their carrier planes and eventually avenge that terrible day at Pearl Harbour.

It was, indeed, a day of infamy, and a major setback for the Allies ability to take the offensive against the latest partner in the despicable Axis alliance.

In accordance with Axis tactics the Japs launched the attack while the Jap envoy was discussing terms with Roosevelt.

That was true, as stated in Roosevelt's address the next day to Congress. However, it did not appear that Japan was discussing terms, but purely stalling for time as the attacks on American and British targets were already taking place whilst the Japanese Ambassador to the United States had been delivering a message of 'refusal to negotiate' to the American Secretary of

State.

It must also be recorded that, in preceding months, America itself had been desperately stalling for time to build up its inadequate defences and weapons in the Pacific region, as their planning and intelligence had indicated that they would be capable of mounting an offensive, should it be necessary, in the spring of 1942. The outcome was inevitable - they were too slow, badly prepared, and too late.

As we did not hear them say 'war' we will not hear their cry for peace.

I wonder where that notable quote came from. I would think that my father would have had just that turn of phrase at such a momentous and infamous moment in history, and all in Britain and especially America would certainly have echoed the words. Very succinct and to the point, it was now all out war with all the Axis sympathisers. Great Britain and her Allies would now be clear who all their enemies were and could plan accordingly. The road to outright victory had just commenced, but the outcome would continue to be long and bloody with the sacrifice of hundreds of thousands of innocent souls who would not see the war end.

Monday 8
U.S.A. & Britain declare war on Japan.
The following is President Roosevelt's address to Congress:

'Yesterday, December 7, 1941 - a date which will live in infamy - the United States of America was suddenly and deliberately attacked by naval and air forces of the Empire of Japan.

The United States was at peace with that nation and, at the solicitation of Japan, was still in conversation with its Government and its Emperor looking toward the maintenance of peace in the Pacific. Indeed, one hour after Japanese air squadrons had commenced bombing in Oahu, the Japanese Ambassador to the United States and his colleague delivered to the Secretary of State a formal reply to a recent American message. While this reply stated that it seemed useless to continue the existing diplomatic negotiations, it contained no threat or hint of war or armed attack.

It will be recorded that the distance of Hawaii from Japan makes it obvious that the attack was deliberately planned many days or even weeks ago. During the intervening time the Japanese Government has deliberately sought to deceive the United States by false statements and expressions of hope for continued peace.

The attack yesterday on the Hawaiian Islands has caused severe damage to American naval and military forces. Very many American lives have been lost. In addition American ships have been reported torpedoed on the high seas between San Francisco and Honolulu.

Yesterday the Japanese Government also launched an attack against Malaya.

Last night Japanese forces attacked Hong Kong.

Last night Japanese forces attacked Guam.

Last night Japanese forces attacked the Philippine Islands.

Last night the Japanese attacked Wake Island.

This morning the Japanese attacked Midway Island.

Japan has, therefore, undertaken a surprise offensive extending throughout the Pacific area. The facts of yesterday speak for themselves.

The people of the United States have already formed their opinions and well understand the implications to the very life and safety of our Nation.

As Commander in Chief of the Army and Navy I have directed that all measures be taken for our defense.

Always will we remember the character of the onslaught against us.

No matter how long it may take us to overcome this premeditated invasion, the American people, in their righteous might, will win through to absolute victory.

I believe I interpret the will of the Congress and of the people when I assert that we will not only defend ourselves to the uttermost but will make very certain that this form of treachery shall never endanger us again.

Hostilities exist. There is no blinking at the fact that our people, our territory, and our interests are in grave danger.

With confidence in our armed forces - with the unbounded determination of our people - we will gain the inevitable triumph - so help us God.

I ask that the Congress declare that since the unprovoked and dastardly attack by Japan on Sunday, December 7, a state of war has existed between the United States and the Japanese Empire.'

~~~~~

(Reproduced from the FRD Library Digital Archives, On-line Documents, Selected Public Paper of FDR, 'Declaration of War with Japan Address to Congress', December 8, 1941)

~~~~~

On receiving the news of Pearl Harbour, and following the reported telephone conversation with President Roosevelt, Prime Minister Winston Churchill had, in confidence, been immensely relieved that America was now in the war. Although there would be the tremendous sadness of losing Malaya, Singapore and Hong Kong to come, the massive stress of nearly nineteen months of German attrition had instantly been removed by the Japanese attacks, and Churchill's immediate reaction was one of '...the greatest joy'. There would be many setbacks, but Churchill knew that there could only be one conclusion - defeat for the Axis alliance.

The Japs, attacking American & British possessions in the Pacific have done terrific damage, sinking a number of American ships, inc 2 Battleships.

Britain was now at war with Japan. The Japanese had attacked Malaya and Hong Kong, while their forces were carrying out devastating strikes on American bases in the Philippines, Guam, Wake Island and Midway Island; all strategic targets in the Pacific designed for use by the ruthless new opponent in the war of attrition - Japan.

No air raids reported locally.

Tuesday 9
Japs attack Thailand we are fighting Jap forces in Malaya.

It would soon be known that Thailand had signed a 'Treaty of Alliance' with Japan, acknowledging Japanese support given when they were previously being attacked by French Indo-China.

The news that Japanese troops had landed on the Malayan Peninsular was a serious and bitter blow for Britain. It would be the start of a humiliating defeat for all our forces in the Far East. Our resources were inadequate; the planning for an expected invasion was inadequate, and the Japanese were extremely aggressive. It was probably the inadequacy of our Air Force in that region, lacking the quality and quantity of our fighters and bombers based in Britain that enabled the Japanese to have a quick and decisive victory. Although they fought with extreme bravery, the RAF and Allied ground forces were overwhelmed by the speed and aggression of the invading hordes. The Japanese were tough, uncompromising and brutal in their methods when defeating the British and Commonwealth forces, and the road to eventual victory for the Allies would be long, tortuous and bloody. It would only finally end when the atomic bombs were dropped on Hiroshima and Nagasaki in 1945. During that intervening period, the Japanese fought to the death, and were a cruel and sadistic enemy, causing many brave men to give their lives in ferocious fighting in all theatres in the Far East.

Never again would tens of thousands of our Allied forces return to their families and homes, as they now rest in peace on former battlefields; now silent but not forgotten in those distant lands. For those who did return, memories of battles and vile prison camps would tarnish and torment them for the rest of their lives.

~~~~~~~~~~

So far nothing has been heard of the American navy.

When eventually the carnage at Pearl Harbour and in the Philippines was recorded, the figures were the following:-

21 ships of the American Naval Fleet had been sunk or badly damaged.

188 aircraft were destroyed.

159 aircraft damaged.

2,403 military and civilian personnel were killed.

1,178 military and civilian personnel were wounded.

For America it was a devastating introduction to war. However, Britain now had a powerful ally and would now be able to become the aggressor in all theatres of war, but that would last for nearly four more tough and terrible years.

~~~~~~~~~~

The Japs have had no opposition altho' we have a few ships out there.

Those 'few ships' were to become even fewer. The Royal Navy was about to suffer another catastrophic blow.

~~~~~~~~~~

There were no enemy air raids reported locally.

Wednesday 10
The 'Prince of Wales' & the 'Repulse' sunk in the Pacific.
A bitter blow.
The 'P. of W.' has only been completed since April and has not yet had a big engagement. We are now wanting to hear further news.

HMS 'Prince of Wales'.
(Source: David Page, navyphotos)

Previously involved in the sinking of the 'Bismark' in May, and the damage having been repaired as a result of the action, the Home Fleet battleship HMS 'Prince of Wales' had fulfilled its task to take Churchill for a secret rendezvous with President Roosevelt in Newfoundland. With that successfully completed, she was assigned to the Mediterranean theatre of operations to protect convoys.

In late October 1941, under the flag of Admiral Sir John Phillips, the 'Prince of Wales' sailed for the Far East in recognition of the deteriorating situation concerning Japan. Together with the aging battle-cruiser HMS 'Repulse', their task was to serve as a deterrent to counter possible Japanese hostility. That policy was not successful as the Japanese attacked Pearl Harbour and other Allied targets, including northern Malaya, on the 7th December.

In convoy with four destroyers *(Force Z),* the two capital ships moved to intercept Japanese landing fleets, but had been unable to locate them, and were forced to return to Singapore. However, the fleet had been seen by a lone Japanese submarine and

HMS 'Repulse' commands attention from a tug.
(Source: David Page, navyphotos)

thereafter shadowed by aircraft and submarines, until on the 10th December, off Kuantan, Malaya, they were attacked by hordes of Japanese bombers and torpedo planes. Lacking surface radar, the ships were taken by surprise, and in the attack that followed they were initially able to dodge many of the torpedoes and bombs launched at them. Eventually, however, both ships suffered several devastating and fatal strikes and were soon sinking.

Russians still pushing Gerry back.
We are chasing them in Libya.

There were no enemy air raids reported locally.

Thursday 11
* *Germany & Italy declare war on America & America declare war a few hours later.*

The formality of declaration had been made. That it was necessary to do so remained insignificant, as it was obvious that America was now at war.

But, as a statement of intent it did not bode well for the Axis powers in their coming battles with the growing and powerful Allied forces.

2,300 officers & men saved from P. of W. & the Repulse. 600 missing.

The stronger hull of the 'Prince of Wales' enabled the ship to stay afloat long enough for the majority of the crew to be saved, although it is sad to relate that a few hundred lost their lives. Regretfully, the very much older 'Repulse' sank quickly, and many perished before rescue was possible.

The record shows that 436 men from the 'Repulse', and 327 from the 'Prince of Wales' died when the ships were lost. It was a vivid reminder of the strength and intensity of aerial attacks, and a further reminder of the limitations and vulnerability of battleships.

We are doing very well in Libya & should clear this up very soon.

The Axis forces were now in retreat, and Tobruk had been relieved.

By this date, Rommel had been informed that he would not be receiving further supplies until January 1942, and he had no option but to withdraw the remnants of his 'Afrika Korps' Divisions - now depleted and battered from constant battles. It would take a few more skirmishes to finally remove Rommel's forces besieged in Bardia on the 2nd January, also Sollom on the 12th January, and finally, on 17th January 1942, the last remnants of the defenders at Halfaya Pass were taken into captivity. By this time Rommel had to withdraw to hold the line at Marsa Brega near El Agheila.

The bravery of the besieged Allied defenders and the efficiency of command during the eight month siege of Tobruk had been an incredible achievement. As Rommel withdrew, virtually to his starting point of the campaign, he would respond later in 1942 with an offence, capturing Tobruk and forcing the 8th Army to withdraw back to Mersa Matruh, and then to El Alamein. It was there that Rommel was halted, and the tide finally turned in favour of the Allies. Bernard Law Montgomery and the 8th Army would be his nemesis.

Russia still pushing Gerry back.

The Soviet counter-offensive continued to gather momentum, as it struck hard into the heart of the German forces. Further advances were made as the month progressed.

Although my father made no further entries in his diary - almost certainly as a result of the Japanese attacks on Pearl Harbour and the Philippines - the Soviet counter-offensive had progressed significantly, which was confirmed on the 14th December by the German forces evacuating the town of Kalinin.

On the 18th December, and presumably as a result of the reversals being experienced by many of the German units, Feldmarschall von Brauchitsch resigned, and Hitler himself assumed personal command; concentrating especially on his armies under severe pressure on the Eastern front.

Continuing the German retreat from Moscow, German forces of the Middle Group prepared new defensive lines more than 100 miles to the west of the capital where, following direct and unequivocal orders from Hitler, they had been told to stand and fight further Soviet advances.

As the year ended, the Red Army increased the pressure on German forces by continuing the counter-offensive in the area around Kalinin, whilst in the eastern Crimea, German troops evacuated Kerch and Theodosia. Finally, on New Year's Eve, German forces halted all further attacks against the beleaguered Crimean fortress of Sevastopol.

The year was at an end, and the likelihood of Stalin's prediction began to gain substance. The final years of the war would prove to be prophetic for the Germans. They were going to be destroyed.

In the Battle of the Atlantic, the year was drawing to a close. The sinking of the battleship 'Bismark' on her maiden voyage in May had persuaded Hitler to withdraw all his surface raiders to safer waters where they remained threatening but impotent until the end of the war. Also notably paying dividends was the capture of 'Enigma', which had given Allies the ability to intercept the coded radio messages of U-boat signal traffic.

In the second half of the year, the contrast in losses was significant. It showed a marked reduction in the number of Allied ships lost at 169 ships (720,159 tons), which was still a horrendous number, but an improvement on the destruction of the first six months. Throughout the year, U-boats had accounted for 432 of the 525 ships sunk in both the north and south Atlantic. Significantly, on the plus side, 35 U-boats had been sunk; 7 million tons of shipping was being built in the USA, and Britain had launched 1.2 million tons of new ships. In the year of 1941, Britain had withstood the destructive power of the U-boats in their 'Wolf Packs'. 1942 would be a different story.

The Luftwaffe continued to attack with small raids after the 11th December when the diary entries finished. During the night of the 20th/21st, incidents were recorded at Panfield adjacent to Braintree, and Southend.

While other areas throughout the country reported small raids by German raiders attacking at low level with bombs and machine guns, no further raids were recorded locally in 1941.

~~~~~~~~~~

On the 23ʳᵈ December, Prime Minister Winston S. Churchill and President Franklin D. Roosevelt held a joint press conference in Washington DC to seal the alliance between the two great nations in their fight for a free world.

~~~~~~~~~~

That final entry concludes the diary recording the year of 1941. From the early part of the year, suffering raids and bad news, then further into and later in the year when certain optimism occurs, we can see the reaction when my father realises that his predictions of an early finish to the war had been more than optimistic. Maybe for that reason, and the realisation that the war was going to continue for a great deal longer, he ceased, to my knowledge, to keep further record of the progress of family, work, and war happenings – or perhaps he was like millions of others, just busy.

Travelling

However, in the back of the diary, there are a few business notes with the odd names of people he had to contact and places he had to go. Also, the day of a journey to London by train with the times of trains from Kelvedon and Witham to Liverpool Street marked as options.

There is, interestingly, his log of petrol used for a few months, headed simply *'Petrol'*.

They are:

		August
19 journeys		*Witham*
5	*" ½ mile*	*Petrol*
		Sept
27 journeys		*Witham*
3	*" ½ mile*	*Petrol*
		Oct
25 journeys		*Witham*
4	*" ½ mile*	*Petrol*
		Nov
24 journeys		*Witham*
1	*"*	*Kelvedon (Firm)*
1	*"*	*Colchester (Firm)*

As we are all aware, petrol was one of the most valuable commodities apart from food and war materials, and at that time during 1941 the destroying of ships by U-boats created a critical situation for the survival of Britain. Recording those journeys became very important to anyone fortunate enough to own a car.

Conclusion

In my father's 1941 diary, I have travelled the world during desperate times; I have experienced my family's early life, with their small triumphs and troubles, and I have learnt greater humility; for theirs were real events that happened during that year of turmoil.

During my limited research I have lived and experienced the world at war, which has very much been a self-motivated knowledge enhanced by the reporting of a few learned historians. I have been intrigued and surprised how fact has differed from the reporting of events by the media as they occurred, and how many of the observations were influenced by events each day. For millions of people like my father, theirs was a real war, full of destruction, death, loyalties, duty and sadness. But while many paid the ultimate price in death, there were those who survived to live in a more enlightened world.

This has been the diary of one of those fortunate enough to realise the relief of peace, and in his small way, help shape the future of Britain. I hope that I have given some credible additions to Peter Anderson's diary and shed some light on his short but relevant observations.

The final footnote:

Finally, after the war, Peter Anderson was able to settle to a quiet family life. By that time (I had arrived in 1943), he was established in his vocation and looking forward to the future. Following his 'official' retirement in 1973, he joined me in our fledgling operation, Titon, his second working life! His retirement was put on hold and he toiled on for another highly productive and rewarding thirteen years. It was satisfying time for him, and one that he would see through to the point of Titon becoming a Public Company, which today is still quoted on the London Stock Exchange.

Father enjoyed life - he smoked, occasionally had a glass of Drambuie, absolutely never swore, loved his family, and we loved him. He passed away from us in October 1987 and is remembered with the greatest of affection by us all.

Thanks Dad.

Bibliography

'Raiders Approach' , Squadron Leader H.T. Hutton, Gale & Polden Ltd. – Aldershot, 1956.

'Beware of the Dog – At War', John Ward, JoTe Publications - Belper, 1997.

'The Bomber Command War Diaries', Martin Middlebrook & Chris Everitt, Viking, 1985

'The Blitz – Then and Now – Volume 2', Editor: Winston G. Ramsey, Battle of Britain Prints International Ltd., London, 1988.

'The Blitz – Then and Now – Volume 3', Editor: Winston G. Ramsey, Battle of Britain Prints International Ltd., London, 1990.

'Johnnie Johnson – Spitfire Top Gun' Part One, Dilip Sakar, Ramrod Publications - Worcester, 2002.

'RAF Bomber Command – and it's aircraft 1941-45', James Golding & Philip Moyes.

'Pattle: Supreme Fighter in the Air', E.C.R. Baker, William Kimber – London, 1965.

'Rommel', Desmond Young, Collins, London, 1950.

'Blitz Over Britain', Edwin Webb & John Duncan, Spellmount.

'Rudolf Hess-Myths and Reality', Roy Conyers Nesbit & Georges Van Acker, Sutton.

'Air Raid', Michael J. F. Bowyer, Patrick Stephens – Wellingborough.

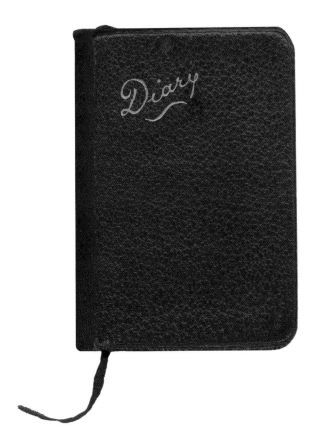